JEWISH PARTISANS

A DOCUMENTARY OF JEWISH RESISTANCE IN THE SOVIET UNION DURING WORLD WAR II

VOLUME II

COMPILED AND EDITED BY
Jack Nusan Porter

WITH THE ASSISTANCE OF
Yehuda Merin

Translated by the Magal Translation Institute, Ltd.
and by Ann Abrams, Esther Ritchie, and Esther Kluger.
Based on original Russian, Polish, and Yiddish Sources.

©1982 by **Jack Nusan Porter**

University Press of America, Inc.

P.O. Box 19101, Washington, D.C. 20036

Printed in the United States of America

ISBN (Perfect): 0-8191-2538-5
ISBN   (Cloth): 0-8191-2537-7
LCN: 81-40258

Permission to publish granted by VAAP, the copyright
agency of the USSR; Binyamin West, editor of the Hebrew
version of Part I; the World Union of Volynian Jews in
Israel; the Federation of Volynian Jews in the United
States for Part II; and the various authors.

Part I originally published as part of Partizanska
Druzhba, Moscow, USSR, Der Emess Publishing House, 1948
and later as a Hebrew version, translated and edited by
the late Binyamin West, Heym Hayu Rabim: Partizanim
Yehudim B'brit Ha-moatzot B'milchemet Ha-olam Ha-shniya,
Tel Aviv, 1968.

Part II is taken in part from K'oranim Gavahu: Partizanim Yehudim B'ya'aret Volyn (Like Pines They Grew:
Jewish Partisans in the Forests of Volyn, Giv'atayim
and New York, Summer 1980, edited by Natan Livneh.

DEDICATED TO MY TWO YOUNG SISTERS

I NEVER KNEW THEM.
THEY MUST HAVE BEEN A TERRIBLE THREAT
TO THE NAZI MACHINE.

Chaya Udel Puchtik
(Age 4, Killed September 23, 1942)

Pesel Puchtik
(Age 2, Killed September 23, 1942)

THE TEN COMMANDMENTS OF THE HOLOCAUST

Jack Nusan Porter

1. Thou shalt remember everything and understand nothing.

2. Thou shalt record everything -- memoirs, diaries, documents, and poetry.

3. Thou shalt teach it diligently to thy children for as Rabbi Emil Fackenheim has said: the survival of Israel is now a sacred duty.

4. Thou shalt teach it to the Gentiles and to their children because thou art often at their mercy.

5. Thou shalt not heap abuse upon the children of the ungodly. Though the wicked are to be punished, their children must be forgiven.

7. Thou shalt not judge the victims. Thou shalt not place one set of idols (the heroic) above another (the cowardly). They are to be judged equally before the Lord. As Reb Eli Wiesel of Sighet has said: there is a time to remain silent, so therefore know when to be silent.

8. Thou shalt not lose faith. Amidst all thy doubt and confusion, I, the Lord your G-d, am here among thee.

9. Thou shalt not dwell heavily upon the sadness of the past. Rejoice for thou hast survived while thine enemies have perished.

10. Thou shalt not turn away from thy brothers and sisters; instead, reach out and build a paradise on earth so that life and love can prevail.

TABLE OF CONTENTS

PREFACE

A nation, especially its young people, needs heroes. No child wants to believe that his parents were cowards or that they went -- to use a tiresome and by now vulgar phrase -- like sheep to slaughter. Soon after the Eichmann trial, a decade and a half ago, we were deluged with books and articles on the Holocaust. Some blamed the victims. Some defended them. Today this debate is futile in the extreme. The question becomes: what are the motives of the writer, not the martyr?

For the Jews, World War II was massive in its scale of death and power, towering and complex in its elemental balance of good and evil, majestic and stirring in its multi-leveled simplicity. Everything can be found within its confines...if only one wants to look for it. It one wants to find cowards, one can find cowards; if one wants to find collaborators, one can find collaborators. If one wants to find weakness and degradation, one can find that also. However, if one wishes to find heroism, one can find that in great measure. If one wants to find rebellion, one can find rebellion; and if one wants to find strength and nobility, one can find that as well.

I want to look for the defiant and for the heroic. I want to look for resistance...of all stripes: passive, active, spiritual, moral, military, and political. I have looked and I have found it. The documents in this section serve as testimony. I have a deep personal interest in them: my parents were both active in the underground movement in Volynia, western Ukraine, in the Kruk detachment mentioned in these articles, from 1942 to 1944.

When one talks to Jewish partisans, few of them, strut and boast of their achievements. Most will tell you their fascinating tales and then remain silent. They will fill you with chronicles of revenge and then they will weep. They will tell you to pass on their tales to future generations.

The first half of the book originally appeared in Moscow in 1948. Its Russian title was <u>Partizanska Druzhba</u> (Partisan Brotherhood) and was compiled by the Jewish Anti-Fascist Committee and the Moscow-based Der Emess Publishing House. This committee, composed of the cream of Jewish writers, poets, and intellectuals, had as its primary duty the task of gaining world-wide support for the Soviet Union during the days when Russia stood almost alone against the Nazi onslaught. After the war, their task widened to include the gathering of material on the vital role Jews played during the war.

Under the megalomaniacal paranoia of Stalin, anti-Semitism was whipped up in the post-war years, 1945-1953. Jewish war veterans, some crippled, were mocked in the streets: "Where did you get those fancy medals, kike? In a crap game? Did you buy them on the black market?" It was during such a time that was to see the purging of Jewish leaders and intellectuals, the closing of Jewish schools and cultural centers, the infamous "Doctor's Plot" and threat of mass pogroms, that the original editors of <u>Partizanska Druzhba</u> worked feverishly to publish these documents. They succeeded just in time because soon after their 1948 publication, many of them were killed or jailed. The Der Emess Government Publishing House was closed, and the book was suppressed.

Miraculously, a few copies were preserved, and fifteen years later, Binyamin West was allowed to see a micro-film copy that the Lenin Library had in its archives. From this copy, West made his translation; and from this same copy, Magal made its translation into English.

So, one must thank the Lenin Library, and one must also thank the Russian people, the Russian army, and the Russian partisan leaders for their devotion and their valor in saving the lives of many Jews in Eastern Europe. I know that this statement will not rest easy with some readers. The Soviet Union today is seen as a villain, but I speak of the Russian people and the Russian soldiers, not the Russian leadership. One must always make that distinction.

These writers are not scholars. They speak as they do for two reasons: first, it is war and this is fighting propaganda, and two, they wish to prove to Jew and non-Jew alike that Jews were neither "cowards" nor "traitors" but loyal citizens and devoted patriots.

These selections are among forty-four testimonies gathered by the Israeli journalist, Binyamin West, in his book Heym Hayu Rabim (They Were Many: Jewish Partisans in the Soviet Union During World War II), Tel Aviv: Labor Archives Press, Department of Soviet Jewry Affairs, 1968. Miriam Migal and the Magal Translation Institute, Ltd. of Tel Aviv did the translation.

* * * * *

The second half of this book was collected more recently, in the past five years or less, and deals specifically with my own family and friends and with a particular region in Volynia, Ukraine, the partisans and the family camp in the area of Horodok, Manievich, Lishnivka, Kamin-Kashirsk, Rafalovka, Griva and Povorsk. This section was edited and compiled together with my cousin Yehuda Merin of Ramat Gan, Israel. It dovetails nicely with Part I.

What is intriguing about this second section is that it is reminiscent of the movie Rashomon. One views the German-Ukrainian "action" (the mass killings of Jews) from various perspectives and then the response -- hiding, going into the forests, and slowly organizing into fighting forces. It was on September 22 and 23, 1942 that an action took place outside Manievich that led to the killing of twenty-five members of my immediate family, including my little sisters, Chaya Udel, four years old, and Pesel, two years old. My mother hid and was saved; she later met my father in the forests and they worked in the "family camp" and the fighting units of Kruk, Max, and others. The Jewish "family camp" is a unique and fascinating aspect of Holocaust history, and I am happy to present various perspectives on it in Part II. I, by the way, was born later on December 2, 1944, after the area was liberated by the Russians.

* * * * *

This volume should be seen as a continuation of Volume I; the two books complement each other. At a time when some misguided scholars are saying that the Holocaust never happened or happened in ways different then we are led to believe, it is refreshing to

hear these voices. The people here actually participated. They are, in a sense, living legends. In
another generation, their voices will be stilled, never
to be heard from again. The recent world gathering of
Holocaust survivors poignantly brought home the message
that time is running out. It is up to us, and especially those of us who are the sons and daughters of
survivors to carry on, to continue the legend, because
soon, very soon, the only thing left will be these
stories, these living legends, for us to hold on to.

                      * * * * *

     These two volumes owe a great deal to many people.
I have mentioned some of these people in the preface to
Volume I. I would now like to add the names of those
who not only helped "build" this book but also those
who contributed financial assistance to make these two
volumes possible. If I have forgotten someone, please
forgive me. The list is so long.

     * To Yehuda Merin for compiling many of the inter-
       views in Part II.

     * To my editor and proofreader, Abby Solomon, who
       labors over nearly everything I write and
       always finds a way for it to read better, my
       deepest thanks.

     * To the translators of this volume: the Magal
       Translation Institute, Ltd. of Israel for Part
       I; and to Ann Abrams, Esther Ritchie, and
       Esther Kluger for translating the Hebrew and
       some Yiddish into English. Ann Abrams is,
       however, responsible for most of Part II. I
       am truly grateful to her.

     * For the maps, my thanks to Marta Braiterman for
       a difficult job well-done. She not only drew
       the maps, but translated them from Hebrew as
       well.

     * To all my friends at Communication Graphics in
       Brookline, Massachusetts for their efforts and
       skill for all the work they have done for me.
       They are a patient group of people, and I am
       grateful to make their names public: Jerrine
       Larsen, Dudley Glover, Norma Larsen, Patricia
       Gould, Susan Gould, and Janice Thalin.

* To all the people who consented to interviews and to their families.

* To VAAP, the Russian Copyright Office, for permission to publish Part I of this volume and all of Volume I.

* To Jack Elbirt and the Federation of Volynian Jews of the USA for permission to publish sections of Part II.

* To the following supporters:

Celia and Avrum Stzundel
Jacob Sredni and Family
Dr. Samuel Porter and family (in memory of Boris Porter and Chana Seltzer Levenson)
Hinda Porter
Leonard Lieberman and Family
Benjamin Lande and Family
Jacob Karsh and Family
Sophie and Lou Kaplan and Family
The Schoenfeld Family
Young Judea of New England
Barney Porter
Sarah Singer
Marie Kargman
Dov (Berl) Lorber
Shulamit Goldman
The Snow Family (Mina Snow)
Abba Klurman
Charlie (Sasha) Zarutski
Morris and Sophie Kramer
Harry Steinbaum (in memory of Michel and Bella, and their two children, Pessie and Avrom; Mordechai Steinbaum from the town of Vishgoradic, Russia; with loving remembrance from their son and brother, Jacob)
Rubin Kirzner (Slivka) and Family
Avraham and Berl Finkel

And finally, to those who purchase copies of this book for themselves and their friends. Lastly, to my wife Miriam, son Gabriel, my mother Faye Porter, my brother and sister, Shlomo and Bella Porter, to my in-laws, Joseph, Reli, and Lea Almuly, and to all my friends. Thanks. And, thank you, dear reader.

Jack Nusan Porter
Brookline, Massachusetts
March 2, 1981

PART I

Jewish Partisans
in the Soviet Union
Latvia, Ukraine, and Byelorussia
1941-1944

THE KOVPAK MEN

P. Y. Braiko
Hero of the Soviet Union, Major, a Former Commander of a Partisan Battalion

Sidor Kovpak was one of the chief organizers and central commanders of the partisan movement in World War II. He was twice awarded the supreme title: Hero of the Soviet Union.

He was born to a poor peasant family in the village of Kotlava (Poltava region) in 1882. From 1941-1944 he fought as a partisan together with Commissar S. Rodniev, behind the lines of the enemy occupational forces -- first on the steppes of Bryansk (Byelorussia) and later on the right shore of the Dneiper, at Polesia; he crossed the Desna, the Sozesh, and the Pripet rivers at the head of his fighters. In the summer of 1943, his battalion was sent on a mission to the Carpathian Mountains and destroyed on the way a large supply of oil intended for the fascist armies on the Ukranian front.

In 1944 Kovpak was wounded and had to return to the Soviet Union. His duties were taken up by Lieutenant Colonel P. Vorshigura in the unit called "The First Kovpak Ukrainian Partisan Division."[1] (See Editor's Notes at the end of Part I.)

In the fall of 1942, Kovpak's famous battalion was given the task of crossing over to the right bank of the Ukraine and Byelorussia. This occurred after the battalion had carried out a great many operations in the woods of Bryansk. In those days Sidor Artiomovich Kovpak's name had become a household word all over the scorched lands held by the Germans. Ukrainians, Byelorussians, Jews, and people from other nationalities flocked to him. Every one of us started his career way down in the ranks; only later, when an individual's aptitudes, know-how, and military ability had been established, was he promoted to a responsible position.

Gregory Loubienisky

When Gregory Loubienisky arrived at our company, we had heard nothing about him -- he was just like any other man. He was tall, well built, with dark hair and eyes; he wore glasses because he was short-sighted, though he did not use them all the time. Apparently his eyes hurt him. He was well educated and had graduated from the faculty of history or literature. We asked him to join our transport platoon, but he refused. So we had him join one of our platoons as a fighter.

Winter came. Our battalion had reached the region of Ovnekovo and was moving to the southwest, carrying out some smallscale missions and engaging the enemy forces in frequent skirmishes; in the course of these we learned something about partisan warfare. Our military experience, however, was complemented and enhanced through the day-to-day analysis and discussion of our operations. During one such analysis session -- I was then chief of staff of the Krolievsk Company -- we found out that the commander of one of the subsidiary units had panicked at a critical moment. It was left for Loubienisky to save the unit from defeat. There are situations where the absence of a preordained commander brings to the fore a "natural" one. The men who took part in that fight realized that Gregory Loubienisky, who had justifiably taken over the command, was a man of great willpower and ingenuity. The men who fought alongside him had faith in him. I thought to myself "Well, we may as well entrust him with the lives of our fighters."

I had many occasions to see Grisha Loubienisky at decisive moments. He had the knack of quickly grasping the gist of a situation. Before long I was to make him company commander and some time later, platoon commander.

We came back from Byelorussia, crossed the Polesia, and the regions of Zhitomir and Kiev. We went out from Knyaz -- a lake near Kiev. In the village of Blitsha in the Ovnekovo region we blew up a number of bridges on the river Irfein. The Germans threw into the battle against us a battalion of young soldiers, who were soon to be called "good-for-nothings" by Kovpak. This battalion, which numbered six hundred soldiers, began its attack in the woods from the direction of Ovnekovo along the right shore of the river

Terterev. They sent ahead two armored cars that suddenly appeared close to our positions in the sector of the third battalion and opened fire. In the wake of the armored cars came the German attack.

Our fourth battalion held defensive positions on the right flank of our third. When the Germans began pressing hard upon the third, we decided to strike back at the rear of the attackers by outflanking them from the right, rolling them back to the river in order to wipe them out. The task was entrusted to the second and third companies. The latter, containing Loubienisky's fighters, kept pressing them without letup. The Germans started jumping onto the ice. Soon the thin ice gave way and they went under.

We were drawn to Loubienisky not only because of his courage, but also because of his great education. We had no newspapers or books, so we had a great appreciation for any interesting story. Loubienisky was an excellent storyteller. He presented every complex thing in a simple, popular manner. His listeners took a liking to what he said.

But the Germans did not calm down. They concentrated great forces and started chasing us. We had to cross the Terterev and after a number of crossings camped at the village of Nova Krassnitza close to the railway tracks running between Chernigov and Avroch (North-central Ukraine).

Everything went well till the latter half of the next day. On that day our patrols told us that the Germans had concentrated great numbers of infantry in the neighboring village. We could quickly have pulled out of that place and moved away, but that very night we expected some planes from the Soviet Union, which were to bring us ammunition and take back our wounded for treatment. So we had to stay.

The German attack came soon after we received news of their intention to mount it. We had to join battle before we could dig in. The fighting was conducted under difficult conditions which were inconvenient for the deployment of our forces. Aside from their overwhelming manpower, the Germans also used mine throwers. The severest blow was aimed at the third company, which included, as I have already mentioned, Loubienisky's unit. This unit bore the brunt of the main German attack. Before long, the company was beaten, leaving only Loubienisky's unit with its twenty fighters to face an attack by an entire German battalion.

At that time I was at the other end of the village, engaged in a fight against the Germans. When a runner came up to us and told us that the third company had been beaten, I sent a reserve company to the aid of Loubienisky. This improved things a little for him, but the situation still was very critical. The Germans kept up their attack without giving Loubienisky's men a chance to dig in. The battle had been going on for three hours, well into twilight -- it had been a clear, sunny day in March. The men had been bled white, but they kept on fighting. Loubienisky kept his ground with astonishing determination. We looked forward to the arrival of the Russian planes. And then, from far away, came the persistent din of plane engines. The fight, conducted under such difficult conditions, had been justified in the end. At that spirit-raising moment, news came that Loubienisky was wounded. I at once sent a carriage to bring him to the plane, which had landed meanwhile, in order to evacuate him to a hospital on Soviet soil.

A mine splinter had entered Loubienisky's chest. Dossia Ostchenko, one of our bravest nurses, had bandaged his wound while the fight was going on, but the wound was a serious one, resulting in quick death.

We had lost one of our best comrades, a distinguished fighter, and a brave commander.

Misha Robinov

I want to tell you also of another partisan, Misha Robinov, who, like Loubienisky, was in my consideration the incarnation of nobility, attained at times by the great sons of a nation.

Michael Elhanan (Misha) Robinov was extremely young. He was born in 1921 in the small town of Timkobichi, in the Minsk region. He had finished only ten grades when he joined the army. When the war broke out he was a sergeant. His company was surrounded by the Germans, but he succeeded in escaping and, like many others, found his way to us. He at once asked to join our reconnaissance company.

I was in charge of picking out the men best fitted for patrol duty. I asked a great deal of them.

This energetic little guy seemed to be the right man
for the job. His quick, precise movements showed
outstanding drive and nervous energy. It would seem
that Misha Robinov liked the job of being a soldier and
did not flinch from danger.

I worked diligently and consistently with my
reconnaissance men to prepare them for their job. I
took a liking to Misha Robinov right from the start.
When I went about training him, I realized that I had
made the right choice. The other scouts also liked
him. But unfortunately they soon began to suspect him
of being overbearing and supercilious. Some partisans
had gone on a patrol mission and had not fulfilled the
task entrusted to them. When debriefed, they did not
tell the truth. Robinov, who had been with them on
that mission, came up to me and told me what had really
happened. This was not to the liking of his comrades,
but I decided to use this incident as a lesson to all
those going out on patrol duty. I told my men, with
considerable emphasis, that reconnaissance in war was a
sacred job, especially in guerilla warfare, and that
loyalty and falsehood could not dwell together. The
men understood what I was driving at. They also
stopped being angry at Misha when they came to realize
that there was no justification for suspecting a daring
and intelligent fighter like him of wanting to lord it
over them -- that such thoughts were not fitting for a
man who had no fear of danger and was ready to risk his
life on highly dangerous missions.

I asked my men not to shy away from the enemy,
even when outnumbered. Misha Robinov proved once and
again that he knew what military daring meant. I do
not remember any attempt on his part to shirk a mission
-- on the contrary he would always volunteer for the
most serious and daring missions.

I decided to take him on as my liaison man: I was
in need of a scout with initiative and courage. Misha
Robinov went through the entire partisan war with me
till the end. He did not know fatigue. Sometimes they
would wake him at night and tell him "Misha, we've got
to move!" And he would answer without hesitation "I'm
ready!" Readiness for battle ran in his blood. He
never asked for more men to go than were needed for any
action. He would get the details of the mission, mount
a horse, and move out. Armed with an automatic rifle,
a pistol, and many cartridges, he would get to places
which seemed to be accessible only to a mouse.

During the battle that raged in the village of Nova Krassnitza, when Loubienisky's company was almost entirely cut off, it was necessary -- before sending reinforcements -- to find out everything about the situation. That called for a man of great daring. I looked around to ask who would do it. "I am going," said Robinov -- and disappeared. He reached the other end of the village at a fast clip, and, under a hail of machine gun bullets and mortar shells, crawled to where Loubienisky was conducting the fight, received the necessary information, and came back. He was a very fast runner.

The more I got to know Misha Robinov, the more I came to rely upon his accuracy and ingenuity. When I sent him on a mission to the battalion staff, I would not tell him exactly what to say. I would merely say "Tell them what is necessary," and Robinov would give them only the most essential information.

In May 1943 we had to cross the railway tracks between Gomel and Kalinkovichi (Byelorussia). The Germans had thrown great forces against us. The battle went on till morning, but we could not get to the railroad tracks. We were nearly surrounded by the enemy: part of the company was on the other side of the tracks, entirely cut off from the main forces. Two companies of the fourth battalion engaged the Germans in battle. When it became evident to the battalion staff that it was impossible for us to cross the railway tracks, they decided to pull back to minimize losses. Robinov came back running from the field staff, holding in his hand the order to withdraw. It is easy to say "withdraw" when there is no contact with two companies, cut off by the enemy.

"I'll go to them and tell them to pull back. Please let me!"

"Where do you want to go? They are cut off."

"That's nothing. I'll get over to them and get them going."

Robinov had to report back to the battalion staff, but he started to talk me into sending him to the cut-off companies. He did his best to persuade me that anyone could get to the field staff, which was not the case with the encircled forces. I agreed to what he said. Robinov ran towards the Germans.

In that terrible hail of rifle and mortar fire, I realized that I had given Misha a difficult and dangerous task. I kept listening to the firing and looking forward to his return. I was afraid he wouldn't make it, but I also had a feeling that Robiniv could not fail -- it wasn't like him; he wasn't cut out for _that_. In war, personal success is tied up with daring and self-confidence. Forty desperate minutes passed, fraught with great concern for the man out there among the bullets and the shells. Then all of a sudden he appeared, followed by the second and third companies. It turned out that he had found a gap in the German encirclement and could not only _get_ to the two surrounded companies but also get them _out_, without having to fire a shot at the enemy.

The German high command now began to trumpet the liquidation of the "Kovpak Gang" and the killing of their chief commanders, Kovpak and Rodniev. But before the Fuhrer got down to the business of awarding medals to his generals and officers for their brilliant exploits, Kovpak's men were again behind the enemy lines, in southern Ukraine. Our appearance at a place where the Germans had never dreamed of seeing us at all was heralded by our blowing up the bridge over the railway track connecting Tarnopol with Vlotchisk, on a road which till then had been beyond the range of partisan activities and had served as a main artery of supplies for the enemy forces deployed in the direction of Orel-Kursk.

The German command did all it could to prevent the infiltration of partisans into the Carpathian region. The enemy turned against us eight mountain companies, including two "Norwegian" ones, an SS Galitshina division, and several SS battalions. That was the beginning of a series of cruel battles, in which we were invariably outnumbered. On the second of August, our battalion, surrounded by Fascist armies, was engaged in battles in the region of Mount Sinichka. The Germans kept bombing with a dogged determination to break through to our field command and the vehicles in its possession.

In these battles Misha Robinov proved once again to be a matchless warrior. During one German bombing of the peak, he came to me running under a hail of artillery and mortar fire.

"What's new at the HQ?" I asked him.

"The commissar has issued an order to hold on to the peak at any price. Runners have been sent in all directions. Tonight we have got to break out of the encirclement."

A few minutes later the runner of the second company came to me and, in a shaking voice, announced:

"Comrade Kapitan, the second and third companies have eva-cuated the heights and are now on the retreat. The company commander is in need of reinforcements. The Germans have received new forces. They are crawling up towards us like so many insects."

I could send no reinforcements, so I decided to go to the company and stop the retreat.

"Comrade Kapitan, permit me to join you," said Robinov.

"You have got to run back to the field command!"

"No, at such a time they don't need me up there," he insisted. "Will you permit me?" Without waiting for an answer, he followed me.

When I arrived at the battle scene, I found the second and third companies pulling back down the slopes of the heights in their retreat. The first and fourth companies, however, were still holding their ground. The summit of the peak had not been taken, neither by us nor by the Germans. Poising for a new attack, the Germans kept pouring artillery and mortar fire on the heights.

There was no time for hesitation. I ordered the commander of the second company to take the summit at once, then called upon the commanders of the other companies to do the same thing.

When the German shelling stopped, we launched a counterattack against the enemy battalions. A hail of machine-gun fire was directed at the summit. The absence of return fire had encouraged the Germans. When we were only about fifty meters from the summit, the enemy mounted an attack on our forces. The second company opened fire. The Germans halted their advance and hugged the ground. Upon a signal from me, companies two and four attacked the enemy from the flanks. The Germans were confused and began to pull back.

Shouting "hurray," companies two and three joined the attack.

Misha Robinov, who was with me in the field, ran with his feline dexterity to the second company at the beginning of the attack and joined the fighters. Within one minute, he was at the head of the company, conducting a running battle with the retreating Germans. They opened up with mortar fire, but they could not stop our advance. After a few minutes, the Germans were thrown back from the heights, leaving on the slopes behind them heaps of dead bodies. I halted the advance of our fighters, as we could not afford to follow the routed enemy for long. The main battle was over. Only sporadic mortar fire came from the enemy's direction.

Robinov sped back to me, paying no attention to the enemy mines. Suddenly a shell hit the ground close to Misha. He fell to the ground, then rose to his feet, went a few steps forward, then fell down again. When I reached him, the nurse had already bandaged his wound. Beside her stood a number of fighters. Robinov was breathing hard, and a gurgling noise came from his throat. Blood ran in thin streaks down his chin from the nose and mouth.

"Is the wound serious?" I asked with concern. The long eyelashes of the nurse moved close together, and she whispered:

"He was hit by a splinter. It penetrated a lung."

I looked at Misha's face, into his blurred eyes. They expressed anxiety. I at once understood what he was worrying about -- this wise young man was afraid we would leave him in the mountains. I said:

"Misha, don't be afraid. Everything will be all right. Until the wedding, the wound will heal --it will heal. We will again dance together."

I tried to soothe him. I looked at his face, which had paled, and into his wet eyes, which had lost their vaunted brilliance, and I thought to myself "How this man has changed!" I gave orders to carry him to the sanitary platoon where the doctor could look at his wound. There might be need for an urgent operation.

During the night we discovered a gap in the enemy lines, and our battalion could finally untangle itself from the encirclement. We carried our the wounded on stretchers we had hurriedly made out of tent material.

Toward morning, there was an improvement in Misha's condition. He was able to speak and even to smile. After a few hours he announced "Why should four men exert themselves for me, when I can go on foot with the help of one or two comrades?"

"Are you crazy?" rebuked the nurse. "Lie down and keep still!" But Robinov would not listen to her. He sat up, leaning on one of the fighters, stood for a moment, and started to walk.

Though severely wounded, Misha regained his strength after a few days, and his wound healed on the march. When I think of this "miracle," which also happened to many other wounded men, I cannot help wondering at the immense vitality of the Soviet fighters.

Toward the end of our careers as partisan fighters, Misha was promoted to liaison officer. He was constantly active, full of life, as he had been since I first met him. He had taken part in all the operations of the Kovpak battalion. His glorious exploits against the German occupation forces eventually earned for Michael Robinov some medals -- "The Red Star," the "Slava Order," Third Class, and the decoration of "To the Partisan --Homeland War," Second Class.

Robinov sped back to me, paying no attention to the enemy mines. Suddenly a shell hit the ground close to Misha. He fell to the ground, then rose to his feet, went a few steps forward, then fell down again. When I reached him, the nurse had already bandaged his wound. Beside her stood a number of fighters. Robinov was breathing hard, and a gurgling noise came from his throat. Blood ran in thin streaks down his chin from the nose and mouth.

"Is the wound serious?" I asked with concern. The long eyelashes of the nurse moved close together, and she whispered:

"He was hit by a splinter. It penetrated a lung."

I looked at Misha's face, into his blurred eyes. They expressed anxiety. I at once understood what he was worrying about -- this wise young man was afraid we would leave him in the mountains. I said:

-12-

"Misha, don't be afraid. Everything will be all right. Until the wedding, the wound will heal --it will heal. We will again dance together."

I tried to soothe him. I looked at his face, which had paled, and into his wet eyes, which had lost their vaunted brilliance, and I thought to myself "How this man has changed!" I gave orders to carry him to the sanitary platoon where the doctor could look at his wound. There might be need for an urgent operation.

During the night we discovered a gap in the enemy lines, and our battalion could finally untangle itself from the encirclement. We carried our the wounded on stretchers we had hurriedly made out of tent material.

Toward morning, there was an improvement in Misha's condition. He was able to speak and even to smile. After a few hours he announced "Why should four men exert themselves for me, when I can go on foot with the help of one or two comrades?"

"Are you crazy?" rebuked the nurse. "Lie down and keep still!" But Robinov would not listen to her. He sat up, leaning on one of the fighters, stood for a moment, and started to walk.

Though severely wounded, Misha regained his strength after a few days, and his wound healed on the march. When I think of this "miracle," which also happened to many other wounded men, I cannot help wondering at the immense vitality of the Soviet fighters.

Toward the end of our careers as partisan fighters, Misha was promoted to liaison officer. He was constantly active, full of life, as he had been since I first met him. He had taken part in all the operations of the Kovpak battalion. His glorious exploits against the German occupation forces eventually earned for Michael Robinov some medals -- "The Red Star," the "Slava Order," Third Class, and the decoration of "To the Partisan -- Homeland War," Second Class.

MY COMRADES IN ARMS

M. G. Sly
Former Commander of a Partisan Unit

The partisan group under my command, which toward the end of 1942 was dropped by parachute over the Yelin Woods in the vicinity of Chernigov (Ukraine) close to the front, numbered only thirty men. Its appearance behind the enemy lines brought us new volunteers every day. By March 1943, my company numbered about 300 men. Two months later I had become the commander of a large unit.

The unit comprised four companies, had considerable military provisions and equipment, a huge quantity of arms, and even field guns. Like that of other partisans, our equipment had come from the Germans. We roamed over 2,500 kilometers behind enemy lines; we were active in the districts of Chernigov, Orio, Zhitomir (Kiev region), Poltava (Kharkov region) and Polesia. We blew up seventy-six German army transports as well as arms and military equipment; we destroyed thirty-eight tanks, 173 vehicles, and thirty-one field guns. As a result of our military operations, seventeen garrisons and thirty-one police stations were put out of commission. In the battles with our unit, the Germans lost about 9,000 soldiers, nearly one full division.

Right from the outset, our unit consisted of men from various nationalities. Its thirteen organizers included Russians, Ukrainians, Byelorussians, and Jews.

Ilya Shaklovsky

Ilya was one of the most resourseful fighters of our unit. Though not young, he was extremely daring. That is why he was soon to be appointed commissar of the Schoras company.

Once, when we were in the woods of Tobichi in the district of Chernigov, Shaklovsky came up to me and said: "May I have your permission, Michael Gordieyvich, to attack the village of Gleibovo? According to the information brought by my patrol units, a number of prisoners of war have been sent out there, and we hae got to release them. In the course of this operation

-14-

I'll take from the German horses, cows, and provisions. Much of what the Germans have commandeered may be found in the village of Gleibovo."

I looked with wonder at Shaklovsky. In Gleibovo there was a ranch full of armed Nazis. In order to reach it, one had to cross the Chernigov-Gomel road. The Germans guarded this traffic artery with reinforced units so that it would not be vulnerable to partisan attacks.

"Are you mad, Ilya?" I asked.

Without batting an eyelash, Shaklovsky started lecturing me on his plan for the attack on Gleibovo. He had thought the plan through; before he asked for my permission, he had worked out all the details of the attack with his chief of staff, Alexeyev.

"With a company of sixty men," said Shaklovsky, "I'll cross the road under cover of darkness, when the German, may he cough out his soul, is fast asleep. As to the way back, we will fly on wings of eagles, on the horses we shall take from the Germans, who will have no time to know what is going on around them."

As the plan of the attack has been worked out by Shaklovsky down to its smallest details, there was nothing left for me but to agree to its implementation.

"Well, go on," I said. As a matter of fact, I was afraid for his life.

That evening, a group of fighters set out under Shaklovksy's command. The night passed. At dawn my worries mounted. Shaklovsky had promised to send me word about the situation at the end of the operation. Nothing had been heard from him so far. Out of sheer anxiety I sent out a group of patrols, but they returned to the camp without having found anything new. In the end, toward evening, news came from Shaklovsky: "Everything is okay!" He himself arrived soon afterwards together with his company. His fighters were mounted on horses. They brought along with them about one hundred horses. They also brought a sizable supply of provisions, followed by a herd of cattle.

Shaklovsky was shivering with cold. I poured him a glass of vodka. He calmed down and told me in detail all about the raid. In order to reach the road, they had to go through the village of Bolshoi Listveyin, about one kilometer and a half from the regional center of Topichaiveh where a garrison of 250 German soldiers was stationed. In the village of Bolshoi Listveyin itself, there was a police company of thirty to forty men. Shaklovsky, at the head of his men, routed the police unit, cut off the telephone and telegraph lines leading to Topichaeiveh, and destroyed a storehouse full of provisions. The company then hurried back across the road and broke into Gleibovo at midnight, quietly dispatching the armed guards.

Once in Gleibovo, Shaklovsky stormed the house which served as the living quarters of the chief of the police and the German majordomo, a man by the name of Kostiok. The chief of the police was killed on the spot, and the talk with the handcuffed majordomo was cool and easy. He pointed out the houses occupied by the German soldiers. The first thing we did was to release the prisoners of war, and they immediately joined us in our operation.

At dawn, Shaklovksy's company left Gleibovo with wagons full of provisions, and a herd of cattle. "The whole thing went as I told you it would," Ilya concluded. "We came back galloping on the German horses. As you see, we rode fast."

I kept silent. Together with Shaklovsky we began looking into the booty. There were many horse-drawn wagons, like a big Ukrainian marketplace. In one of the wagons sat two women and their children.

"What's this?" I asked. "You know all too well that we do not include in the company women and their kids!"

"I couldn't do otherwise," answered Shaklovsky. "I had to bring them along."

It turned out that they could not leave the women by themselves. One of them was the wife of a commander in the Red Army; the other a chemical engineer, Maria Gordon. Both had children. All the time we stayed at Gleibovo we did not know that Maria Gordon was a Jewess. It might be interesting to see how Shaklovsky came to know about it. Before the company left the village, Shaklovsky ordered that Kostick, the local German majordomo, be executed. All of a sudden, both women came running to him. One of them said that she was a Jewess and that Kostiok had known about her and had hidden her. She also said that he had treated the Russian prisoners well.

Shaklovsky checked up on what Maria Gordon told him and found it to be true. Whereupon he not only waived his order to put Kostiok to death, but also ordered him to destroy all German possessions in the neighboring village, to release the prisoners of war, and to bring them along to the Schoras partisan company. Kostiok carried out the order.

Once Shaklovsky heard that a ship was to leave Kiev and sail out on the Dneper to Chernovil. As usual, he came to me with a carefully worked out plan to attack the ship.

"You see, this is their first ship," he said. "All this time the Germans have been hesitating about sailing on the Dneper. Now they've finally decided to do it. I'd like to make it clear to them that this time the risk involved is not worth it to those who call the cards. Grant me permission to do it. Come on, be a friend. I'll be back before you can bat an eyelash ...."

Once again this business of not having time to bat an eye. I decided to joke a little myself and asked, "Are you returning on that ship?" "What for?" he replied seriously. "I'll destroy it."

Shaklovsky did not succeed in destroying the ship, for it was armored. As usual, Ilya had taken with him a rather small company, about sixty partisans. Under cover of darkness the company came close to the Dneper and dug in quietly. In the morning the ship appeared. When it approached the line where Shaklovsky's men had dug in, he gave the order "Fire!" The partisans opened up with machine guns and antitank guns. The Germans had been eating breakfast peacefully, without any thought of an imminent attack. It is impossible to describe the shock they experienced when Shaklovsky let them have it with all the weaponry at his disposal. In this operation scores of Germans were killed, and the ship turned around and scuttled back to the shore it had sailed from. Much to our regret, it succeeded in escaping the blows of our shells.

On the right-hand shore of the Dneper, a group of Germans stood guard over a storehouse. We succeeded in wiping out the guards and blowing up the storehouse. Courage and self-sacrifice were the characteristics of Shaklovsky's exploits as company commander. These qualities stood out particularly in times of crisis. For instance, in the battles against the Germans on the river Teterev, in the district of Kiev, Shaklovsky was cut off from his battalion and surrounded by Germans. He was outnumbered, yet he broke through the German encirlement. He struck at the enemy effectively by ambushing them in places they never thought of. In the districts of Chernigov and Zhitomir, he wiped out several armed enemy columns in this manner. He was particularly successful in destroying hundreds of German vehicles on the roads leading to Chernobil and Dovliatti-Avrotsh.

I have recounted some of the exploits of the company whose commissar was Ilya Shaklovsky. He carried out many operations. In all of them, he was a daring, courageous man.

Isaac Sosnovsky

In Korofa, in the district of Chernigov, lived a Jewish cobbler who was the father of a large family. In the next village, his fifteen-year-old son tended the sheep and goats of the kolkhoz. Every morning at the first light, the boy took the livestock out to pasture, despite the unease that was being felt on account of the Germans' approach to Korofa. Once, on his way back home, he met an old woman who advised him to run away, never to come back to Korofa. "The Germans have wiped out your entire family, and they will kill you, too." The boy turned to the woods. At home, only death was waiting for him. He wanted to live. But one could live only by struggling against the murderers, shoulder to shoulder with the "men of the forest", the partisans, of whom the boy had heard. For a long time he wandered about in the woods, looking for those men, seeking shelter in the accommodating trees by day. He had no fear of animals --he had learned to fear only the two-legged creatures who swaggered around in dark blue overcoats.

He spent many nights searching for "the men of the forest," only to be found in the end by one of our patrols. The men called him Isaac Sosnovsky. He was emaciated and exhausted. They thought it only fitting to let him work on the transports, but he would not hear of it.

"I didn't come to you to save my skin," Sosnovsky asserted firmly. "I want to strike at the Germans."

They had no alternative but to put a rifle in his hands. In April 1943 his company was camping in the woods of Yelin. It was getting ready to cross the river Snob while fighting it out with the Germans. The latter were making all the necessary preparations to encircle us and, for this purpose, had brought considerable forces into the region. In order to check the German advance along the axis of the Torya-Tichobichi line, we stationed at Ivankovka a company made up of thirty fighters. Among them was the boy Isaac Sosnovsky.

On April 12 my brother Ivan Grodiev Kroglienko-Salai set out for the village of Ivankovka to see how the company was deployed. At the same time, about 500 Germans mounted an attack on the village. Under the command of Kroglienko-Salai, our fighters, highly outnumbered, engaged the enemy in a desperate battle. The Germans opened up with deadly fire from machine guns and mine throwers. The entire village was set afire. That was the first battle the boy had ever seen, but he acquitted himself as a hero. Not far from that spot there was a bridge, and Sosnovsky, together with the fighter Selekhov, was entrusted with the task of blowing it up. At the risk of their lives, they succeeded in carrying out their difficult mission, and by so doing they checked the advance of the German invaders.

The fight went on. Isaac Sosnovsky was now put in charge of defending the command post. An enemy mine hit the post, killing two partisans and seriously wounding Kroglienko-Salai. Sosnovsky evacuated the chief of staff from the battlefield: on his way back he kept up the fight until the partisan group he belonged to succeeded in rolling back the enemy in this sector of the battlefield too. In their attack on Ivankovka, eighty Germans were killed...some sixty wounded. Eventually they had to withdraw. While committing atrocities, they mounted another attack on our men with new reinforcements with a view to encircling our company and forcing it back to the river Snob. Under these conditions we had to fall back.

We went through marshlands, floundering and often sinking into the treacherous water. The Germans guessed that we were heading for the river, so they brought tanks and machine guns to the shore, and on seeing us, opened up with all they had. In order to divert their attention, we set up a dummy bridge near the farm of Shapchenko and under cover of darkness began to cross the river near the village of Kirilovka. We had gone eight kilometers into the water when it began to get light. I ordered the main forces to move away toward the forest and, together with a small group of fighters, we went back to retrieve the field gun which had sunk into the water. It took us a long time. Our repeated efforts eventually succeeded in saving the gun. By then I did not know in what direction our main forces had gone and where they had camped. German soldiers and policemen roamed that vast forest. All of a sudden I saw a horseman galloping at a terrific speed. It was Isaac Sosnovsky. Having been anxious about my prolonged absence, Commissar Nagriev had sent him to search for us. We followed Sosnovsky and before long were with the company again. When the Germans learned of our having broken out of their grip, they began chasing us, but by then, it was too late.

After a long night trek, we finally reached the woods of Zlini in the region of Bryansk.

Following that episode, Isaac was made a scout, and what a scout at that! In the forest of Kossiev we were again surrounded by the Germans. For two long days we warded off their attacks, but we could not break through the ring they threw around us. It was necessary to feel our way about; we sent Isaac Sosnovsky, together with comrades Koshiliev and Chernisheyev, to the village of Kossay, where we believed the major forces of the enemy were stationed. The daring scouts went right into the lion's mouth, obtained the necessary information, and came back safely to us.

At the village of Alexandrovichi, four of our scouts encoutered a company of German soldiers who had two armored car with them. Our scouts flattened themselves to the ground and opened fire. The exchange of fire went on for over an hour. Two scouts, Sosnovsky and Wissotzky, crawled up to the armored cars and tossed hand grenades into them. One car blew up, and Wissotzky was seriously injured. Isaac managed to help him; for 400 meters, he crawled doggedly with this wounded comrade on his shoulders until they were both safe from enemy fire.

Once at the village of Golobichi, when three partisans -- Sosnovsky, Koshiliev and Damados -- were on their way back from a reconnaissance mission, a company of Magyars (Hungarian Nazis) came into the village at the same time. Our scouts wore police uniforms, and the Magyars, without suspecting them to be partisans, started calling out to them: "Pan, Pan, come here." Sosnovsky and his comrades went up to them and, at point blank range, opened up with their automatic weapons. Six Magyars were killed on the spot, and the rest beat a hasty retreat.

Whenever I looked at Isaac Sosnovsky or listened to his reports, I always saw before my mind's eye that tortured boy who had come to us in order to strike at the Germans. To tell the truth, I never thought at the time that Isaac would become a real partisan and an outstanding scout. In our unit, he grew up and gathered strength. Three medals were awarded to Sosnovsky -- the man, not the emaciated boy: a brave young man, a robust, gifted scout, a fearless avenger.

"Major"

It started out as a joke, when someone called Isaac Meitin of the quartermaster service "Major." Then it went on all the time -- "Major," "Major." People even began to forget his surname. As for the partisans who kept joining our unit, they did not know that he had any other name.

"Major" was my assistant in the equipment and materials department. He was fifty-two when he joined the partisans. As a matter of fact, he had first been a partisan in the civil war in the Ukraine, but when he heard during the "war of the fatherland," that I was in charge of a partisan sabotage group, he came to me with the request that I "make him a saboteur." "How would that be possible, when you're doing responsible work now?" I chided. "Well, you're right! But as a partisan, I'd like to be an ordinary man," he said.

I thought about the matter for some time and then decided to put him in charge of supplies. At first the major was offended, but he realized that a partisan in charge of supplies and services is not just a caterer.

In the woods of Yelin we were short of provisions. The neighboring villagers were considered partisan

-21-

sympathizers, so we did not want to take any provisions from them. Major suggested that for this purpose we should go to the distant villages. "We've got to live off the police and the traitors," he said, "and there are many of them in the region of Korofa. May I have your permission, Michael Gordievich, to go to these places?"

As a matter of fact, I hesitated to give the major permission to go on. It involved great danger. But later on he succeeded in presenting strong arguments for his case, and I agreed. Of course he gave me his word to be careful. Thus he eventually set forth in the company of twenty partisans, all armed with automatic weapons. Now you can imagine the extent of my anxiety when on the following day, one our patrols brought me the news that in the vicinity of Korofa a partisan group had been wiped out. Thus, it would seem, we had lost the major. I waited, angry at myself for having agreed to let him go on such a dangerous mission. I sent scouts out to search for the missing men all over the surrounding area. One hour followed the other. One day followed another. On the morning of the fifth day, I could not believe at first what I saw. There, in front on me, was the major, sitting in a covered wagon drawn by three horses and behind him a long line of horses, cows, pigs, and even prisoners. The major reported: "I've brought eight wagons full of provisions, plus horses, three cows, and two pigs. We're a little late in coming back, for we did some baking on the way, since we were short of bread and it takes time to build a new bakery. That's why we did what we did."

With great relief and joy, I poured him a large glass of vodka, but the major refused to drink. "How can an old man drink vodka?!"

In the evening the major gave us a detailed account of the raid: At the village of Tichonovichi, his provisions company chanced upon two peasants of that area, who knew well the roads leading to Korofa. During the night they reached the village, disarmed the policemen and killed them, took provisions, horses, cows, pigs, and even baked some bread.

The partisans left the village in the morning by another road. At a distance they saw a company of Magyars (Hungarian S.S. units). The major had enough time to hide the wagons. He left three partisans to guard them and he himself, together with the rest of the partisans, lay in ambush.

When the Magyars came within effective firing range, the major's company opened fire. Four enemy horsemen flew up from their horses, and the others ran away.

Another encounter with the police took place not far from the village of Tikhoya. Some of the policemen were killed and the others escaped. In a third clash, in the village of Antipovka, the major suddenly came upon a German garrison. He could not withdraw, and it was impossible to wait. So the men decided to fight their way through the village. That took about an hour and a half. The German garrison was partly defeated, and the major took twelve soldiers prisoner. Incidentally, they were our first prisoners.

In the partisan unit itself, the major was on excellent terms with Karamazin. This friendship started on a "productive basis." Karamazin was our sausage man, and the major wanted to feed the men properly. Often they would both go out to fetch food in the wagon hitched to the three horses. For this purpose they sometimes went to the Niezin Woods region. Those were hard times, as we had just broken out of an enemy encirclement and did not have anything with which to feed the men. The little supply of food at our disposal we had to throw away in that operation. When the major and Karamazin entered the village, the Germans started firing at them from an armored train. What to do? The partisans were hungry, and the major could not reconcile himself to that fact. Paying no attention to the shells bursting around them, the two friends began to gather provisions. They were inside the house of a farmer when they heard someone cry out: "Run for your lives, the Germans are in the vegetable patch!"

The two came out of the house, jumped onto their provisons-laden wagon, and beat a hasty retreat to their base, firing back at the Germans.

This was our "Major", the man of the supply service.

Naomov

A resident of Koriokovsky, former surveyor Naomov was in command of our sabotage group. His large family -- his wife, two sons, two sisters, father, and grandmother -- had been shot by the Germans. Actually, he had been among those taken out to be put to death, but fortunately the enemy bullets had missed him -- they "spared" him. Naomov was pushed to the ground by the falling bodies of those shot beside him. He fell and for several hours lay under the corpses of his close relatives. Some time later he succeeded in getting out of his blood-curdling "hiding" place. He looked for the partisans for a long time, and eventually reached us.

The sabotage group also included Levin, Moroz, and Maurosia, nicknamed "Pievouchia" on account of her lilting voice.

Our saboteurs set forth at once in the direction of the railway tracks connecting Bakhmach with Kiev, with the intention of blowing up an enemy transport. They were not lucky this time. During the night they laid mines on the tracks, only to have those mines removed by the Germans the next day. This laying of mines by our men and their removal by the Germans afterwards was repeated a number of times.

What were we to do now? The saboteurs held a "council of war." There were several options. Naomov proposed going back to camp. Maurosia was of the same opinion. But Levin and Moroz were firmly opposed: to return to camp without having achieved anything -- that was a sign of weakness. Naomov held to his opinion: "We didn't succeed this time, but we'll make it later. We cannot stay forever in this damned place."

"Not forever, only until we wipe out a German transport," Levin kept on repeating. "We'll be the laughing stock of the whole camp. They'll say 'There go "good-for-nothing" saboteurs.'"

This argument convinced Naomov. Once more the partisans laid mines, now on two railway tracks, and pulled back to hide on the far side of a hill overlooking the spot. They crouched there waiting, shivering with excitement. Then, like music at a boisterous party, the sound of chugging, so much cherished and awaited, came to their ears. It grew

louder and louder. The men held their breath.
Suddenly came the expected, earsplitting explosion. At
the same time, another train was approaching from the
opposite direction. This one hit the other set of
mines.

In one operation, two transports were wiped out.

It is easy to understand the great joy felt by the
sabotage group upon returning to the camp.

Alexander Kamyensky

As a boy, he had already taken part in the civil
war.[2] In the course of my frequent meetings with
Kamyensky, who was to become one of the important
figures in the country's economy, I had the impression
that he had forgotten about his own clashes in the past
with the "Whites" and the "Greens" in the Ukraine.
However, in the early days of the great war of the
fatherland, who should drop in on me but my old friend,
a man with gray hair. With his first words he tried to
convince me that both of us had to join the partisan
fight behind enemy lines.

"And what about your factory?" I asked Kamyensky.
"After all, you are its manager!"

"Down at the plant, they can manage without me,"
replied Alexander. "You see, Michael Gordievich, who
but us, who took part in the civil war, should be first
among the partisans?"

I remember quite well how Alexander Kamyensky
started on his way as a partisan. At the village of
Breitsh, there was a Magyar garrison at the time.
According to the information we had, the garrison numbered about one hundred men. It stood in our way to
the other shore of the river Snob. Consequently, we
had to strike at it.

One night, Alexander Kamyensky went out to the
village of Breitsh accompanied by thirty fighters. He
had decided to storm his way into the village from the
direction of the river, taking advantage of the hard
ice. But as it was the end of March, the ice had
thawed close to the shores. Kamyensky fetched a board,
put one end of it on the shore and the other on the
edge of the ice. After a few paces on the board, the

-25-

ice went under and Kamyensky and his men sank in icy water. But they managed to outflank the village, and wet and shivering with cold, got on the shore once again. The Magyars were asleep in the schoolhouse. The partisans surrounded the place and opened fire. Having been taken by surprise, the Magyars escaped, many in their pants. Eighteen Magyars were killed and twelve taken prisoner. The partisans burned down the enemy command and took a great quantity of arms. As time went on, Kamyensky's company became bigger and bigger, having been joined by some twenty peasants. He himself was a modest, righteous man, of a quiet nature, but daring and courageous. In the vicinity of Zlinka he destroyed seven police stations, and only afterwards requested me to put him in command of the company.

"I won't be a bad commander!" he said in his simple and direct manner.

Actually, Kamyensky was an excellent commander of his company, which was named after Stalin. One day I received an urgent order to cross over to the right-hand shore of the river Desna. The order came late in the night of September 9, 1943. Time was at a premium, so we decided to start moving early in the morning. On September 10, we began crossing the Desna. First to cross over with him company was Alexander Kamyensky. His men had succeeded in setting up some defensive positions when all of a sudden, as if they had been watching us all this time, German horsemen appeared from the nearby forest. The other companies were still on the left-hand shore of the Desna, and we could do nothing to help Kamyensky and his company. We sat there, clenching our fists and watching the battle.

It was a terrible sight. The German horsemen attacked Kamyensky's company at a fast gallop. We heard all too clearly the automatic rifles and machine guns of the Germans. From that distance we watched as Kamyensky's company held its breath in the face of approaching death. But Kamyensky warded it off just at the last moment, with the firm hand of a competent and experienced commander. He let the Germans come close so as to open up with lethal fire. For a few long minutes it was impossible to tell the outcome of the battle, but suddenly we realized that the German horsemen had fallen back. The crossing of the whole unit over the river Desna went on without a hitch, with not a single casualty to our forces.

Alexander Kamyensky always knew how to find the right men. It was thus that he found one by the name of Arteim, who helped the unit cross the Desna. At the Dneper, too, he hit upon a peasant by the name of Mikyenko, who was to help us in our hour of need. The Dneper, this vast body of water, held a surprise for us. It was so wide, we could not see the opposite shore. Feeling dejected, I stood by the water and stared ahead. Alexander and his Mikyenko came up to me. We met one another. Sensing my low spirits, Mikyenko turned to me and asked, "Why are you so sad, Commander?"

"How can one manage not to be down in the mouth on seeing this wide Dneper? Even a sparrow cannot cross safely to the opposite shore."

Obviously Mikyenko was not of the same opinion. He scratched his head, narrowed his eyes cunningly, and said, "Don't worry, Commander. By the first light of day, we'll all be on the opposite shore. We have our "major" with us, Isaac Meitin."

The major's first concern was how to move our provisions and cows. He went over to Mikyenko, spoke with him excitedly about his "cargo," and began to count the horses, cows, horsemen, and wagons.

"My cows will be lost," said Meitin in a sad voice. "They won't be able to cross the Dneper." To him came Mikyenko's reply, with that same narrowing of the eyes:

"Don't worry. By the first light of the morning, we shall all be over there."

Our guide made only one mistake: the date of the crossing. At dawn, enemy planes appeared and started to bomb us. They kept at it all day without letup. The major, with all his cargo, could not cross over. He had to spend the day in the forest. Mikyenko stayed by him and under cover of darkness helped him cross the river with all his earthly goods.

The partisans in the company under Alexander Kamyensky were on friendly relations with each other. As a matter of fact, similar friendly relations characterized our whole unit. The reason for that was to be found in the warmth and cordiality which characterized the relations of the partisans among themselves. The sense of brotherhood existing between Alexander Kamyensky and his chief of staff, Konstantin Kossyenko, was a model for all the partisans to follow. I know of occasions where one saved the other at the risk of his own life.

IN THE STRUGGLE FOR SOVIET LATVIA

Ottomar Oskalin
Hero of the Soviet Union, Former Commissar
in a Latvian Partisan Brigade

Our partisan company was called "For Soviet Latvia." Its origins were in White Russia, where it numbered only a few fighters. Later, when it moved north to Latvia, it soon grew into "The Latvian Partisan Brigade." It was then under the command of Wilhelm Levin. I was its commissar.

This brigade included many Jewish fighters, both soldiers and officers, who with heroism and courage fought side by side with us to save the country from the fascist yoke. I shall now proceed to tell you something about a number of them.

Raphael Blum

Blum was the commissar of the second company and, some time later, the commissar of the expanded partisan brigade. Comrade Blum, "The Bespectacled Politruk," as he was called by the partisans, played a guiding role in our life and struggle. He was a young man with a technical education, a gifted newsman, and a singer. When the war broke out, he volunteered for the Red Army. Later the Komsomol[3] center in Latvia sent him over to our brigade for political orientation.

Upon arriving at the partisan camp, Blum took a rifle in his hand, and his personal example whipped up the people's enthusiasm in their struggle against the Nazis. On the most dangerous missions, you could see from a distance his tall body, which stood out even among us Latvians who are well known for our height. He was always to be found in the first rows of the fighters, never flinching in the face of whining

bullets. This naturally brought him love and popu-
larity among the partisans.

"I've grown so used to bullets," he would say with
a boyish smile, "that I carry forever a bullet in my
shoulder. Even a scalpel could not separate us from
each other."

This "token" (the bullet) Blum had received upon
crossing the Latvian border along with ten other partisans, in the direction of the Lyubian forests. They
kept marching on for eleven days and nights, making
special use of the protective cover of darkness. On
that memorable march, they occasionally came face-to-
face with Germans as well as Latvian Fascists.[4] But
the group always succeeded in storming its way through
the enemy forces and established friendly relations
with the peasants of the Lyuban district. Blum was an
oft-invited guest at the villagers' celebrations, where
he was received with unmitigated pleasure on account of
his wonderful voice and vivacious personality. In this
manner he succeeded in finding his way to the hearts of
the village youth, and thus we were able to obtain the
information we needed for our struggle. These youths
were ready to come along with us through thick and
thin. When a battle was going on, Blum would sprint
from one fighter to another, encouraging this one with
a joke and showing the other how to take deadly aim.

"You've got to know," he would say, "that every
partisan bullet is a digit in our account with the
Germans. Each figure has to be put in the right place,
like a digit set down by a competent bookkeeper. And
the more accurate our digits, the greater the sum total
will grow in the final reckoning."

The brigade commander and his colleagues had a
great appreciation for the exploits of Blum. He himself was very modest. Whenever there was talk about a
new heroic deed of his, he would put a stop to it with
the following retort:

"As a matter of fact I thought fighting would be
much more difficult, but it turned out to be easy. I
often wonder whether I haven't been born for just this
sort of thing: to be a partisan and to settle the
account with the fascists."

Blum had good reason to take revenge. Once, while
sitting around talking of various things, Blum suddenly

picked up a pencil and started adding up all the catastrophes he had gone through on account of the Hitlerite tyrants. His father, his stepmother, (and the best of stepmothers at that), a sister, a brother, two female cousins, and a number of distant relatives ... "We had all lived on such friendly terms with each other ... and they have wiped out such a family."

Here is a characteristic feature of Blum's altruism. When the partisans were being inoculated against typhus and there wasn't enough vaccine to go around, he stepped aside in favor of the other partisans. Eventually, Blum himself came down with typhus fever and was about to die. But his immense desire to live tided him over the danger, and he came back to our lines, fresh and vigorous again.

Toward the end of July 1944, we began to hear the artillery of the advancing Red Army; we had been looking forward to them for so long. Blum went out with a group of partisans and drove back the Germans and their collaborators from the region of Bayersville, then put up red flags in every corner. The Red Army forces which reached this region a few days later found it clean of enemy forces.

This is only a brief outline of Raphael Blum's life. When you watched his behavior under fire, you could see that he was a born fighter, a well-tempered soldier, who had spent all his life in carnage and incessant fighting. But that is how he looked in the midst of fighting. When relaxed, he was a young man full of the joy of life, good-natured and sharp-witted, with a touch of romanticism.

For his achievements he was awarded the order of "War of the Fatherland, First Class," the "Partisan Decoration, First Class," and the decoration "For Victory over Germany."

After the war he returned to his former occupation, exchanging his rifle for a writer's pen and becoming the editor of a Latvian paper called "Soviet Youth." As editor, he worked as tirelessly as he had done in his partisan years, which he considered the highlight of his life.

Leib Kassel

I would like to tell you about another outstanding partisan in our brigade, the chief of staff of the Third Company, Leib Kassel, who was nicknamed "The Landlord of Zhigori."

Kassel really earned this nickname. He virtually held in his young hands the entire region of Zhigori, a vast, vital and strategic area in Latvia. The name "Zhigori" became well known to the Nazis, connoting railroad derailment, blowing up of bridges, and incessant ambushes.

Until the outbreak of the war, this young man, a Komsomol member, had worked in a weaving factory. When the Germans occupied Riga (the capital of Latvia), he was among the last residents to leave the city. Together with a group of young workers, he traveled through Latvia and Estonia, up to Leningrad. After the Latvian Division had been organized, Kassel joined it as a volunteer and took part in all its battles. Twice wounded, he later went over to the company of Latvian partisans.

Seven times a plane carrying Kassel and his six partisan comrades attempted to land in the district of Abrien in Latgalia, only to return without landing. The Germans had learned to recognize its distinguishing signs. On the eighth attempt they succeeded in landing, but the partisan group that Kassel was to join had in the meantime been beaten. Thus, the partisans found themselves in unknown territory; they were strangers to both the place and the people. But partisans usually do not lose their head; they dispersed at various points in the district and began to fulfill their mission unaided.

Leib Kassel arrived in Zhigori and started operating with great enthusiasm. He had a highly variegated task: to prepare the local population for the expected arrival of the Red Army, to activate the peasants toward the ultimate struggle with the German invaders, to draw the inhabitants toward joint action with the partisans, and to organize the security forces.

"I look back with satisfaction on those days," Kassel once told me. "They were good days. They taught me to hate the enemy from the depths of my soul and to develop a strong love for the Jews. They enriched my knowledge of nature and of life. I had spent all my former days in a town and could not distinguish between a pine and a birch. As a partisan I learned, like an animal, to recognize tracks in the marshes or in the grass; to determine the nature of sounds coming from a distance, to crawl like a snake, and to run like an antelope." Kassel would not take pleasure in speaking about himself. He was a modest man. But the distinguished orders of "The Red Flag," "The Partisan Decoration," and "For Victory over Germany" pinned to the chest of this man proclaim his exploits. One of these exploits may be related here as a case in point:

It happened near Kachanovo late one May night in 1944. Kassel and a group of fighters had come on a visit to this village, which was the administrative center for the region. They decorated the entire village with red flags. The enraged Germans mobilized one full division to wipe out the company, some 12,000 soldiers against 100 partisans! Kassel did not think much of that. He knew the woods around this region like the palm of his hand. He spread out his partisans behind tree trunks over an area of one square kilometer with the order to open fire on every fascist they saw. The Germans began to move shakily in the forest, step by step, thinking it to be full of partisans. Kassel's fighters shot the enemy soldiers one after the other, at the same time outflanking the enemy and appearing at his rear. In this way a great many Germans fell without a single loss to the partisans. The Germans, with their overwhelming numbers, took to their heels. The operation was carried out with remarkable skill, and it will live long in the annals of our partisan struggle as an example of matchless bravery and remarkable tactics.

In his exploits in the woods, Kassel, in the company of his fighters, would call at villages which had been scenes of the outrages of the Germans and their Latvian collaborators. In the course of such "visits," the partisans would attack police stations or the administrative quarters of the districts. They would release prisoners destined for hard labor camps and hold court-martials for the traitors of the people. Once, when Kassel and a group of partisans were holding a court-martial of this kind against Kolak, a traitor, a large unit of German gendarmes came into the village. The partisans did not lose their head; while their comrades, who stood guard at the outskirts of the village, fought it out with the Germans, the court-martial went on according to partisan protocol. However, when news came that the guards were incapable of keeping their ground much longer, Kassel ordered his men to shoot the traitor and leave the village.

As already mentioned, Kassel knew how to organize his information service in the best possible manner. The peasant girls would put at a predetermined spot, packages of cheese, butter, and eggs, with messages attached to them. For their part, the peasants brought along potatoes and, in separate sacks, maps of the surrounding area. The shepherds would bring along packs of German printed material, together with SS printed material, and receive from Kassel leaflets for distribution among the local population. Thanks to such organization, Kassel knew all about what was going on around him. He would systematicaly send this infor-mation to Moscow, three times a day, to central Army headquarters and usually within three or four hours after receiving his information, the high command would send in planes to bomb the places and the factories he had marked out for them.

On several occasions, Kassel went deep into the rear lines of the enemy. Once he even reached Riga, dressed as a German officer, in order to establish con-tact with the people of the ghetto, among whom was his own father. When Kassel approached the city, one of the guards recognized him, but before the soldier could do anything, he shot the fascist dead and jumped onto a car that came along. He immediately put his gun to the temple of the driver and streaked out of danger ....

Sasha Gurari

"Assoufi" was the nickname of the Jewish boy Sasha Gurari in our brigade. The story of his life is a multi-colored account. In the early days of the war, the ship in which he was sailing after he had left Leningrad hit a German mine and sank. The waves carried Gurari to the island of Dago in the Bay of Riga. There, the Germans arrested him and put him in a POW camp. Sasha told the Germans that he had been born in the Ukraine, thus saving himself from a quick death. For two long years he suffered in this camp, and in August 1943, he eventually succeeded in escaping.

Our reconnaissance men came upon him one summer night when he was asleep in the field. Before long this boy, with such dreamy, tender features and short stature, had turned into a fearless fighter; he fought like a lion.

Once Gurari, with the commander of our group and a number of partisans, went out on a mission to wipe out a gang of SS. The mission was carried out properly, but it cost us many casualties; out of the entire company, only the commander the Gurari remained alive. Since Gurari's wounds were superficial, he carried the commander on his shoulders, took him up into an attic he found along the way, and dressed both the commander's wounds and his own; they both stayed there for the night. In the morning, our reconnaissance men found them and brought them back to our camp.

I remember another incident which is so characteristic of Gurari's ties of friendship. In one of the battles against a strong group of SS, Partisan Istomir, a close friend of Gurari's, was wounded. Gurari went on fighting with his usual fierceness and courage. When the fighting ended and the Esesarges had run away, we did not find Gurari among us and were greatly concerned for his life, thinking that he had been killed. While searching for his body, we heard some firing in the area, and a few minutes later saw Gurari running in our direction from the woods holding a smoking rifle in one hand and a ... cap full of strawberries in the other!

"It wasn't easy bringing back my strawberries from those mongrels," he said, breathing heavily, his eyes looking for his wounded friend. Then he went over to Istomir and started feeding him the fruit he was holding in his hand. Istomir looked at Gurari with a deep sense of gratitude and apparently felt better. Gurari was so pleased, so moved, that he started dancing around.

"That's it! I knew that all you needed was strawberries."

Sasha Gurari was a colorful personality in our company. He was very particular about his clothes and walked around in highly polished boots. He even washed with scented soap, which he knew how to come by under any circumstances. He had a strong liking for Ukrainian folk songs, as well as sports and wrestling.

His skills in sports helped him in his hand-to-hand fighting with the fascist enemy. Like a panther, he would dash at his prey. In one battle, against a punishment squad, Gurari accounted for eleven German soldiers and saved the company from encirclement.

During his career as a partisan, Gurari was wounded three times, but he never stopped fighting. For his achievements in battle, he was awarded the order of "The War of the Fatherland, Second Class."

Zina

Gusta Jacobson, or "Nurse Zina" as she was called in our company, was liked by all. She was a medical nurse, but when necessary she picked up a rifle and fought shoulder-to-shoulder with her comrades.

This fragile young woman adapted with unusual ease to the difficult conditions of the partisans and their struggle. I often had occasion to see her in battle. She was a fearless young woman, cool and hardy. She would evacuate the wounded under a hail of bullets, and many partisans owe her their lives.

I well remember one particular incident: in the midst of a battle, our machine gun stopped firing. We had counted heavily on that machine gun. Zina told us that she would try to find out what was the matter. It turned out that the machine gunner had been seriously wounded. She bandaged his wounds, replaced him behind the machine gun, and resumed the firing until she herself was replaced by another partisan. Such was "Nurse Zina" in battle.

While the men were resting, Zina would often think up all sorts of entertainment for the company. Before the war she was a scout instructress and knew a lot of games, songs, and legends. At present, she is working at the Komsomol youth center in Riga, and you can often meet her there, along with several elderly bearded men who sit there with her for hours. Such visitors usually make one wonder, since they do not look like Komsomol members at all. But "Nurse Zina," who is now once again Gusta Jacobson, tells the inquirers:

"These are my partisan friends, the dearest men of all ...."

Gregory Garchik

In the pageant of Jewish partisan fighters in the Riga region, one particular commander stands out in my memory: "The Black Bandit with the Golden Teeth," as he was called by the Germans. He was known far and wide as a fearless partisan, and the Germans put up an award of forty liters of vodka for catching him alive! Such a prize meant a great deal in those days. Not many people could whip up enthusiasm to catch him, even for such a reward, for it was impossible to catch him anyway. Garchik was an expert at lightning-speed, hit-and-run raids. He had an uncanny sense of orientation and was adept at disguise.

Thanks to this latter skill, he often succeeded in getting far behind enemy lines. Once we were surprised to find an officer wearing a German uniform in our camp. The partisans could not understand how this could happen, but were soon relieved to find that it was none other than Garchik himself.

Once, Garchik and his adjutant Stanislav put on SS clothes and went about as ordinary citizens. On their way, they saw two German officers, dressed as hunters, coming out of a car. Garchik and Stanislav went up to them and engaged them in conversation. A few moments later the two men had shot and killed what turned out to be a German general and his adjutant.

Here is another incident. A reconnaissance man brought the news that some 350 Germans and two armored vehicles had come into the village next to the forest where Garchik and his soldiers were stationed, in order to collect bread and cattle. Garchik's company had only fifty fighters and could not engage the enemy in open battle. They hid on the outskirts of the forest; when the Germans came out of the village loaded with provisions and leading a large herd of cows they had taken from the peasants, they opened up with all the fire power at their disposal. The Germans took to their heels, some even jumped into a nearby river, leaving behind all the provisions and cows they had taken. Garchik gave back to the peasants the cows and the bread that the Germans had taken from them. This incident had a great impact on the peasants' attitude toward the partisan movement; within a short time about 600 new volunteers joined our companies.

On another occasion, Garchik and his company arrived one night at a village and thought to get some rest after a long and tiring march. At midnight, they learned that the Germans were approaching. Upon entering the village, the Germans were received with partisan fire from all directions. Most of the Germans were killed, but seventeen were taken prisoner and brought to the company field command.

Garchik was an experienced soldier. He had taken part in the battle with Finland as a commander of a skiing group. In the early days of the war he served in the Red Army, was taken prisoner, then escaped and reached a partisan company. He spent ten months fighting with us. During this period he accounted for some 60 Germans, blew up a score of enemy tanks and 400 trucks, and took about 200 prisoners. For his exploits in the partisan movement, Garchik was awarded the order of the "Red Flag."

* * * * *

In our brigade there was a young man by the name of Cohen. I forget his first name. He was born in Yelgava and worked as a diver. Being jovial and quick witted, he was soon nicknamed "Witty Cohen" by the partisans.

On a certain mission, the company to which Cohen belonged had to cover a distance of thirty kilometers. The going was tough. The men were tired from previous fighting, and they expected more. Seeing the sinking spirits of the men around him, Cohen decided to inject some life into the tired fighters. All through that seemingly endless thirty-kilometer march, he told them jokes. The partisans said later that Cohen's jokes took their minds off this dangerous and weary trek.

Cohen was not simply a merry young man. During a battle that the partisans started immediately after that long trek, Cohen killed four Germans with his own hands; this time he was not joking. To our regret, however, he himself was killed in that same battle ....

* * * * *

The six partisans I have written about here do not cover the entire list of Jewish comrades who fought in

-37-

our brigade and provided examples of courage and fearlessness. I shall forever remember the names of Ahron Khayat and Alexander Heidosa, who blew themselves up in order not to fall into the hands of the enemy; also the names of Sima Friedlander, Alexander Galperin, Bracha Kretzeir, S. Galfend, and many, many others who died heros' deaths in the fight for our Soviet fatherland. In every instance, the Jewish partisans showed they knew what they were fighting for; they were excellent comrades and fearless soldiers. In the battle against the fascist monster, they pitched in with all their spiritual strength, with all their fiery hatred for the enemy.

In conclusion, I would like to add that the Soviet government awarded me the highly coveted order -- "Hero of the Soviet Union." I proudly wear another order -- the "Golden Star": not with pride alone, but also with humility, realizing that the gold of this star has been steeped in the blood of heroic partisans. Among them, the Jewish partisans occupy a distinguished place.

IN WHITE RUSSIA

P. P. Kapusta
Major-General, Former Commander of a Partisan Unit

In July 1941, while getting my battalion out of enemy encirclement, I was seriously wounded in the leg. I could not move and had to stay behind the lines of the German forces. For two days I was hidden by the peasants of the village of Starya Falici, and then they moved me by cart to the small town of Starya Dorogny, where the doctor dressed my wound. From there I was later taken to the hospital in the city of Slotsk.

Before I was taken prisoner, I heard Stalin on the radio, calling upon the Soviet people to set up a movement of partisans to fight behind enemy lines. Thus, while at the POW camp, I began carefully, but conscientiously, to gather a group of people who thought the same way I did. We set ourselves the task of escaping from the camp and hiding in the woods, with a view to setting up a partisan company there. In the spring of 1942, our plan was put into operation. We escaped from the German camp under a hail of bullets and slipped into the woods. The roads were rugged and movement was difficult. We headed for the woods of Staritsk. We were fourteen men, including a Jew by the name of Zubariyev. In the forest of Staritsk, among the first to join us was Leib Gilchik, an inhabitant of the Kopil Region. When the Germans occupied the region, Gilchik headed for the woods in search of the partisans. His wife, a Russian, and his children stayed behind in Kopil. When the Germans heard that Gilchik had gone into the woods, they killed his wife and children.

First of all, it was necessary to get the men well armed and equipped. Zubariyev and Gilchik helped me a great deal in this task. The former proved to be a first-rate scout and the latter, an outstanding commander. Both knew well the region where we had started to operate. We had no maps, but the familiarity of both Zubariyev and Gilchik with the region filled in the gap. They knew every path in that area, including the woods. Before long, Zubariyev had brought the intelligence service to such a level that I knew what was going on over a radius of sixty kilometers. On no occasion did he lose his way in that vast region, nor was he late in delivering a message, nor did he deliver inaccurate information.

Zubariyev was very young, only twenty years old, and remarkably diligent. He knew how to acquire authority among the partisans as well as with the local population. The latter supplied him with valuable bits of information. In the beginning, when it was highly essential to acquire military equipment, the local inhabitants showed Zubariyev several places where we could find caches of arms.

Leib Gilchik was older than Zubariyev. He was born in 1907. Like Zubariyev, he was very alert, had his own way with the hearts of people, and had a friendly countenance. I entrusted Gilchik with the task of establishing contact with the inmates of the ghetto of the small town of Kopil. With the help of the ghetto's eldest man, Kogan, it was possible for Gilchik to gather the youth around him. Furthermore, he even got into the ghettos of the towns of Neizwische and Kleichek and succeeded, after meticulous preparation, in releasing thirty persons from them.

At first I thought to distribute the ghetto people among the partisan companies, but I dropped this plan

and asked Gilchik, who had a great sense of respon-
sibililty, to form a new and independent company out of
them. For its initial equipment we allotted a few
rifles, assuming that the recruits themselves would
take care of getting additional arms. For the position
of company commissar, I appointed Senior Air Force
Lieutenant Razobiyev. And so, within a short time, our
company had grown into a 140-man unit, nearly all of
them Jews. The men of the company proved that they
knew how to get more arms and proved that they could
use them too.

No longer prisoners of the Germans, we were now a
fighting company of fourteen men, heading for the
woods. All of a sudden, we were attacked by a large
group of gendarmes and policemen armed to the teeth.
They did not succeed in driving us out of the woods and
eventually retreated, sustaining heavy casualties.
Soon it was known all over the region of Slotsk that a
large partisan unit was active in the forest of
Staritsk. Volunteers began to flock to us, and by May
1942 I had become the commander of a brigade called
"Voroshikov."

We did all we could to establish contact with the
other partisan groups operating in the area. With the
help of Vassili Ivanovich Kozalov, chairman of the
Presidium of the Supreme Council of the Soviet
Socialist Republic of Byelorussia and later commander
of a partisan company, we succeeded in establishing
contact with Moscow and with the headquarters of the
Byelorussian partisan movement. Kozalov also helped us
in making the necessary arrangements for publishing
leaflets to distribute among the local population and
in organizing Komsomol groups.

In order to give my unit greater mobility, I
divided it into a number of companies, each headed by
an officer under my command. We then went on to draw
up a plan for attacking the town of Kopil. However, we
did not succeed in carrying out this plan, since the
Germans soon brought in a large force against us, with
further reinforcements sent in from time to time. My
grapevine brought me information that SS companies had
been sent over to Slotsk and Kopil in order to wipe us
out. And, indeed, on May 1, 1942, at seven in the
morning, the SS troops mounted an all-out attack on our
unit. My companies were spread out all over the region
of Slotsk. The brunt of the attack fell on two companies under the command of Gilchik and Donayev. The

outnumbered partisans engaged the attackers three times in hand-to-hand fighting. Nikolai Vassilyevich Donayev was killed in this battle, but the Germans suffered heavy losses, including more than 740 killed. They also lost three field guns, three tanks, and fourteen vehicles. Gilchik's company proved its military mettle in this battle. The task entrusted to it, of not letting the enemy get into the woods, was fulfilled.

Before long news reached us from our scouts that the Germans had received new reinforcements. In those days we were suffering from ammunition shortage, so I decided to move to another location, more suited to our struggle. We thus went to another forest near the small town of Peisochnoya. The persistent efforts of the Germans to drive us out of the woods were doomed to failure and, suffering heavy losses, they discontinued their activities against us. Our units, however, went on with their raids on German garrisons, blowing up enemy convoys and bridges and destroying factories which were engaged in war materiel production for the Hitlerite army.

By order of the "hangman" Kuba, Hitler's deputy in Byelorussia, all the police forces in this area were mobilized to strike at the "Kapusta Gang" and wipe it out. Zubariyev, director of my "grapevine," knew how to obtain the correct information in time. On December 8, 1942, at four in the afternoon, the Germans were to mount their attack upon us. I deployed my forces so that one fighting unit was sent out about two kilometers ahead of our main force. This unit would engage the enemy in battle before the time they had set for it and before they could come close to our main force.

Gilchik's men bore the full brunt of the battle. Advancing toward them were the 64th SS battalion and two police battalions. The fighting continued for a long time. The partisans stood their ground, vowing not to withdraw. They fell to the last man, having fulfilled the task they had been entrusted with. German prisoners later told us that the Hitlerites eventually wiped the group of partisans, but they could find not a single round of ammunition, or even a single rifle, indicating the partisans had fought to the last bullet. As we learned later, two partisans who had succeeded in eluding the enemy buried their partisan rifles and machine guns in the snow, then put an end to their own lives, as befits loyal Soviet patriots.

Gilchik's company was to move a distance of eighty to ninety kilometers in order to reach its objective and cross the road between Brest and Moscow, which was heavily guarded by the Germans. This march seemed to me both dangerous and difficult, so I decided to go with the men myself. Under cover of darkness we reached the railway tracks, with Gilchik and I traveling at the head of the company. Suddenly we were discovered by enemy guards. Our men took cover and we opened up with all the firepower at our disposal, killing all the guards. Our booty included a number of machine guns, hand grenades, rifles, cartridge cases, tents, all of which we took back into the forest.

* * * * *

That is the end of my reminiscences of Zubariyev, Gilchik and their company. In May 1943 I was given the task of relocating to the region of Bialystok, in order to spark partisan struggle behind enemy lines.

It was necessary to pass through numerous points in the enemy's rear line, over an area of approximately 1,000 square kilometers. We succeeded in crossing five railway tracks and twelve roads after eight battles with the enemy. On the way between Baranovich and Loninyech we destroyed an eighteen-kilometer length of railway track, blew up a number of fortified German gun emplacements, and wiped out police stations which happened to be on our way.

Upon reaching the forest of Leipeishansk, I divided the fighting force into three companies and gave each one a well-defined task. When we went through the district of Bialystok, we found hardly any Jews in the entire area; the majority of the Jewish population had been wiped out. We then went about organizing underground groups of Communist youth. There were only a few Jews who had been saved by the non-Jewish population. We received highly valuable information from the local people and passed it on to Moscow.

The Germans had terrorized the entire population. Often they would send among the people traitors and spies posing as partisans, so that we had to act with extreme care. Nevertheless, in every area we had a liaison man, a loyal citizen, who carried out all our instructions.

In conclusion, I would like to say a few words about a liaison woman, one of the best. She was a young woman, short of stature, modest, well built, who spoke German well. She was a resident of Bialystok, where she lived under a false passport and called herself Maria Ivanova Rozovskaya. Her real name was Liza Chapnik. Only two years after the German invasion, she decided to devote herself to the fight against the fascists. In order to help us in our struggle, she found work at the German command.

A brigade commander of my unit, Nikolai Witzikhovsky, received an order from me to set camp near Bialystok. He moved with great care through a forest not far from the town. Then word came that there was a trusted person in Bialystok, a young woman, who was in close contact with the local underground. That was Liza Chapnik. Witzikhovsky could thus entrust her with the task of getting the information he needed and to find among the German personnel people who would be willing to carry out our instructions. This highly complicated task was efficiently fulfilled by Liza Chapnik.

The Red Army was nearing Bialystok. The retreating Germans had reached a state of disintegration. With Chapnik's help we could find out what they did before they left the town, especially the places where they had laid mines. We got the plan in time to hand it to the Red Army commander who was approaching the town. Thanks to this information, our army also succeeded in finding military equipment and enemy storehouses.

THREE FIGHTERS OF MY UNIT

Y. Y. Melnik
Polkovnik, Former Commander of a Partisan Unit

The unit under my command was organized in the days when Sidor Kovpak, who had been fighting in the Somsk area, moved over to the woods of Bryansk. At this time it was suggested that I join Kovpak's struggle in that region, set up new partisan groups, and strike at enemy communications.

Comrade Kovpak helped me very much in organizing my unit. He put at my disposal a partisan group from his unit that had considerable experience in local fighting conditions. With the full help of this group, my first fighting units were organized: "For the Fatherland" company, "Red Partisan" company, and "Death to Fascism" company, which together numbered 300 fighters. Our base was to be in the Khinailsky Forest. The village of Lumyenko in the Lampol region turned into something like headquarters for us. It was from here that we started our struggle against the German invaders.

Not only fighting operations fell to our lot. For instance, the Hitlerites sent our skilled youth to Germany for forced labor. We took a variety of measures to prevent such practices. We would attack the Germans who accompanied them and liberate the young men, who would then join our companies. We killed the Germans without mercy, at the same time caring for the people of the districts through which we used to pass in our fight against the German hordes. Thus, we were to distribute to the local inhabitants some 10,000 tons of bread, 141 tons of sugar, thousands of head of cattle, 3,800 sheep and pigs, besides a great deal of salt, which was in great demand by the peasants.

In the beginning we worked in small groups, but before long we had grown into a large unit. As time went on, from October 25, 1942 to March 26, 1944, our unit had covered more than 6,000 kilometers. We fought the Germans on the soil of eight regions, crossed thirty-eight rivers, including the Desna, the Dneper, and the southern Bug. We also crossed forty-eight railway tracks. In the 114 battles we went through, our unit accounted for over 12,000 enemy soldiers and officers, derailed eighty-two regular trains and armored trains and shot down five enemy planes.

From these figures alone, it is possible to have an idea of the self-sacrifice, courage, and daring of all the men of my unit. In the following accounts, however, I shall speak of the exploits and heroism of only three partisans: a telegraph operator, a doctor, and a reconnaissance man.

Telegraph Operator Joseph Isakovich Mali

I had met Joseph Isakovich Mali in Stalingrad. This small, lean man was working as a telegraph operator at one of our military units. The men of this unit always spoke of him as a skilled technician. When it was decided that I fly over with a group of comrades behind enemy lines, I immediately thought of Mali and asked him directly:

"Are you ready to drop behind enemy lines?"

He answered briefly and to the point: "I am!"

Upon reaching the rear of the enemy forces, we gathered in the woods of Khinailsky. Before long, Mali had established two-way communication with Russia. He worked tirelessly, with remarkable coolness and precision. He was always alert and calm. Our unit went on expanding, and it was necessary to equip all the companies with radio transmitters. Comrade Mali took it upon himself to train telegraph operators from among the partisans. In 1942, under difficult fighting conditions in the woods, Joseph Isakovich held courses for wireless operators; and, indeed, in three months --November, December, and January -- he succeeded in giving proper training to five women operators. Some time later these operators were allocated to the companies under Naomov's command, and they were to render great service to the fighting forces in the regions of Somsk, Poltava, Kirovograd, Odessa, Vinitza and Zhitomir.

In February 1943 I received orders to move on to the district of Chernigov, north of Kiev. Mali came over with me. On the day that followed our arrival at the specified place, which was nine kilometers from Kholmi, a regional center in the region of Chernigov, my intelligence service found out that one full Magyar division was stationed in the town, while the nearby villages contained police battalions. I instructed Mali to contact Moscow in order to pass on to the Ukrainian headquarters our request for military equipment. That was a tough job. The request had to be made in such a way that the Germans would not be able to decipher it and consequently find out the spot where we expected the equipment to be dropped by parachute. For two full days, with no rest or sleep, Mali kept working on the final form of our request. In the end he found a way out, and the message was sent. Before long the planes appeared over us and dropped the military equipment we had asked for.

On our second crossing of the region of Shavtovka, we were once surrounded by large enemy forces and

-45-

forced to move into open country. Here we came under heavy German attacks; but even under these conditions, Mali worked with his usual precision. We had a number of transmitters. Mali organized work on these transmitters and regularly sent out our messages to the "Big Land" (Central HQ in Russia). While on the move in this operation, under the most difficult conditions, we lost three transmitters. Mali always kept his in excellent working condition, and we always had contact with the fatherland. In our third crossing, in October 1943, Mali was also to render us great service through his regular radio communication.

In battle or when on the move, a transmitter would go on the blink. Mali knew how to repair it in a short time. Once a transmitter component broke and communication stopped. Using the transmitter of a nearby company, Mali devised a new part. Contact was established once again in the camp. On another occasion, when we could get no batteries from the "Big Land," Mali used an accumulator from a broken down car and thus kept the transmitter working. Mali asked me to instruct our fighters that upon destroying enemy vehicles, they should do their best to keep the engines intact.

Joseph Isakovich Mali stayed with us for nearly two years. He accompanied the unit throughout all the fighting. For that, he was awarded the "Order of the War of the Fatherland, Second Class," "The Red Star," and "The Partisan Medal, First Class."

At the end of partisan warfare, Mali stayed on in a military unit. I am certain that he kept on working with his usual conscientiousness and loyalty. He will always remain in my memory as a man of impeccable character and loyal in his duty.

Dr. Yaakov Bolach

When we were on the move in August 1943, two doctors joined our forces. I forget the name of one of them, but the other was called Yaakov Emmanuelovich Bolach. He was fifty-five years old. Both doctors escaped from the town of Kirch by the skin of their teeth, the Germans having wiped out more than half the Jewish population. Bolach was of great benefit to us. He healed the sick and operated on some of the wounded. He knew how to fight typhus. We improvised a primitive

bathhouse on the river Obart. We dug out a hole in the
ground, put inside it an iron petrol barrel, and
covered it with wooden boards. In this bathhouse it
was also possible to disinfect clothing. We did not
have a single case of typhus. Our doctor provided
medical aid not only for the fighters but also for the
neighboring inhabitants, putting in endless hours of
work. At times he would help women in childbirth in
the villages where the Germans had stopped all medical
services.

The "Big Land" could not provide us with the
necessary amount of medicines. We made up for the
shortage by obtaining the necessary items from German
hospitals and pharmacies. Nevertheless, we sometimes
lacked medicines and supplies, particularly bandages.
For this latter purpose we sometimes resorted to
parachute cloth. Bolach's out-patients from the neighboring villages, who owed him a great debt of gratitude, began to provide us with bandage material,
sometimes made of high-quality linen.

Yaakov Emmanuelovich had a vivacious, pleasant
nature. In the evenings he would come over to us at
headquarters, to the campfire, where the fighters and
their commanders usually gathered. When he arrived,
joy would spread all around us. I often joined him in
the dancing to bring joy into the hearts of the young
men. The difficulties and the pain involved in partisan warfare did not snuff out his joy of life or
lessen his love for the people.

Scout Yevgeni Volyansky

In the early days of 1943, when our unit was
encamped in the region of Khinailsky Forest, we
received great help from Red Army Lieutenant Yevgeni
Volyansky. He was born in Zhamrinka. Since October
1941, Volyansky had served in one partisan company
after another, which had been organized from among the
Russian soldiers who had escaped enemy encirclement.
He was sent over to the scouts' company as its deputy
commander.

In the Desna region, the Germans stood in the way
of the river we wanted to cross and actually encircled
us. We had to find a way out. At the head of the
patrol group was Volyansky. Four of our attempts at
reaching the river were thwarted by the enemy; and it

-47-

was only thanks to Volyansky that we succeeded in breaking out of the encirclement without any casualties, even without being detected by the enemy.

The Germans attached great importance to alcohol factories. They used alcohol for their tanks and vehicles. It was only natural that the partisans would want to destroy these plants. Once, while stopping at a regional center in the area of Chernigov, I sent the Chevony company to the village of Kriski on some military mission. Volyansky was among its men. There was an alcohol factory in that village. The dauntless scout not only found out where the distillery was, but also supplied the fighters with accurate details on how to get to it and how to dispose of the guards. Volyansky himself took two comrades along with him, slipped into the factory building, laid explosives, and blew up the alcohol tubs.

On another occasion, when we were camped near the Prifiat River, Volyansky went out with a group of partisans to the railway tracks running between Gomel and Kalinkovichi. These tracks served as a main line of communications for the German army in the Bryansk front. Naturally, the tracks were heavily guarded by the Germans. After thorough reconnoitering, Volyansky crept up to the tracks with the men, at a point four kilometers from the Goleniche station. A passenger train went by, followed by an eight-man German guard. Volyansky waited for the guard to move away and then went to work with his men on the tracks. He laid two demolition charges at a distance of twenty meters from each other. The partisans were hardly through when an armored train was seen chugging its way from a distance. The partisans moved away from the tracks, slipping into the nearby woods. Still trying to catch their breath from the intensive effort, they heard two ear-shattering explosions. Fragments of both train and tracks went up into the air. The tracks were put out of commission for five days.

On other occasions, Volyansky and his scouts would slip into an enemy-held village, find out all about the German forces there, and come back to base to draw up the plan for the attack.

Yevgeni Volyansky was awarded the "Red Flag" order, the "War of the Fatherland" order, First Class, and the "Partisan Medal," First Class. After our companies had ceased their operations behind enemy lines,

Volyansky expressed his wish to fly over to the Carpathian Mountains where he could resume partisan warfare against the Germans. His wish was granted. For his military exploits in Czechoslovakia, he was awarded a Czechoslovak decoration.

VICTOR SPUTMANN

Y. Kuzshar
Hero of the Soviet Union, Major-General, Former
Commander of a Partisan Unit

In the spring of 1943, a special-missions company was formed in our unit. The man appointed as its commander was Victor Sputmann, a young officer who had long proved his military mettle. For that he had thrice been awarded state decorations. There was no important military operation in which he did not take part along with his partisans. In everything he did, he showed not only courage, but also understanding and ingenuity.

Here is one of his exploits. In early June 1943, there arrived at Rechitsa a German division, including tanks and armored cars, two battalions of gendarmes, and even airplanes. Our unit was encamped at a distance of twenty-five kilometers from Rechitsa. On the eve of the enemy arrival, our men succeeded in downing a reconnaissance plane. In it they found a map showing the exact location of our company and the headquarters of our unit. It was evident that the Germans would launch a heavy attack on these spots, which were now known to them. With the help of our own combat reconnaissance and intelligence teams, we succeeded in finding out the date of the planned German onslaught --June 13, 1943. On the night of this day, our partisan unit left its camp and, after a forced march, took positions behind the line that was marked out on the enemy map.

At exactly six in the morning, the Germans started shelling the spot we had evacuated. Before long this shelling was complemented by an attack mounted by German infantry and tank units. We laid strong ambushes along the roads flanking the woods and sent out a fighting outfit of lookouts to the village of Uzhnosh. When the Germans appeared, the outfit fired at them and forced them back to the outskirts of the forest. The Germans, having recovered from the initial shock, went after the lookout outfit, but they were forced back once again by the fire of our ambush.

In order to collect their dead and heavily wounded, the Germans sent out a large infantry unit. At the same time, the partisan ambush had received significant reinforcement. Thus half an hour after the first shot had been fired, a great battle raged between some 3,000 fighters on both sides, using automatic rifles, machine guns, and mine-throwers. Before long, the field guns joined the battle.

At the head of his company of sharpshooters, Sputmann controlled the central sector of one side of the forest. At this sector the Germans poured a dense fire from mine-throwers. Sputmann's unique familiarity with the place made it possible for him not only to stand his ground, but also to prevent loss of life among his men.

After the first German attack had petered out, Sputmann moved his men fast from the outskirts of the forest to a distance of about one hundred meters inside it. The company had hardly taken its new position when enemy mines started exploding at the outskirts of the woods, at the exact spot where the partisans had been before. The explosions died down after some time, and Sputmann ordered his men to go back to the outskirts of the forest, where the ground had been deeply marked by the exploding German mines. At the same time the enemy directed its mines and artillery fire into the forest, where the partisans would have met a bitter end had they stayed.

The Germans launched another attack. They went in close lines, walking upright, feeling certain that there was no one to oppose them at the end of the forest. When they came to a distance of about fifty meters from us, Sputmann and his men opened up with a crossfire of machine guns, rifles, and mine-throwers. The Germans fell back. Four times they attacked the outskirts of the woods, leading two charges at the spot. After Sputmann's counterattack, they eventually ran away. Despite the large concentration of German infantry, arms, tanks, and armored vehicles, one end of the forest still remained in our hands.

Full of resentment, the Germans burned down the village of Uzhnosh and filled up the wells with earth. But they were soon to retreat, leaving behind them hundreds of dead and wounded.

TYPICAL BIOGRAPHIES

Y.A. Belsky
Hero of the Soviet Union, Former Commander of a Partisan Unit

As one who took part in organizing a partisan movement in Byelorussia, I was often behind enemy lines in the districts of Minsk, Polesia, Mogilyov, and Pinsk.

The partisan movement was small in its early days; the first groups organized consisted of ten, fifteen, and twenty men each. The future commanders of the units personally picked out the men, gathered information, and saw to the provision of supplies and arms. In the vicinity of the Rok district, aided by the chairman of the Chovet Polessa kolkhoz, I organized a partisan company made up of twenty-eight men. For its commander I appointed the Jew Bredyekovich, who had formerly been a postal employee. The company still had no arms, so I gave Brednyekovich one of my pistols and he set out, at the head of thirty hand-picked fighters, to get arms for the company.

By the approach of fall there were scores of such companies. But the situation in general was not clear to me. So I sent one of my aides, Roman Katznelson, to Minsk in order to bring over Brenson, whom I had come to know in the course of our working together some time before. I met Brenson and Katzenelson in the winter in the district of Lubyanski and sent them on a long reconnaissance mission: to find out the forces that were trying to work with us and to indicate what could be done for a more comprehensive organization of the partisan movement. They called at seven districts: Slutsk, Staro-Dorshesk, Djerdjinsk, Zasslabel, Pokovichev, Rudansk, and Minsk, and also visited the town of Minsk itself. They were gone about a month and a half, doing propaganda work besides reconnaissance.

-51-

They called upon the people to carry out resistance operations behind enemy lines.

Then one day I heard that Katznelson died a war hero.

In October 1941 we got ready for our first operation. We formed a striking force of about 180 men out of three companies and put it under the command of Davidovich, the commander of one of them. And thus, though greatly outnumbered, we attacked the German garrison.

The battles we waged attracted new men into our fighting units. We set up a chain of workshops for making and repairing arms. Each workshop was manned by ten to fifteen workers. In these workshops we had 110 craftsmen in all. The Germans bombed us, but many of the bombs were duds, so we took out their powder and used their explosive charges. In May 1942 we received a transmitter and could thus send out the announcement that we had some 5,000 partisans active in our region.

At about this time I met in the woods two people, barefoot and in tatters, a man and a young girl. The man, whose name was Abraham (I forgot his family name.), had been a photographer in Gomel. He was about forty-five. The girl had been a high-school pupil in Sutsak, and was called Mania Mintz. They had escaped from the Germans into the forest, where they fed on potatoes boiled in a German steel helmet. Mania could walk only on her toes, as the soles of her feet were bleeding. I brought them to one of our companies.

We allocated Abraham to our supplies platoon. He was entrusted with the task of carting supplies to the company from the neighboring villages. This was highly dangerous, as he was likely to fall into the hands of the Germans. Often he would move under a hail of bullets. But he did not flinch. Mania, for her part, worked in the kitchen for nine months, then asked to be given a combat task. She was attached as a demolition fighter to the Gastilo company and took part in many combat missions.

I appointed Alter Kostanovich as my adjutant. He had been left behind enemy lines to organize the partisan movement. His wife was killed by the Germans. Accompanied by one partisan, he destroyed and burned an enemy truck, killing the ten German soldiers who were

in it. I could not think of a better adjutant. He did
not seem to sleep at all. He stationed the guards and
lookouts in their positions. In battle he patrolled
the area and was responsible for establishing contact
with the neighboring companies. He did everything
fast, accurately, and without fear.

Physician Nahum Schweitz entered the woods in the
early days of the war. In the district of Glosk he
joined a partisan company under the command of
Stolyarov. It was here that I met him in December of
1941 and had him transferred to Davidovich's company.
He healed and operated on the sick and wounded of both
the partisans and the neighboring population, even
serving as obstetrician in emergencies. At the same
time he trained the cadres of medics we so badly
needed. Before long Schweitz was put in charge of the
sanitary service for the entire unit.

Simon Reznik, an ordinary fighter in July 1941,
was later made commissar of one of our companies. He
was only twenty-five and took part in at least four
battles, destroying twenty firing positions near
Lomovichi, blowing up the bridge on the river Orissa,
and destroying the Palichi station. He was wounded in
1944 and airlifted to the "Big Land."

Schulman, the commander of one of our companies,
came to us in 1942. Till then he had been hiding in
the woods for about one year. At first he served as an
ordinary fighter, but he soon established himself as a
daring partisan who won the respect of his colleagues
and thus was appointed commander of his company. He
was given the task of blowing up railway tracks. Some
time later he set up a company of saboteurs under his
command. His company accounted for many German trains
destroyed on the tracks running from Bobroysk through
Yassin to Ossipovich.

The following is a typical account of one Jewish
family. To my regret, I cannot remember its name. At
the time we knew the people by their first names only
and that is how we remember them. Till the outbreak of
the war, this family had lived in Orechiya, in the
region of Starodozhya. Later on the family was brought
over to us. Abraham, the head of the family, was put
in charge of supplies. His wife worked in the kitchen.
Their son, Georgi, was a mounted scout. Under our
instructions, he twice accompanied convoys headed for
the "Big Land" through the front lines. On his second

mission he stayed there and joined the Red Army. Abraham's sixteen-year-old daughter, Ida, worked at our headquarters. When later we established contact with the Red Army, we sent her to school.

In 1941 I met Khinits. In that year the Germans had killed his wife. He took part in many battles and sabotage operations as an ordinary fighter. Later on he set up a new company and was made its commissar. He personally accounted for eighteen dead Germans. He kept fighting until 1944.

There were many Jews in my unit, both fighters and commanders. Here I have mentioned the names of only a few. But the stories of their lives, their fates, and their participation in the partisan movement are typical of all the sons and daughters of the Jewish people who, along with the other peoples of our Soviet fatherland, rose up in arms against the enemy during the difficult years of German occupation.

TWO PARTISANS

V. Klukov
Hero of the Soviet Union, Former, Deputy-Commander
of a Partisan Unit

Young Zelig Kadin was seriously wounded in one of the battles. A fascist bullet had shattered his hand, but Kadin did not leave the company. He only moved from the platoon of sharpshooters to that of demolition fighters.

Zelig's wound took a long time to heal. The shattered bone of his hand did not join well, but he kept taking part in combat operations. Holding a grenade in his hand, he would go out in the company of his comrades to face the enemy, charging ahead and killing Germans. Months passed, and the bone in Zelig's hand did not heal. So we decided to send him back into the Soviet hinterland. The parting was hard on all of us, and we often remembered our "Zeikeh," as we fondly called him in our company.

* * * * *

Simon Yudovich joined the partisan company in
September 1942. He had succeeded in escaping from a
German POW camp. I came to know him well in August
1943 when I was appointed deputy company commander, and
Yudovich was appointed commissar of the sabotage platoon. Being aggressive and full of drive, he at once
adapted to his new job and elicited both respect and
friendship from the men of the platoon. Even while
serving as a commissar, Yudovich kept up the hard task
of saboteur.

I remember well one event in particular. It happened in early November 1943. The company had used all
the explosives at its disposal. Only seven kilograms
were left, enough for one demolition operation. So far,
we had accounted for ninety-six blown-up trains and had
a strong desire to show a hundred for the October
celebrations. But how to do that? We decided to
switch over to using one kilogram mines. Such mines
were usually laid on the tracks a short time before the
approach of a train, a highly dangerous operation to
the life of a saboteur. One slip would mean premature
explosion. We used these mines to blow up three more
trains. The blowing up of the hundredth was entrusted
to partisan Sobolyev. But he did not succeed. After
the mine had been laid, something went wrong and it
exploded. His entire left hand was lost, along with
four fingers of his right hand.

Only a few days remained to the celebrations of
the October Revolution. The honor of blowing up the
hundredth German train fell to Yudovich. Under cover
of darkness he went to the specified spot. Back at the
camp we waited for Yudovich with mounting impatience.
At long last he appeared. He approached us with the
long-familiar glint in his eyes. The comrades
surrounded him and congratulated each other on the
hundredth enemy train, a present of the saboteurs and
the entire company in honor of the celebrations.

This account of Simon Yudovich may well be
concluded by an outline of his character in combat: in
the course of the partisan company's struggle, Yudovich
proved to be a patriot loyal to his fatherland; he took
part in many battles against the fascist invaders and
himself accounted for seventeen dead Germans. In
fighting he showed courage, fearlessness, and
leadership.

As commissar of the sabotage platoon, Yudovich often led the sabotage operations on the railway tracks. He himself derailed eleven German trains containing soldiers and equipment. His sabotage work accounted for eleven engines, seventy-six railway carriages full of soldiers and equipment, and over 320 killed and wounded German soldiers and officers. In addition, he took part in destroying fourteen German trains carrying soldiers and equipment on the tracks running between Kovel and Rovno, in the western Ukraine.

COMMISSAR NACHUM FELDMAN

A. Fismyeni

When Nachum Feldman was fourteen years old, he left Kormi, the small town in which he was born, and went to the town of Gomel in White Russia. Even then he was a good tailor and thus was soon to find work at the shop of a local craftsman. After the October Revolution, Feldman began a new life. He dedicated his life to the skilled-workers movement and began to study. Before long he joined the Bolshevik party.

In 1918 the Germans occupied White Russia and the Ukraine. Huge fires lit the skies over the small towns and the villages, and the blood of peaceful citizens flowed like water. Feldman joined a partisan company together with a group of Gomel inhabitants and soldiers who had come from the front. The company was formed in the village of Feodorovka (region of Gomel), and there its headquarters were set up; hence its name: the "Feodorovian Partisan" Company. Its commander was a former railway worker, Yakovlev. In those early days the partisan struggle was still taking its first steps, but the Feodorovian company, which numbered only forty men, struck hard at enemy installations. It was in this company that Feldman acquired the experience that he would need many years later.

When the Red Army started to get organized, Feldman volunteered, joined the First Gomelian Proletarian Battalion, and took part in the battles on the western front. Later on he was to reach Warsaw along with the Soviet cavalry corps.

More than twenty years passed. It was now 1941.
The great war of the fatherland had begun. The enemy
was at the gates of Minsk. In the backyard of the
house where Feldman lived, there was a gathering of
neighbors and friends. The weather was hot, and the
air was filled with the smoke of the numerous fires
that were raging around. The rolling of artillery fire
was coming nearer and nearer. All were apprehensive of
what the next hour might bring. Feldman said: "Anyone
not connected with the defense of the town must leave
Minsk for Moscow immediately on the main road."

Along the wide asphalt road they walked, ashen
with struggle, thirsty for water, carrying on their
shoulders packages of meager household utensils. Enemy
planes zoomed fast above them, and the thousands of
wandering refugees -- women, children, and old men
marched on the burning asphalt. When dawn broke, they
were approaching Borisov. At the same time the Germans
dropped paratroopers, thus blocking the way of the
escaping refugees.

With the passage of time Feldman was to witness
many formidable events, but this first encounter with
the enemy left an indelible mark on his memory. The
Germans fired indiscriminately at the defenseless
people. They killed old men, women, and children.
When the carnage had subsided, they gathered the survivors and forced them to run back to Minsk.

Feldman survived. When the firing started, he had
jumped into a ditch. He had crawled to some shrubs
along the road and escaped into the nearby forest. As
a veteran partisan he immediately began to think of
fighting the enemy and the need to rally the people and
get them organized in partisan companies. Nachum
Feldman returned to Minsk. For some days he went into
hiding in the home of a friend. To appear on the
street was out of the question: many people would
recognize him. In those days the Hitlerites issued an
order that all men between the ages of sixteen and
fifty had to have their names registered. Feldman did
not show up for registration. One day he secretly went
out on the street to find out who had remained in the
town. He was caught by a German guard and sent to a
concentration camp. At first this camp was in a
faraway cemetery not far from Minsk. Later the partisans were moved to Drozdi, where the garbage dumping
grounds had previously been. And from Drozdi, they
were taken to the Minsk ghetto.

Feldman knew many of his fellow prisoners in the fenced-off neighborhood, and he looked for men ready for the struggle ahead. He was to find them. The Party's underground committee in the ghetto was composed of sixteen comrades. Its secretary was Nachum Feldman.

With the help of ghetto people whom the Germans took out to work in the town, Feldman and his friends succeeded in establishing contact with the workers of the Voronov printing house. The latter called a meeting between the underground group and a printer who worked at the German department. Through this printer they got type, paper, ink, and the parts of a printing press. The thirst for true information was so great, and the ghetto people were in such a pressing need for a live word, that the underground group decided first to put out a bulletin.

In October 1941 a meeting took place between Komsomol member Kaplan and the writer Smolar, a brave and experienced man of the underground. Kaplan introduced Feldman to Smolar. Before long the ghetto underground group had established contact with the Party underground committee in Minsk and willingly accepted its authority.

But even before contact was established with the Feldman group in the ghetto, working relations had been established between the town committee of the Party and the partisan companies operating in the forests around Minsk. These companies were in need of aid and support. They needed men, clothing, and medicines. The underground committee suggested that the Feldman group provide equipment for the partisan companies. In many workshops Feldman had supporters who rallied to the call of the underground people. The wallets of the workers served for hiding medicines, bandages, pieces of cloth, and the like.

In accordance with the instructions of Smolar and instructor Michael Gebelyev, men were taken secretly out of the ghetto to join the partisan companies. Arms were also collected from the inhabitants and smuggled to the partisans. Some of the arms were captured from the Germans. But all this was not enough for Feldman. Together with Communist Joseph Lapidot, he decided to set up a new partisan company.

In the beginning it was necessary to set up a base in one of the neighboring forests for the company in

the making.   During the long nights of the fall, he
thought the plan through.   For the first reconnaissance
Feldman picked out fifteen men, putting them under the
command of his son, Victor, who was only sixteen years
old.

The group left the ghetto unharmed, but the reconnaissance operation did not succeed.   For about one
week Victor and his men wandered about in the region of
Dokor, only to return without having accomplished
anything.   But the lack of success did not weaken
Feldman's will.   In the ghetto there were rumors that
strong partisan companies operated somewhere in the
regions of Zaslabel and Quidanov.

"We must first set up a base close to them,"
thought Feldman, and once again sent his son out on
reconnaissance.

But now he sent along with him a young woman,
Natasha Lifshitz.   Before the outbreak of the war,
Natasha had been studying in the ninth form.   Now she
was to be revealed as a daring young woman who soon
adapted to the hard and dangerous task of a ground
scout.   Lately she had gone thrice on missions to
Minsk.   On one of these missions she was caught by the
Gestapo, but she bluffed her way out.   She took them
along to a house where she told them she lived.   She
knew that the house had a backyard open on both sides.
She slipped away through this backyard, leaving the
Gestapo guarding the entrance ....

Natasha first accompanied Victor on a reconnoitering mission when they both were still inex-
perienced.   For five days they kept looking for the
partisan groups -- in vain.   They returned to the
ghetto empty-handed.   Upon hearing that the "Pokrovsk"
company was active beyond Dokor, Feldman once again
sent out three men: Komsomol member Arotsky, vivacious
and liked by one and all, along with Pessin and Tumin.
They had succeeded in reaching the village of Lushitzi
when they came upon a company of policemen.   Battle
broke out between the two unequal forces, and two
ground scouts were killed.   Wounded Tumin buried himself in a heap of snow and some time later made it to
the ghetto.

However, the unsuccessful attempts did not weaken
Feldman's determination to move his men out of the
ghetto.   He went about making further preparations with

greater thoroughness. Despite the alertness of the Hitlerite guards, people left the ghetto on the tenth of April, heading ostensibly for their daily chores, under the leadership of Commander Israel Lapidot and Commissar Feldman. On reaching the road to Slutsk, the people divided into groups. Some time before, guides had been posted along the road to show them the way. Thus, by being passed from one guide to another, they found their way to their destination in the distant forest.

The group headed by Feldman consisted of twenty men. They had gathered together, surmounted all the difficulties, and were only a few steps from the meeting with the second part of the group, led by Lapidot. Then, all of a sudden, German mounted guards loomed up, charged at the Jews, and killed sixteen of them. Feldman was forced to go back to the ghetto with the few men who had survived the attack.

What spiritual strength, what self-control and persistence were required of Feldman so that he should not sink into despair in the face of all the losses and failures. Since Feldman did not succeed in establishing contact with Lapidot and his group, he once again met with Smolar and members of the underground committee of the Party in that town. This time the committee took it upon itself to see that the men were taken out of the ghetto. At kilometer nine, the Feldman group was met by experienced guides who directed the men to the forest of Starosilsk, where the company base was to be set up.

There were neither tents nor earth huts. Everything had to be built from scratch. At the same time, the people started their combat training. Till the end of May 1942 the Feldman company was busy collecting arms, preparing provisions, going on reconnaissance missions, and establishing friendly relations with the inhabitants of the surrounding villages. That area was the fighting grounds of other partisan companies as well. Sometimes the Feldman partisans would join them and have their first taste of battle against the enemy.

The relations with the ghetto and the urban committee became stronger and more viable. More people joined Feldman's company. On the first anniversary of the war, on June 22, 1942, the underground committee sent Simon Gregoryevich Ganzinko to the Feldman com-

pany.   Wounded, he had been taken prisoner by the
Germans and brought back by Natasha Lifshitz. Ganzinko
was appointed company commander and Feldman, company
commissar.   Firing in the woods never ceased, and
Ganzinko taught the men how to shoot.   Feldman,
Ganzinko, and their friends began to make careful preparations for their first combat mission.   For this
eventuality the company had already gathered some sixty
rifles, eight machine guns and countless cartridges and
grenades.

Shortly before the attack was mounted, Feldman
went around the camp and told his friends: "Well,
brothers, tonight we go out on the road. The saying
goes that every beginning is hard, but we shall come
through all right."

On the grounds of a former kolkhoz, not far from
Kidanovo, the Germans had set up a large ranch. It was
decided to destroy this ranch. In it was stationed a
very strong garrison.   In three groups the partisans
closed in on the German stronghold. Ganzinko gave the
sign by firing his pistol, and the waves of partisans
charged at the enemy. The German garrison was taken.
Some time later, after the ranch had been retaken and
rebuilt by the Germans, it was once again attacked by
Ganzinko and Feldman.

The partisans later launched several attacks on
the German farm near Rakov, and many times they
derailed German military trains, drove back convoys,
and wiped out garrisons in villages and small towns.
The company, having been honed to a sharp edge in con-
tant fighting, now bore the name of the indefatigable
Bodyenny.

In mid-1943 the Feldman-Ganzinko company received
a large shipment of explosives. Now it was possible to
carry out sabotage operations on a much larger scale.

...It was the beginning of 1944. Along the entire
front the Red Army was chasing the retreating enemy
forces. Before the attack on Minsk, it was necessary
to cut off all railway communications on the tracks
running between Stobichi and Quidanovo. The high command entrusted this task to a brigade named after
Stalin.

In three companies the partisans set out for the
railway tracks.   The Feldman-Ganzinko company found a

base for itself in the forest of Iyovinechk after it had covered fifty-eight kilometers in a single day. In the evening the Feldman-Ganzinko men arrived at the predetermined spot. From a distance they could see a German convoy, consisting of tanks and other heavy equipment. They had no time to mine the tracks. They had to act fast and wipe out the convoy at any price. Feldman gave the order "After me!" Grenade in hand, he ran out to the tracks to meet the convoy. Anti-tank grenades flew in the direction of the engine. Until this encounter Feldman had accounted for fourteen blown-up convoys. This one would be the fifteenth. The heavy German engine was blown from the tracks, followed by the carriages, one after the other. The entire tracks were demolished.

The Feldman company kept up the fight until all of White Russia was liberated from enemy forces. In the course of its military operations, the company accounted for over 2,500 dead Hitlerites and hundreds of derailed enemy railway carriages.

THE LARMONTOV COMPANY

S. Davidovsky

In September 1942, after the German hordes had reached Stalingrad and driven a wedge in the foothills of the Caucasus Mountains, a company named after Larmontov mounted a heroic attack on the large village of Kaminomosteskaya in the Kabard Region. The partisans crossed the Malki River, stormed the village, and drove the German garrison out. The company blew up the command of the German tank unit and carried out other important operations. In the village streets and on the shores of the Malki River were strewn some four hundred German corpses.

The razing of Kaminomosteskaya, which lay at an important crossroad near the front, caused much worry to the Germans. They sent punishment squads after the partisans.

The twenty-fifth anniversary of the 1917 October Revolution drew near. To celebrate the day, partisan groups, along with the Larmontov company, launched an attack on the populated center of Khabas, forty kilometers from Makislovodsk, where there was a German transit base. The attack was of course preceded by large-scale reconnoitering missions. Besides the Larmontov company the partisan companies of Nagornozilsky and Baksansky were involved. The access to Khabas was so difficult that the mounted partisans had to reach the place on foot.

On the night of November 2, 1942, the partisans, holding onto each other's hands, descended the jagged slopes leading to Khabas. They split into three groups and, on reaching the predetermined spot, opened fire. The Germans first pinned the partisans down with machine guns and mortar fire. Then, at the head of a partisan group, Company Commander Gregory Davidov stormed the German command. Shouting "Halt!" at the German sentry, he killed him with a pistol shot. On the roof of the command building there was a group of German officers. Some ten anti-tank shells were enough to blow up the entire command building.

The fighting went on for over two hours. The German garrison was wiped out. On the walls of the houses the partisans hung handwritten leaflets devoted to the twenty-fifth anniversary of the October Revolution. The leaflets asked the population to keep up the struggle against the Germans and closed with the words: "We have struck at the invaders. We are striking at them now and will keep on striking at them till they are wiped out completely." A short time later German reinforcements arrived. They were made up of a sniper unit which pushed our company back. In this battle, machine-gunner Vanya Kussinko was outstanding in the hits he scored. He was wounded four times. Sixteen-year-old girl partisan Motya, who until the outbreak of the war had been working at the molybdenum complex, lifted the wounded partisan and carried him on her back for a distance of two kilometers. Other outstanding comrades were Alexander Romninko, Feodor Bogato, Prokofi Kolesnikov, and partisans who had taken part in the Russian civil war following World War I. The partisans laid mines in the way of the retreating Germans and later hid in one of the ravines.

For one whole day the Germans combed the valleys, the paths, and the mountains, but they could not find the partisans. In order to launch the attack, the company had to cover some 200 kilometers on the way to

Khabas on such steep mountains as Mt. Kinzhal, Mt. Kashtan, and Mt. Kartman, close behind the German front. In their ascent the partisans held on to the tails of their horses, and in the descent they used ropes and belts. The conditions became extremely bad at the foothills of the Caucasus Mountains. The region of the Baksansky ravine contained a large population which was forced to leave with some 40,000 head of sheep and goats and a huge amount of ore: wolfram, and molybdenum. All that could have fallen into the hands of the enemy. The Germans occupied the vehicle store-house and dug in on the slopes of the Albrus. After they had established control over the population centers of Zayokovo and Gongolina, they tightened their siege of the ravine in Aksansk. There was only one way out: to overcome the snow passages at Don, Bashi, and Khuzruk, which are nearly impassable in winter. After two days of efforts to hold their ground on the summit of a cliff, the men started their descent. During this passage it was essential to keep proper distance between the men. The fall of one into the abyss would bring others along with him. Close watch had to be kept over the movement of snow masses. In this manner, for five days and nights, some 20,000 people were to pass through these treacherous regions -- one long, endless chain of partisans and local inhabitants who had left their settlements. The company covered fifty kilometers in these ravines and descended to Svanyetya. From this point the partisans went into Mingarlin, then to Kizliar, and the outlying territory behind enemy lines.

In Kizliar, Gregory Davidov-Koltunov was appointed leader of the southern group of the partisan company. This group was assigned the task of destroying the unpaved roads and the enemy communication lines on the railway tracks of Ordzhonikidza. After many battles between the partisans and the Cossak armies (probably the traitorous Cossak troops that collaborated with the German forces), the partisan commander wrote: "These men fight like lions." The fighting took place under extremely difficult conditions, on the sands of the Kizliar steppes.

The Larmontov company was international in its composition. Shoulder-to-shoulder fought Russians, Kabardians, Armenians, and Jews. Among the fighters were many who belonged to the independent professions. Outstanding in battle was the engineer Urshavsky and the professor at the local spa, Andreyev. Despite his age, Andreyev never parted from his rifle.

Of particular interest is the biography of company commander Gregory Davidov-Koltunov. As a child he had studied in the cheder[5], in the town of Starodov in the district of Chernigov. In his adolescence he graduated from a drama school and for some time acted in a Jewish theater. Later, he was director of the arts department in the district of Ivanovsk.

THE COMMANDER OF THE BOIBOI UNIT

V. Grassimova

Leningrad is the city of a myriad of heroic exploits. It has been entered in the annals of the great war of the fatherland as a unique city, whose millions of inhabitants hovered between life and death for over two years. People in years to come will continue to extol the brave inhabitants of this important city, its glorious fighters, and the faultless men of the Red Navy.

But there was another force, another brilliant army, whose exploits are worthy of being entered in the book of glory concerning Lenin's city; the partisan force in the Leningrad region. It was the men belonging to this force, in those dark days when the destiny of this large city was being determined, who neutra-lized large enemy forces by holding them in a tight vise of partisan warfare, bled them to exhaustion with their iron will and resourcefulness, undermined their morale, and annihilated them. Suffice it to say that in order to fight the partisan companies operating in the Leningrad region, the Germans had to throw some 40,000 of their elite troops into the battle, particularly in the decisive days of the fight to capture the city. At the time apparently, almost the entire region was in the hands of the occupation forces. It seemed that at the outskirts of the northern capital, Hitler's men were about to begin their victory celebrations. These celebrations, which they so eagerly looked forward to, had been hysterically hailed by the fascists newspapers, leaflets, and broadcasts. But those very fascists, with their premature bragging, kept asking apprehensively: What are the partisans up to in the region of Khavoynin? Of Phystov? What region would they capture now? Where is the Boiboi company operating at present? And the Grozny company, where is it?

In all these grim and disquieting questions that the Germans asked about the intentions and actions of the partisans, one name kept recurring on their lips, the name of Partisan Commander Boiboi -- Dimitri Ivanovich Novkovsky.

Now, after the war, when you see Dimitri Novkovsky at the head of a large industrial plant in the Soviet Union, in his spacious and well-lighted office at a large desk, it is difficult to visualize him in the partisan struggle, with his thick growth of hair, yellowish beard, leather coat, and fur cap. That is how he looked in those days, which were not so long ago.[6] Behind this man lie years of hard fighting, interminable shortages, hunger, cold, sleepless nights. And now he sits, a very quiet man, bright eyed, clean shaven, smiling.

Engineer Novkovsky began his military career in the early days of the war. In those days he had already decided to join the ranks of those who fought behind enemy lines. Before long this quiet man of the industrial sector, who had been born in the region of Chernigov, was to make his appearance in the woods and the marshes of the forbidding northern district. But the man was strong of spirit and did not give in to the hardships of the bleak environment. As a Bolshevik, he showed no weakness even for a single moment.

In the beginning only a few dozen people belonged to the company commanded by Novkovsky. But with the expansion of its combat activities, more men joined its ranks, especially after the local inhabitants came to realize that Novkovsky was their staunch defendant. Hundreds of people flocked to him: people who had left downtrodden and ruined villages or had escaped from enemy-occupied towns. But in order to win the full confidence of the local people and to serve as an emblem of persistent struggle against the invaders, the company had to wage further battles against greatly superior numbers of enemy forces, battles of glory and heroic exploits.[7]

Even in the early days of its formation, the Boiboi company, then numbering only about eighty men, attacked a German punishment squad made up of 400 men.

This disparity in numbers between the two fighting sides called for a high degree of resourcefulness, courage, skill, and even cunning on the part of the partisans, as physical strength alone would not suffice. There was a need for a great measure of sacrifice and even self-effacement, a quality which characterized the people of the Boiboi company under their commander. That was the first encounter of a company made up a newly formed fighters with an enemy armed to the teeth. The operation was set for the twenty-fourth anniversary of the Red Army.

This brilliant operation, carried out on a pitch-dark February night in 1942 according to the plan drawn up by Novkovsky and under his command, is interesting for its combination of cool calculation and revolutionary, passionate courage. And that, in effect, was a characteristic feature of Novkovsky's spiritual make-up.

News had reached the company that the German command was sending a large punishment squad to the region of the village of Tiorikovo. The company had also learned of the task that had been assigned to this squad: "To burn down villages and ruthlessly wipe out the entire population, including the children." The partisans also learned that the punishment squad would be under the command of the tyrant hangman Fashisky, who had become notorious for the acts of cruelty he had perpetrated in White Russia and the Ukraine. The partisans refrained from direct encounters with the numerically superior forces. Then the fighting started with a trivial and unexpected act, though it showed a great measure of self-control and resourcefulness.

It happened that nine armed German soldiers were approaching a barn full of hay, carrying pitchforks on their shoulders, to get some fodder. In the same barn were a number of partisans, including Novkovsky. A single shot would have alerted the entire area. Apparently there was no way out. The commander whispered an order to catch the fascists. We lay there waiting. "When the Germans came near, we caught them without a single shot," reminisced Novkovsky with a broad smile on his face. We extracted from the Germans detailed information about the deployment of the punishment squad in the village of Tiorikovo. They also devulged the information that the squad would start its attack on the following day. Last but not least, they gave the partisans the password to Tiorikovo, "Pan Fascisky."

Novkovsky found that he could not afford to lose a single moment. He had to strike at the Germans while they were still unfamiliar with the place and could be taken by surprise. In the evening the partisans tore up a white overall, tied on their sleeves white arm bands similar to those worn by the German police, and went out on carts to Tiorikovo. To the sentry's challenge of "Halt!" they answered "Pan Fascisky." Thus the partisans could get into the village. Once inside, they quietly deployed for the next move, as they knew where to find the enemy. Novkovsky went to the schoolhouse which, according to the information supplied by the partisan scouts, housed the command of the garrison. The men in this building had not gone to sleep. Novkovsky tossed an antitank grenade through the window. According to the predetermined plan, that was the sign his comrades had been waiting for. The village shook under the noise of the explosions. The barracks went up on flames. Desperate howls, shrieks, and curses shouted in a foreign language came from inside the smoke and flames. The Germans who attempted to escape from the burning houses were cut down by the well-aimed partisan bullets -- the wounded were killed with the butts of the rifles. The commander of the punishment squad, "Pan Fascisky", whose name had been of such a great help to the company, was captured alive.

In this first battle, the Boiboi company killed some 200 Germans and took fifty-two prisoners. Its booty was also sizable: field guns, machine guns, vehicles, radio transmitters, etc.

The news flashed through the villages and small towns of the Leningrad area: "Our men are striking at the German beasts." But that was only the "first swallow." Following the fighting in the village of Tiorikovo there came an attack on the village of Sivieri and others on the villages of Stanki, Krochi, Zvebke, Prochi, Kreizshi, etc.

Regular army battalions were often aided by the partisans. On one occasion, the enemy attacked a Soviet army battalion stationed at the village of Korchi. The battalion was greatly outnumbered, and though the situation was desperate, the fighters and their commanders heroically repulsed the enemy attacks. When the Boiboi company heard of this, it ouflanked the attacking German unit and, just when the Germans were drunk with the prospect of the approaching victory, landed a sudden blow on them. The Germans threw down their weapons and beat a disorderly retreat.

Forged by the fire of continued fighting against the Germans, the feeling of partisan brotherhood became stronger in the company from day to day. Surrounded by the enemy, separated from the "Big Land" (Russia), the partisans came to the rescue of each other at the risk of their own lives. Novkovsky could thus be found carrying his best friend and military aide in his arms and donating blood to him. Prokhorov, his daring friend, was to save Novkovsky from certain death on many other occasions. An outstanding feeling of brotherhood tied together these two courageous men....

Cruel are the laws of war. The struggle against the enemy called for great sacrifices. When the company attacked the village of Zvibo, the first to charge was the platoon commanded by Kozhornin. This unit wanted to carrry out the task it had been given, to burn down the storehouse with all its military equipment and to kill the general staff. The Germans attempted to pin the partisans down with hand grenades and machinegun fire. Nevertheless, the mission was carried out; both the storehouse and the German command went up in flames. But the redoubtable commander, Kozhornin, was fatally wounded and died on the battlefield.

Novkovsky's fearless comrades went shoulder to shoulder with him into battle. His consistent and firm willpower forged them into one united fighting force. His close friends were Prokhorov, Kozhornin, Biluzyorov, Nikitin, Petrov and Lavrentiev. His name and those of his aides will ever be dear and close to the hearts of the kolkhoz farmers in the region of Lenigrad.

The Germans burned down the village of Prochi for its relations with the partisans. But the latter were soon to get into the outpost that the Germans had built on the ruins of the village, where they apparently felt secure. The avengers of the people threw antitank grenades at the outpost, and the village that the Germans had burned down became their own burial ground.

In celebration of the Red Army anniversary, the German garrison at the village of Tiorikovo was wiped out. In honor of the First of May, the partisans struck at the German garrison in the village of

-69-

Kreizshi. On that international holiday of the workers, the dauntless fighters accomplished many heroic exploits.

* * * * *

In the woods and the marshes of the Leningrad region, the "victorious" Germans were being constantly harassed by the partisans. In only two months and ten days-- from the 20th of February to the 30th of April 1942 -- the Boiboi company led seven sorties against the enemies and killed a great many German soldiers.

During this same period, sabotage groups blew up the railway tracks running between the stations of Viajo-M.T. Sakh and Shibkovo-Poroslav, derailed a German military train between the stations of Morino and Polostank, cut telephone communications on the lone connecting Prochi to Gorky, and captured a great deal of booty and many storehouses.

Here is an excerpt from a letter found in the pocket of a killed German soldier:

"We are fighting in the heart of partisan country. It is my duty to tell you that many friends who arrived here with me are now among the dead or wounded. It is better to be at the front than here. There I know the distance separating us from the enemy. Here the enemy is everywhere; he is all around us; he is watching us from every nook and cranny; and his bullets usually find their targets."

Thus were the Germans, who had lorded it over the area, to feel the punishing hand of the partisans. As for the local peasants, they could get goth aid and protection from them. Communists Novkovsky did not spare any opportunity to prove to the peasants that he was their faithful protector, theirs and that of their cause. On one occasion, word got to the company that the fascist robbers had entered a village lying in partisan territory and had taken all the livestock and poultry. The company, headed by one of its commanders, soon arrived at the scene, wiped out the robbers, and returned all the loot, down to the last chicken, to the owners. This incident was illustrated in the cartoon that appeared in Boiboi's own newspaper, drawn by the young and talented partisan Nikitin, depicting birds flying out of the laps of dead Fritzes (Germans).

* * * * *

All the facts concerning the murders perpetrated
by the Germans were thoroughly examined by the company.
Evidence of torture, murder, and theft was entered in
special certificates signed by partisan representatives
and the kolkhoz people. Here is one such certificate
concerning the cruel acts of the fascists, as written
down at the scene of the crime:

We, the undersigned, have written this cer-
tificate concerning the murderous àcts of the
German fascists in the village of Karpova.
The certificate has been written by Molin,
head of special platoon of the Boiboi
company; Nikitin, head of the general staff;
Petrov, member of Krassny Krotief kolkhoz;
Feodor Petrov, Michael Gregoryev, and
Yevdokya Petrov:

On the night of the April first, a group of
robbers belonging to the SS punishment squad
broke into the village of Karpova, headed by
German officers. They found the inhabitants
fast asleep and set fire to all the houses
and other buildings in that place. In addition, they mounted a machine gun and opened
fire up and down the village. Besides their
barbarian acts they killed the woman
Vassyleva Marfa, aged sixty-five, and fifty-
one-year-old Gabrielov Michael. The entire
village, comprising twelve houses, was burned
down. The survivors of this brutal massacre
are now leading a life of poverty; they are
living in three wooden bath houses..."

(Signed)
Head of the Special Platoon
of the Boiboi Company
Chief of Staff
Kolkhoz Members

These criminal acts did not go without reprisals.
With firmness and ingenuity the partisans picked out
the traitors among the local inhabitants, an operation
which called for a large measure of equability and
self-restraint. Novkovsky recalled how partisans
dressed as German officers came to a village head, who
was a traitor. It was necessary to finish off this

-71-

traitor quickly, for he knew the hiding place of the partisan company. On seeing these German officers on this friendly visit, the head of the village offered his services to these "officer masters" and accompanied them to the path in the woods that led to the partisan headquarters. Needless to say, this was his last trip.

The bewilderment of the traitor's wife increased when, some hours after her husband had gone out with the "German officers," there came the Germans whom the head of the village had promised to show the way leading to the partisans. They had arrived too late. The man who could have shown them the way lay dead in a secluded path in the woods. The partisans applied the same treatment to other traitors.

All these activities enhanced the authority that the company wielded over the local population. Like a lodestone, the company drew to its ranks the best of the village people who were suffering under the yoke of occupation in the Lenigrad region. The company soon grew to such proportions that it was necessary to divide it into units according to regions. Along with the stepped-up momentum of the attacks the company launched against the Germans, there came the idea of setting up a partisan territory under Soviet rule behind enemy lines. In the summer of 1942, the partisans drove the Germans out of this vast area, which comprised about 2,000 villages. The Germans were forced to evacuate all the points they had captured in this territory. On the soil thus cleansed from German filth there streamed once again the usual Soviet way of life. Here, behind enemy lines, returned the kolkhozes, the schools, the activities concerned with information and culture; newspapers and leaflets, and celebrations were held in honor of Soviet holidays. In addition, an unbelievable operation under German occupation was carried out by Novkovksy: through the front line he sent about 200 carts laden with food supplies to the beleaguered city of Leningrad. On the way, many carts joined the expedition. Everyone tried to add something, the last onion, the last egg, but the main thing was "to send food to the people of Leningrad," Novkovsky was to sum up later.

Such was this Company Commander Novkovsky, a commander who generated respect and faith and allowed the people to participate in his exploits. This approach gave him the strength and courage to go through difficult situations with unflagging zeal.

Once, while saving himself from the Germans who had
suddenly appeared nearby, he was to wander in the
woods, lightly dressed and seriously wounded, for
twelve days, tired out, hungry, and frozen with cold.
But he held his own in the face of death.

In these modest words Comrade Novkovsky said of
himself "I was born to a working Jewish family. My
father learned to read and write by himself, thus
remaining uneducated for the rest of his life. The
outside world was an invincible barrier to him. He led
a hard life, a life of degeneration; but we, his
children, are doing creative work which is both
interesting and valuable. My brothers work at large
aircraft industries, and my sister is a newswoman."

"But I am not speaking of my own lot," adds
Novkovsky, "or of the fate of my relatives, although
even in this is reflected all that is new and important
in human life in our country. When I saw burned-down
villages, tortured children, violated women, I realized
and kept in mind only one thing: it is worthwhile to
sacrifice everything so that all this should never happen again; so that emancipated humanity should never
allow the warmongers to raise their heads. Of all this
I thought when I sat with my friends around a campfire
in the depths of the forest or when I hid within
impassable marshland. These were also the thoughts
that passed through the minds of my fellow partisans
who took part in the national war."

Editor's Notes

1. This short biographical sketch is taken from the Soviet Encyclopedia, 1951 edition.

2. The civil war in Russia after the October 1917 revolution. The "Whites" or "Bella Gwardia" supported the Czar; the "Greens" were the Communist forces.

3. Komsomol was the youth group of the Communist Party.

4. Latvian collaborators.

5. Jewish day school.

6. This was written in 1948.

7. Again, one must understand the minor exaggeration that the "heroic style" of these memoirs engenders.

PART II

Jewish Partisans
in Volynia and Polesia, Ukraine
1941-1944

IN THE FAMILY CAMP UNDER MAX'S COMMAND

Pesel Librant (Bronstein)

Long before the first "action,"[1] an attempt to organize and flee to the woods was made. Once, by chance, in Asher Halperin's house, in the restaurant downstairs, I ran into a group of men: Asher Halperin, Shmerel Paul, Avraham Slivka, my husband, Zev, and others. They did not allow me to be present at the meeting. I asked my husband for an explanation, and he told me that they were planning to escape together with the boys, without women. I told him the children and I wanted to accompany him. To my sorrow nothing came of this escape plan. Most were captured during the first action and the rest of the 370 Jews were shot in the "Horses' Graves."[2] A miracle happened to my husband -- he wasn't captured.

My husband, my son, and my brother worked in the sawmill next to the woods, and they began to plan an escape. On the last Friday before the liquidation of the ghetto, my husband and son parted from me and from my other three children. Bitter crying began. "Why us? Why do we have to die?" My husband hugged them and said, "Please don't cry, children. You are dear to me, and I will not abandon you." And, indeed, he went to the sawmill with my oldest son, Yaakov and returned home the same night. Meanwhile, there was a commotion on our street. Jews were being rounded up from every street. Representatives of the Judenrat also appeared and said, "This is the end for us all."

My husband began looking for separate hiding places for each one of the children. One could grab onto the huge tree in the yard, one could go underneath the stairway. I was against this and said that we had to hide together, and we started to go up on the roof. We lay stretched out, motionless, and all we heard was the forced gathering together amidst beating and cursing, of the Jews in the street.

The next day (on Shabbat) at dawn, I went down with my son Yaakov, who hadn't left me and I saw them assembling the Jews amidst shouts and threats; gradually there was quiet in the street. We heard until late at night only the drunken voices of the Ukrainian and Polish murderers who were celebrating their victory by drinking whiskey. Suddenly, we heard whispers, "Pesel, Pesel," and it was Faygeh Puchtik (Merin)[3] who had been hiding inside a cask in the stable; she came with us up on the roof. Later we heard a little girl's cry and the cry of Itka Rozenfeld, who was led off by the police. They had been hiding but were discovered. Itka tried to calm her small daughter. "This is our fate," she said.

The next day at four A.M., at dawn, we climbed down from the roof and began to leave the town. We crawled across the railroad tracks and went into the woods. We hid among the bushes the entire day. In the evening, on the way to the house of Slovik, the Polish forester, we met a farmer from the village of Manievich who was amazed that we had been able to escape. He gave us a piece of bread, but we greatly feared that he'd hand us over to the police force.

Upon our arrival at Slovik's home, barking dogs confronted us and Slovik came out to meet us. He did not tell us that there were other Jews hiding at his place; only later did we see my brother Shmuel's daughter, D'vorah Sherman, who had managed to escape. And also, there were Chava and Hershel Kuperberg and their daughter, Raizel. They had been hiding in a farmer's attic. (The Germans searched there, stabbed around with their bayonets, and injured the girl.)

At sunset Slovik led us to a shed in the middle of the woods, where we would stay through the night. In the morning my brother-in-law, Dov, and another person arrived and took us to the woods.

At the place to which we were led, we met the Michal Brat family with their four children, the Shmaryahu Guz family with their two children, and the two sisters Dinah and D'vorah Zilbershtein. Slovik instructed us to remain in the place throughout the day. In the evening he brought us to another hiding place. When I wanted to know why he was transferring us from one place to another, he replied: "You must believe me, if I had not transferred you, you would have been caught. Because the police searched your hiding places." He allowed us to collect potatoes from his fields and warned us not to take any from other fields.

With the passing of time, after many hardships and prolonged wanderings, during the rainy and snowy seasons, we were brought to the camp that was next to Max's fighting unit.

The Organization of the Family Camp

Max's family camp was separate from the fighting unit, about four kilometers from it. The guard duty and internal schedules were set up in accordance with the partisan commanders. Avraham Puchtik served as the camp's commander.[4]

I remember an incident from a time I was on guard duty with "rifles", with Yankeleh Guz, when a reconnaissance unit from the fighting units -- Kartuchin's, Naseikin's, and Max's -- started to approach our camp on horseback. When we heard that riders were approaching, we called to them to halt, and we asked them for identification. They were favorably impressed this manner of guard duty, and they mentioned us in their dispatches. Standing on guard duty was an obligation for all those who could use weapons, women, men, and youths over the age of twelve.

The first stage of our getting organized continued for four months, and we were sustained by pilfering from the fields and cellars of the Polish peasants. One day, partisans from Max's unit came by and told us that we had to move to the woods by the village. One peasant was supposed to give us shelter for awhile, until we reached the woods. But the peasant left us in the forester's house (it was winter) without food and frozen from the cold. Only after ten days did Itka and Rachel Brat arrive with two partisans who brought us bread and led us to the partisan camp. We did not know the camp's routine, and we began to "get organized," cooking potatoes, etc. And then Max appeared and started shouting: "All misery is on my head!" and ordered our removal from the camp.

They began to look for a suitable place for us, and they "settled us" on a piece of ground amidst swamp and marshes. We started digging bunkers. Water began streaming into them. We covered the walls with cowhide.

Gradually the camp became productive: a herd of cows and oxen grazed -- a source for meat and milk; we

prepared young pig meat and smoked meat sausages that
we gave out to the camp and to the partisans. We baked
bread and made toast for them.   For me civilian camp
then was without any shortages.

The family camp's residents would go out to the
fields of those peasants who were liquidated, according
to a list by the partisans, and would harvest and
gather the produce from their fields and gardens.   The
Jewish fighters would frequently come to the family
camp, bringing with them clothing, food, and all kinds
of goods that were important at that time.   The young
partisan men's attitude toward us, and especially
toward the children, was warm and friendly.   They, too,
benefited in the camp from the homey atmosphere, which
they needed so much. Here they changed sheets which we
laundered for them and washed themselves in the bathtub
that was set up in the <u>zimlaynka</u>.[5] After a short time,
the camp was spotted by Germans who discovered it from
their planes. We left the place. German tanks began
to attack the the camp, bomb it, but they didn't enter
it.   Upon our return we found the <u>zimlaynka</u> destroyed,
but, amazingly, most of the cows survived, scattered
about the woods and local villages.

During my entire stay in the woods, although I
prepared dishes of sausages made out of pig meat, etc.,
I never tasted this meat. While I cooked I would tie a
handkerchief around my mouth and had someone else taste
the dish.   I remember when we were moved from the woods
to a fighters' camp, they cut up pieces of pig meat for
everyone.   Max found out that I didn't eat pig meat.
He threatened that if he found a piece of pig meat in a
dish he would kill me. The children got frightened and
passed the piece of meat behind their backs when we
were searched.

On Passover eve, 1943, we received flour from the
partisans. We prepared dough and rolled it out with a
bottle on a board and baked <u>matzah</u> on the campfire in a
frying pan. The men <u>davened</u> by heart in a <u>minyan</u>.[6]
During the entire holiday we prepared dishes from potatoes and didn't eat <u>chametz</u>.[7]

On Yom Kippur eve we made candles out of wax,
using linen thread as a wick, and in this way we com-
memorated the memory of the martyrs. Mostly everyone
fasted.   That same Yom Kippur I had given a jar of
borsht and chopped meat to my twelve year old daughter,
Zisel.   She was then grazing the three hundred head of

sheep. At dusk she brought all the food to me "It's a commandment to fast on Yom Kippur," she said. We observed all the holidays in a special way, and prayers were said by heart, as much as possible.

I remember a Jewish refugee, one of the refugees from Manievich, who got sick and died after he had received "treatment" from a peasant. The camp's Jews gave him a Jewish funeral and wrapped him in linen material for a shroud. Any piece of material like this was then a rare commodity. Several other Jews died, including Hershel Kuperberg and Kahat Finkel, who Max himself killed and then hid, as we didn't know for a long time that he had been murdered. His son, Avraham Finkel, searched a long time for him until he found him, shot.

Often we sat together at the campfire, telling stories about the past, and here and there would be a joke or a song in Yiddish, Polish, Ukrainian or Russian. The youths and the children would begin, and the adults sometimes joined them. I remember Avraham Gorodetzer, who would sing songs in Yiddish filled with humor and joking, but he always ended with a sad song; then a silence would take over and gradually everyone left for a night's rest.

Children in the Camp

(For Avraham Merin, in blessed memory)

In our camp there were more than twenty children, the youngest three years old. They included children orphaned of both a father and a mother. These children, although they had "matured" and behaved as adults in every way, were in need of some "family care," such as bathing, haircuts, and more. (Shimon Mirochnik, who was in the fighting unit, brought me scissors from an "operation" as I had asked.) We cut their hair, and washed their clothes, and gave them showers in a bathtub set up with a barrel from above, with the water warmed up on a boiler. We women helped one another, knitting gloves, socks, and scarves. Chava Puchtik, especially, excelled at this. But, sadly, there were those who evaded all types of work.

It is especially worthwhile to mention Zisla Brat, who had a strong position, because her two daughters, Ida and Rachel, were in the fighters' camp. She took care of everyone, especially the orphan children, and demanded an equal share of the staples or clothing that the partisans, mainly the Jewish ones, brought for the camp's residents. I once heard her say to her partisan daughters: "Take care of the orphans. We, thank God, have a father who takes care of us."

I also remember the first "hot meal," (soup made out of flour) which she served us when we arrived at the woods, frightened and frozen from the cold.

I also remember the good deeds of Avraham Merin, the son of Yosef and Mindel. He was the only one from his family to survive, and he reached our group after walking through the local woods and marshes with Zecharya Viner for a long time. (They were both killed, as soldiers in the Red Army, close to the victory day).

One evening, as we sat frozen from the cold in a zimlaynka, he took off his jacket and covered my son with it. When I said to him, "Aren't you cold, too?" he replied, "It doesn't matter, these are small children and I'm able to tolerate it." Avraham excelled at preparing all kinds of medicines and ointments from plants. He actually saved my foot that had been completely swollen, with an ointment made out of pig fat and the sap of a pine tree. The ointment really worked wonders and helped many people who suffered from "tzerks," pus-filled infections that resulted from our declining sanitary conditions.

Leaving the Woods and the Soviet Homeland -- and Going Home!

In the winter of 1943, we got reinforcements for the camp. The Slovik family, headed by the Polish nobleman who had saved hundreds of Jews, was forced to leave its home, and came to our camp. First, Kapzik (Casimir), the son, arrived and then the entire Slovik family. It was thought that Slovik's deeds and actions had been followed for quite awhile, but he was mainly forced to move because of the Banderovtzy, who harassed the Polish settlers.[8] We received them joyfully and with open arms. He and his family got along well with the Jews, who had only appreciation and gratitude for him. (After the war the family received an agricultural farm from the Polish government and lived near the otryad[9] commander, Max, who rose to the rank of general and mayor.)

We left the woods when the Red Army arrived in our region. Our house in Manievich was burned down with the entire row of Jewish houses on our street. At the beginning of 1943, we had seen the flames of fire from the woods and were actually glad. We went to the nearby town of Rafalovka. We settled into the home of Simcha Brat, who had survived with his family, two daughters and a son; Michael and Zisel were also there with their four children, Itka, Rachel, Moshe, and Leah'la.

Once, late at night, when we were all sleeping closed up in the kitchen, we heard knocking on the door. We became very frightened. There had been many incidents of Banderovtzy murdering Jews who had returned from the woods. We were unable to identify the voice. Was it that of my husband, Velvel, who had been conscripted into the army? Kola, the partisan, who was with us at that time, moved cautiously with a weapon in his hand and opened the door. And there in the doorway stood a tall soldier on crutches. With difficulty, I saw that it was my brother-in-law, Avraham. The children at first were very frightened, but then became happy. I began to take care of him in order to rehabilitate him, physically and economically. His disability enabled him to move about freely on the roads and take "business" trips.

At the end of 1944 we succeeded in leaving, in a legal manner, for Chelm, Poland, as we wanted very much to go to Israel. We all went. Simcha Brat took provisions for the road -- a cow and a harness of horses. I brought two sacks of flour.

We arrived in Atlit in November 1945.[10] We could breathe easily. We had finally, truly, come home. My family and I moved to Kibbutz Ramat HaChovesh. My daughter, Shoshana joined a youth group at Kibbutz Yagur in Israel.

A PARTISAN'S TESTIMONY

David Blaustein

On Friday, 22 Elul, 5712, the night of the slaughter, I decided to flee from the town, come what may.[11]

I had previously heard that a number of Jews from Manievich and Griva were already in the Bir Woods, next to the villages of Lishnivka and Griva. I crossed the Lutzah, the main road, and the Sosnova road -- a road that went through Shlomo Verba's yard.

Zev Verba's mother, when she saw me leaving, asked that her son Zev go along with me. On the road, I met up with Urtziya Chazon, who was serving as a policeman. I arranged with him to direct us as if we were going to the sawmill. En route, the boy Zev Rabinowitz joined us. At first I tried to send him away, as his appearance was so very wretched. But he refused to leave, so I allowed him to join us.

As I crossed over the the eastern side of the town, I saw Shmaryahu Zafran and Yehoshua Kanonitz. We were a group of eight in all. We walked in the direction of the sawmill and, from there, to the Krasin road. We crossed over the fence of the "Praktaniya" and started running in the direction of the towns. On the way, some more people from Manievich joined us, and we ran about four kilometers into the woods. At my own initiative I assumed command of the company, and I showed them how to gather together all the food and divide it equally. Everyone listened to me. Thus, I took for myself, the only gun with its six bullets that had belonged to Yehoshua Kanonitz, in blessed memory.

I asked specifically for everyone's agreement to obey me, and they agreed. In the late night hours, we reached the yard of the landlord Sandutzin. There we filled our bellies with carrots and took provisions with us for the road. We continued in the direction of the village of Lishnivka. There I met the peasants who had had some contact with the Jews who were already in the woods with Kruk.[12] At last I received a number of messages, including one saying that they wanted contact with me, because I had served in the Polish Army in the cavalry and had become very familiar with all of the forests in the area due to commercial relations with the local peasants.

When I arrived at the village of Lishnivka we were a group of sixteen to eighteen men, including Pinchas Tina, Yitzchak Kuperberg, Asher Flash, Yosef Guz, and Chunek Wolper.

I asked the liaison peasant, Makri Maz, to deliver a message to Kruk, saying we were waiting next to the bridge over the Stock River. During the day, I attended to the confiscation of bread from the shepherds in the fields.

The following night, we met with the company from Lishnivka by the bridge. The brothers Abraham and Yisrael-Hersh Blaustein and others informed me that Kruk was preparing to abandon twenty of the comrades, because their fate would be bitter without arms and, even more important, without familiarity with the region. Yitzchak Kuperberg came up to me and kissed me: "Only in times of trouble," he said, "is it possible to recognize a human being, and that is you, David."

The messengers returned to inform Kruk of our arrival. Kruk himself arrived and led the entire group to the edge of Nabroski, deep in the woods. There we decided that a portion of the men would go out together with our men to gather some food for the group, without revealing its whereabouts. Kruk had good reason to do this. According to him, an embarrassing incident had occurred in Troyanovka because of a Jew who had been captured by the Germans and had led them to the hiding places of all of Troyanovka's Jews.

We got ourselves organized in the woods. A month later I told Kruk that we had to move to another forest, because the peasants "smelled" that Jews were living there. It is worth mentioning that the only arms in our possession were Yehoshua Kanonitz's gun and a few "utrizim" (sawed-off shotguns). Kruk brought us to the woods surrounding the village of Sarchov. There we counted more than thirty people, mostly from Manievich and the local villages. There were also a number of women among them. I approved Yitzchak Kuperberg's request to bring back his parents and sister who were in Koninsk with Slovik,[13] and I sent a number of men with him. They later brought back with them Chava, Hershel, and Elka Kuperberg.

The group of Jews with Kruk and Yosef Zweibel numbered in the tens, consisting mainly of the Zweibel and Rozenfeld families and the Lishnivka Jews. In the Sarchov woods, we made an effort to collect food in anticipation of the coming winter. We would dig pits in which to store potatoes and cover them up so that the peasants would not discover them. We dug more than twenty-two pits. We brought the potatoes to new "habitations" in the middle of the woods and covered them with the forest's vegetation for camouflage.

We had in our possession three sawed-off, defective rifles. Kruk agreed that I should come to him to fix them. I reached his camp after a nightlong journey, and the rifles were fixed and ready for action.

On the way, I fired some test shots. The rifles really worked. Upon my return, I found out that a peasant had arrived at the camp on the pretext of looking for oxen. I could see that danger was lurking here; he wasn't really looking for escaped oxen, but rather searching for the hiding places of the Jews. One night after we had returned from an operation, Chunek Wolper was on guard duty. We all lay down to sleep when suddenly, a shot was heard. It was Chunek's shot that saved us. A hail of bullets came down on all sides. I gave the order to flee and disperse, and the company fled. We had with us a refugee from Trespol by the name of Aharleh, whose leg was swollen from an erysipelas he had contacted. We had carried him on his back to the camp, but at the time of our escape he held onto my coat and ran behind me. The power of the will to survive!

We ran the entire night. About three kilometers from Kruk's camp, we stopped. I went to him, by myself, and told him about the attack on us. Kruk decided that it was necessary to also move his camp immediately, because he was certain that the police would follow us. He knew the local woods well, and with his leadership we tread many kilometers into the thick of the woods to a new campsite.

We went out to the villages to find out who the attackers were. It became clear that they had been Germans, together with the Ukrainian police force. There was no doubt that this had been the work of the peasant who had been looking for oxen.

After three months we decided (Kruk, myself, and the others who were armed) that it was important to set up a fighting unit, and that those unfit to carry arms -- women, old people, and children -- in all about 100 people, would organize a family camp that would be under our protection. I went over to the fighting unit. We collected food and clothing for the family camp and from time to time brought them whatever we could.

The family camp was situated close to the fighting unit and began to organize a life it would be worthwhile to describe at a later time. We Jewish partisans gave a lot of attention and concern to the family camp. Each time we returned from an operation we went into the camp, as we brought with us equipment and food.

The fighting group began its operations by coordinating with other units, and we concentrated mainly on blowing up trains. I personally took part in blowing up thirteen trains.

Outside of other operations, we knew that in Manievich there were many who had taken part in the murdering of Jews. We had a list of fifty-six murderers we decided to liquidate, and I admit and confess that with my own hands, I liquidated eighteen. With this I fulfilled the martyrs' will and testament -- to avenge their spilled blood. It was not easy! However, in the beginning we severely punished the murderers, according to our own decision -- that of the unit. Later we had to get permission from Dadya Petya's partisans' headquarters, to which our unit, along with Max and Kartuchin's unit belonged.[14]

We made the effort and also received permission to avenge the blood of the Jews of Troyanovka, who were murdered by the peasants of Gradisk.

I knew the residents of the village due to my business dealings with them, and I requested to join the partisan group under the command of Berl Lorber ("Malenka") and Yisroel Puchtik ("Zalonka"), together with thirty partisans. We liquidated about twenty murderers and left in every house a notice written in Russian, saying that this had been a retaliatory mission for the Jews of Troyanovka, who were caught and murdered by them.

Once when we were on our way to an operation near the village of Stivikva, we found inside a bunker six or seven Jews, men, women, and children, who were all skin and bones. We took clothes off ourselves and dressed them and left them food. I do not know what their fate was, because they were far from our base.

During our entire stay in the woods, individuals who were hiding in the woods or with the peasants joined our family. It eventually numbered more than 100 people and included women and children, young men and young women.

A Good Ending

With the liberation from the woods, a new chapter of wandering began for me: conscription into the Red Army. Many of my friends who were conscripted fell in battle on the way to Berlin. I decided to reach Eretz Yisrael at any cost. In Rovno I made contact with Abba Kovner's group, and I went with their help to Lublin. I volunteered for public work in the Jewish community there, and I was assigned to organize an orphanage.

I began gathering children who had been hiding with Polish peasants; sometimes I had to use armed force to take these Jewish children from them. There were also incidents where the children themselves did not want to leave the peasant's domain. At the inception of the orphanage, there were about thirty children, and several months later, when I left, there were sixty-four. I tried to instill in them a love for Eretz Yisrael through the study of Hebrew, using placards, etc. But this idyll did not last long, because I was threatened by the danger of imprisonment. The men of the "escape" decided that I had to leave.[15] I went to Rumania, got married, and immigrated to Israel with my wife. As of today I am a "lord" in my nation and in my land, and we have three children and three grandchildren. Let them multiply!

STAGES IN THE ORGANIZATION OF THE PARTISAN FIGHTING

Abba Klurman

The organization of the partisan fighting began, in fact, only in the fall of 1942, when Jewish young men went out to the woods and became the nucleus for the formation of partisan units. Word spread through the town that there was an organization made up of refugees from the Soviet rule who had remained in the rear lines when the Red Army retreated.

The reason for these people staying behind was hazy. It was very doubtful that they had stayed behind in the occupied area in order to organize a Soviet underground in the German military rear line, as the rumors stated. I suspected that the rapid disin-

-88-

tegration of the Red Army at the beginning of July 1941, after the unexpected German attack, was the cause for their remaining behind. A local incident is imprinted in my memory that points to the friendship that prevailed or, more accurately, that was nurtured between the Germans and the Russians, especially in the border regions; because of this it is possible to infer that the Russian officers had no idea about the clash with the Germans. In any case they had not planned on preparing staff officers for fighting in the Germans' rear lines after retreating, which they had not dreamed of doing in the first place.

On June 19, 1941 I was taking part in a party organized by Soviet officers for the German officers, who had come to us to attend to moving the Volks Deutsch from the occupied Russian regions to Germany.[16] At the same party, Soviet military officers were uttering threats in the ears of Jewish girls who refused to dance with German officers.

It is worthwhile mentioning that one night before the outbreak of the war, in the city of Brisk on the Bug River, German trains, filled with soldiers, crossed the border, disguised as merchandise for the Soviet Union. The cars were not expected at all. When the war broke out, commando units with improved military equipment jumped from the cars and attacked the city of Brisk. An additional fact is that, at the very least, in the region of my hometown, Kamin-Kashirsk, there was not any prepared organization to deal with the possibility of a war in the rear lines, one of the cardinal principles in the partisan organization; the remaining Russians fled from the ghettos. This occurred, in essence, between the first action and the final liquidation (during the period between May-October 1942).[17]

The plan for the final solution in the areas taken from the Russians by the Germans in 1941, as distinguished from the plan for the final solution in the territories taken by the Germans in 1939, was based on two concrete liquidation operations, the last one being complete.

1) Psychological preparation for annihilation that came about through selective murdering.

2) Complete annihilation in two actions.

This also confirms again and again the fact that the Germans had no trouble finding collaborators in carrying out the annihilation. These included the Ukrainians, who had been the Jews' neighbors for generations. The Germans found in them active collaborators who were ready to carry out the murder of a people. The final plan for destruction of the Jewish population in all the other occupied regions was carried out by removing the Jewish population from their home towns on various pretexts, such as assembling them for "work camps." In the Ukraine and Byelorussia, on the other hand, the Jews were publicly annihilated with the help of the local residents, who did not take the trouble to prepare alternative plans if there were to be mishaps or mistakes in the annihilation operation. One piece of evidence that confirms that there were preparations for massive annihilation is that in July of 1941, four weeks following the occupation, the Jews were put to work preparing the ground, digging pits, etc., near the Jewish cemetaries where, in fact, the murders were carried out.

The Jews -- Combat and Creative Potential

With the grouping together of Jews from all levels, from those who were educated to the lowly maidservant, there was great creative potential. With their strong desire to justify the essence of their existence, this potential was doubled and tripled, helping the fighting units. And there was a nucleus of communal life in the middle of the woods. While there was no agricultural or economic base, every one of the camp's residents carried a load of knowledge and the desire to create, help, and contribute. They also contributed to keeping up the moral framework between the partisan fighting unit surrounding the population.

The beginning of the partisan organization was based on the ethical behavior of the Russians who fled from German imprisonment, the pro-Soviet Ukrainians, or the Poles who did not sympathize with the Germans and had been forced to flee to the woods. One can see in this period the first stage of individuals, or of small groups, who began the armed struggle against the Germans and their allies. Their behavior was different from that which existed in the area. It was an area where all kinds of gangs swarmed whose common denominator was looting and plunder, murder and rape.

The second stage was still based on violence, murder, and rape by the fighters on the civilian population. But there began to be restraint, a slowing down of lawlessness, and gradually there was a governing force from above which took the trouble to unite the ranks of the fighter; it did so successfully.

The third stage was defined by cooperation, tranquility, and humane relations in private and family life. And it was the "Jewish camp" that contributed to this, and as I pointed out earlier, it was one of the significant factors that led to a repairing of relations between the partisans and the local population.

Kruk -- Anti-Semitism in the Midst of the Partisans

One of the central figures in our Partizankeh was, without a doubt, Kruk. And it is not surprising that our opinions about him are divided. On the one hand, he received almost every Jew, even non-combatants, under his auspices; on the other hand he also killed Jews, including youths, because of a breach of discipline (though he also killed Ukrainians for this reason). All in all, he was a primitive man, illiterate, but imbued with an instinctive sense for absolute justice and fine organizational ability. In my humble opinion, there was not a trace of anti-Semitism in him. On the contrary, I would dare say he was, as we nicknamed him, one of the "righteous of the nations."[18] In fact, he also was not a Communist. The combination of Kruk and Jews was formed because both parties were looking for partners for support.

The anti-Semitism among the partisans mainly derived from the Russians' belief in some idea of freedom and equality, at a time when they imagined and remembered the Jews to be merchants and exploiters. It is possible that we felt guilty for following after a Gentile out of indecision and a certain fear. We could have gotten along as well without them.

Kruk killed as a result of the pressure of time. Generally people acted then according to the senses alone, and life or death was a trifling matter, a game, nothing else. Kruk was the one who would order fighters to guard the citizens' camp, when we had left them on their own and mortal danger awaited them. Through his inspiration we also left them a lot of food.

Still, it must be emphasized that it was not Kruk, Max, or Moscow who organized these partisan units but the young Jews discussed in this book.

IN THE FOREST WITH GRANDFATHER

Micha Gazit

And this is what I want to do -- all the survivors of the Holocaust probably do the same -- I want to present a vivid picture and revive all those moments in my life which I still remember from childhood and boyhood.

The 1940's. Europe is fighting and bleeding. Germany is victorious everywhere, and one can feel that the "vision" of a thousand years of the Reich, the reign of the "pure Aryan race," will come true. Not a single country in Europe could oppose the Germans; not a single army could resist the stream of the German armoured forces or their trampling boots. But for us, this was not simply occupation. It was a question of life and death. Our lot was different from that of all other defeated nations that were allowed to live. And what on earth was it we wanted? All we wanted was to be left alive.

I can still vividly remember the escape into the forest. Beaten and frightened, we were like those creatures who fled from a rapidly spreading fire; we ran wherever we could, in all directions. In front of us there were the great Polesia forests, the marsh land, and the rivers streaming through enormous areas. It was a dark and rainy night in the autumn of 1942 when my uncle Joseph sent us strict orders to escape quickly, because the next day we all would be sent away and slaughtered. We left quietly in the dark of the night, under the watchful eyes of the German and Ukrainian guards. We were moving in circles, afraid of meeting people, because the hatred all over the Ukrainian villages was enormous. All that night we walked in the midst of the deep forest toward the meeting spot which my uncle had decided on earlier.

In the early morning we made our first stop. We took slices of dry bread and sugar cubes, which we still had with us, out of our bags. And so we lay all

day long, waiting for new orders tellingwhen to move.
Suddenly good news arrived -- there was a group of partisans gathering in the neighborhood village. (Later
the group was named the Kruk division.) This Kruk knew
my uncle very well; when in trouble, they used to help
each other.   And so the partisans started organizing
their people in the forests.

This first nucleus developed into a company, which
in the course of time became a place of security for
all the Jews who had survived and had run into the
forest.   And in the forests connections were created
between distant people -- strangers became brothers.
Brothers sharing the same fate -- stress, cold, hunger
-- comrades in arms.   This was the covenant of blood
created by the war. Jewish partisans, a symbol of our
new pride, which since the days of the Maccabees had
been buried somewhere deep in our subconscious. Jewish
partisans, the first sign of the renewal of the
people's youth and a sign of good tidings of revival.
This is what I thought and imagined in those harsh
days.   I, a Jewish boy of twelve. But the partisans
did not realize what they really were.

The Jewish partisans fought a battle of revenge.
There was no enthusiasm in those dreary days, death was
lurking everywhere and it was terribly real; you could
feel it close at hand.   The fighting was hopeless and
nobody thought of survival -- only revenge.   In the
long and dark nights, they were marching toward their
missions -- exploding of trains and fortifications,
disrupting of communications, destroying of bridges,
hitting the enemy in the rear.   They were marching in
long lines, carrying outdated arms and wearing rags.
They were walking silently, and only in their faces
could one discern the stubborn bitterness and the
burning eyes thirsty for revenge.

We, the camp of women and children, were
accompanying them with loving eyes and wishes for
success and safe arrival home.   Every parting was like
a last one -- every pressing of the hands was a last
one.   We were anxious, because they were like those
uncrowned Olympic champions whose records spoke for
themselves.   The partisans' records boasted of killed
Germans, of damaged trains and, most important, of the
disruption of the supply-road, so essential for the
enemy -- the main road to Kiev.   Every delay of these
loaded trains bound for the front was a great victory.
The number of graves of our dear comrades was

increasing day by day. This was the price for victory. The forest became very precious to us. Among those thick trees covering enormously wide areas we found our home. This was our rear area, our country. We penetrated into the most secret corners of the forest, into places where it seemed man's foot had never trodden. It was virgin soil into which we injected life.

There lived among us in the forest a wonderful man, an outstanding person. It was Grandfather Shlomo Zweibel, of blessed memory. His glorious beard and his typically Jewish appearance symbolized for us the Jewish tragedy of this war. I vividly remember those days when Grandfather used to wake up early in the morning, when the forest was still dark. Grandfather used to prepare himself for his personal talk with the creator. He would put on the tefilin and talit and would raise his head up high -- he would stand and murmur his prayers in whisper and devotion. And then, in unity with him, the entire forest would wake up.

The birds began singing while circling over the tops of the trees; on the branches sleepy squirrels would spring, drops of cold dew still glistening on their long tails. From beneath the trees a strange and different voice would burst forth, by no means less pure than that above. One could listen to prayers like Ma Tovu Ohalecha, and "God of Abraham, Isaac and Jacob...," "To Jerusalem thy city thou shalt return in mercy"... and "We sinned we offended."

And the trees stood still, like that holy congregation on Yom Kippur, a big and diverse crowd. Back home on Yom Kippur, the crowd was clad in white, and here in brown. And here in the forest too, Grandfather would pass in front of the Ark of the Law, and his lips would utter prayers and psalms. This was prayer never before uttered in such a way and in such surroundings. And I do not know if such a pure prayer will ever be uttered again. During all those years Grandfather's food consisted of potatoes only, because there was no kosher food. He used to retire into the forest, light his small fire, roast his few potatoes, and eat them slowly, as if he were eating delicacies. And he felt replete, more replete than anyone else. How could he? Only God knew.

And when the partisans were leaving the forest for their operations, they always remembered Grandfather

Zweibel and always brought him something kosher, which they had stolen somewhere. They did it because Grandfather was loved by all. Not only did they love him, but they also guarded him as a most dear human being. When Passover approached, Grandfather would contemplate very hard how he could keep all the rituals, those rituals which he kept strictly his whole life. The partisans remembered the holiday, bringing him kosher dishes and fulfilling his special holiday needs. In those remote days there was some consolation in what the partisans did.

Out of the dreariness, in the midst of the daily bloodshed, acts of chivalry of the individual and the group hovered prominently. And it was those deeds which lit the few sparks of light in the darkness surrounding us.

The hardest time for us was the winter, the cold winter of the Ukrainian forests. Typical for the winter were the horrible storms, hurling the forest violently and sweeping out all those creatures who inhabited it in warmer days. And then the heavy snow would fall and accumulate on the branches and on treetops, till the trees themselves would fall down, unable to bear their heavy burden.

And we were wandering within this cold dreariness -- we and the hungry wolves, both of us looking for food, both of us chased, as it seemed, by the same demons. The wolves cherished some special sentiment for us. During our stay near them they did not touch us, they only revealed some "playfulness" toward our food.

And in those cold days the Germans would enter the forest on purpose. They would raid the depths of the forest to find our hiding places and to finish with us. They thought that in the winter it would be easier to starve and freeze us. And then came the days of trial. There were days during which we felt completely lost. We would run in all directions. We would run thousands of miles without rest, passing frozen swamps and mountains of boggy snow, and from time to time we would groan, fall down, breathing heavily, stand up again, and stubbornly move on and on ....

There were nights in which, after running a lot, we would gather in one place, a heap of human bodies, wet and hurt. Nobody would utter a word. We would lie almost unconscious, and only the strong among us would from time to time wake the sleeping, because even a short sleep in the snow could have ended in the everlasting sleep. Sometimes we would sit and sometimes lie down, and the snow would be our pillow. We would also stare at the skies, at the distant glittering stars.

There would be times we would strive to fly high up into those distant and benevolent worlds of enormous light, shining on God's angels who hover in the light and fly close to His holy chair. At midnight the moon would appear and shine brightly. Its face would be sadder than ever, because it was bereaved. The moon would bewail those of her sons who in the past would sanctify it every month and welcome it with happiness and joy. And here in the forests there was nobody to welcome it; now it also was bereaved. And so it would move on and sink into far distances. And you would feel as if you wanted to tell the moon something, to send with the moon a message for your distant brothers, if they survived, if any were still alive. You wished to send them the blessing, "Be strong and of good courage."

But there were also nights without the moon, dark nights of snow and storm. We would grope in the dark without compasses and in no particular direction, walking stooped, horror looking from our eyes and accompanying our steps. From the far distance we could hear the howling of the wandering wolves and echoes of the trees breaking in the wind. The snow would utter deaf rattlings when our feet pressed its white smooth rugs. From time to time we shook the snow from our backs and dried our eyes, which were running with tears of cold.

At the end of the line we could discern Grandfather, his beard frozen in splinters and his back stooped low, bearing the burden of his years. On his back he carried a bag from which a fringe of the talith was dangling in the wind. Did he then see himself as one who wore the last talith in Israel, as one whose talith did not guard him anymore that day, as that day he did not wrap his back to pray? From time to time Grandfather would raise his eyes, as if looking for something, as if hoping for a day which was so far away -- he would look for tomorrow to come and rescue him from this dreary existence which seemed as endless as the galut (diaspora) itself. He would look for his God

who had long ago forgotten to look down at him from
heaven and to see...

Translated by Esther Kluger of Israel

A TOWN IN THE WOODS

Abraham Puchtik

In underground trenches in various places in the
Volynia and Polesia Woods, Jewish "towns" blossomed
during the period of the Holocaust. They were the
citizen camps under the control of Russian and Jewish
partisans.

In the citizens' camp in the Kochov Woods, there
were about 150 souls, sometimes more, sometimes less,
because there were reunions of families or friends.
People came there from ghettos in the Rovno region.
There were entire families, portions of families, and
individuals. Most were men who were fit for fighting
and hardships, but there were a few old people and
children who required help and care.

We dug our bunkers for our quarters. We called
them zimlaynkas These quarters were camouflaged, and a
guard was posted over them, day and night, from the
partisan camp, which was under the leadership of "Dadya
Petya" (Anton Brinsky). Individuals and families with
some kind of weapon were taken in by the partisans.

When we began to set up, the number of partisans
was small and their weapons were few. In time we ac-
cumulated more fighters, some of them having escaped
German imprisonment. Thus, arms that had been taken as
booty from the Germans and the Bolbovtzy (Ukrainian
nationalists) were added to what we had. Our partisan
unit was in contact with other units, and in time of
need we cooperated with one another.

As was taken for granted under those circumstances, the partisans' job was to provide arms, food,
shelter, and means of transportation. The operations
were carried out against the Germans and their allies.
Until the outbreak of the war, I lived with my family
in the village of Holozi in the area of the town of

Manievich. I had had business relations with the local villages. During the Soviet rule I was director of the flour mill near the village of Holozi and as a result, I became an expert in the work of running mills. A number of months after the German occupation, in the autumn of 1941, we were expelled to the Manievich ghetto. We hid with village friends before the first "action" began, and we were not harmed.

We knew that in order to survive we had to flee to the woods. Among those who were fit for this dangerous mission was a portion of my family -- my wife, Chava, my son, Yitzchak, my daughter, Itkeh, and myself. My mother, my sister, and my two small daughters stayed in the ghetto.

We fled to the woods. We built a hut and I got in contact with my village friends. I got food from them, as well as a rifle with ammunition.

We wandered far into the woods searching for the partisans. In one of northern Volynia's spacious forests, we succeeded in reaching a group of Russian and Jewish partisans. Thanks to the rifle, I was accepted into this group. The commander was responsible for getting food for the citizens' camp that was part of his organization. I was among the most active members. My son, Yitzchak, became a part of the fighting brigade.

Concern for food was implicit in the term, "to organize," which meant taking from the villagers. To accomplish this, a group of armed partisans would go out and, in a show of strength, would obtain food, fuel, matches, house and kitchen utensils, and more. At the camp we were concerned with cleanliness, discipline, quiet, and mutual aid. Women took care of housework. My wife mainly attended to child care.

During the partisan operations, certain villages were taken, including the place where "my" flour mill was from the days of Russian rule. The mill was full, and the otryad commander ordered me to operate it for the local villagers, as a portion of the flour was reserved for our people. During the four months of the mill's operation, in the summer of 1942, I managed to collect enough flour for our people for the winter season.

The Bolbovtzy "smelled" the mill one day. We stopped operating it. After a fierce battle, the enemy retreated and we again operated the mill, but after ten days we were forced to leave it. It fell into the hands of the Bolbovtzy who burned it.

The second winter in the woods (1942 - 1943) we had an abundance of flour, four cows, and potatoes, but mortal danger awaited us. The woods were swarming with Germans and Ukrainian police. We had to leave and move onward in order to join up with another partisan unit. We left behind the cows and loaded up our wagons and horses with old people, children, food, and clothing. The rest went on foot and, following four armed partisans, the march set out. We trudged along that entire night, a winter's night, but in vain. We did not meet any partisans. In broad daylight we hid among trees and bushes. That short winter's day was interminable for us. Near us the villagers moved about, engaged in their business, but fortunately we were not noticed.

In the evening we went, four Jewish partisans, to the nearby village of Zelnitza in order to collect provisions. There we found an empty barn. Our men went inside and gathered grain for four full days. There were Bolbovtzy in the area. Other partisans that we met told us that the enemy had not discovered our living quarters and that the cows were still there. We returned "home" to our trenches.

A strong fighter joined our ranks -- D'vorah. She went on the most difficult missions. To our sorrow, she fell because of treason. One Banderovtzy infiltrated our ranks, and he handed her over to the enemy. There was also an incident of a killing based on settling a personal account. The Polish partisan commander, Max, shot a Jewish partisan, Kahat, because in his day, a man by the name of Kahat had killed the commander of the Polish police force.

For some reason there arose in the partisan headquarters a desire for valuables, and an order was issued to give jewelry and ready cash to headquarters. Those who violated the order could expect the death penalty. I, at the risk of my life, was involved in trying to prevent the implementation of this order. I worked at obtaining food for our camp. One day I arrived at the flour mill in Karasin. The mill belonged to a Pole who was murdered along with his family by the Banderovsty. I operated the mill after I received permission to do so. Someone informed on me, charging personal fraud in my job, and a search was conducted accompanied by an interrogation of witnesses. It was then I learned that this had been a case of intentional slander and nothing else.

It was the beginning of spring, and the Red Army had entered the region. From our camp youths were inducted into the Red Army and some of them fell in battle. A few of our people were killed after the liberation by the Banderovsty. We endured many more hardships. But most of the people of the "town" in the woods survived. And some of them, including myself, reached Eretz Yisrael.

THE FIRST DAYS IN THE WOODS

Zev Avruch

One evening (19, Elul, 1942), we decided to flee from the Manievich ghetto, in spite of the mortal danger involved in the escape.[19] Whoever was caught was shot on the spot. Our goal was to reach Kruk, the organizer of a partisan group in the area.

Parting from our parents was very melancholy. They gave us some light valuables, all that they had, mostly threads that we could exchange for bread. We left and had to stop for a moment. We heard the weeping voices of our dear ones. We fled. But the voices followed after us and still follow me till this very day.

My sister, Faygeh, took a chance and approached the house where Kruk was known to be hiding. She was successful. We walked in the dark of night into the thick forest, my sister, Faygeh, my brother, Berl, and I. The fear that took hold of us was an old one. The same fear was with us every time there were people who chased after us and who, from time to time, overtook us. It was similar to that primal fear one feels fleeing in the dark of night in dense woods.

At dawn we reached the village of Lishnivka. Here we met the brothers Avraham and Hershel, natives of our city. In the village there was a peasant acquaintance of ours. He allowed us to stay one day in his barn. In the evening we headed for Kruk's house.

Kruk was a Ukrainian Communist, a native of the village of Griva. During the Soviet rule in eastern Poland, he served as head of the village of Griva. With the retreat of the Red Army, Kruk moved to Kiev. He went through training there, received some kind of arms, and was dropped by parachute near his village. His objective was to organize a partisan detachment from the local residents. He hid in different places, and changed his outer appearance as much as possible. He moved about the villages and tried to persuade the young Ukrainians to join him and organize a partisan group -- but in vain. He had success with the young Jews, but Kruk refused to take anyone without weapons. He postponed fulfilling his plans and meanwhile worked in units. At night when he arrived at his living quarters, he wasn't pleased that we had come to him without arms, but he agreed to take us. In his outer appearance, he was a partisan "to the hilt," dressed in leather clothing and equipped with a rifle, pistol, and ammunition. He also had binoculars in his possession.

We went out to the road. He told us that in the woods was a group of young Jews who had fled from the villages even before the Jews had been moved to the Manievich ghetto and to other ghettoes.

His partisan leadership training began with instructing us in how to gather potatoes into sacks that he had prepared. This seemed strange to us -- to go into a strange field and gather the fruit of someone else's labor. After we had gathered the potatoes, Kruk brought us to the cowshed of a certain peasant. He drew his pistol, and under the threat of killing him, demanded a sheep. Berl, my brother, carried the sheep on his shoulders to the woods. Kruk knew every tree and path in the woods and led us to a place that was surrounded on three sides by uncrossable swamps.

On Kruk's partisan territory we met with families and individual Jews. Kruk appointed himself commander; his first order was for two volunteers to go to Manievich and persuade the Jews to flee to the woods. The volunteers were my sister, Faygeh, who disguised herself as a Ukrainian, and a lad by the name of Yechezkel from the village of Lishnivka who looked like a young Ukrainian.

The two of them arrived at the town, but to our great sorrow, they were late for the designated meeting time. This was on Shabbat, the 23rd of Elul, in the morning. On that day the Jews of Manievich were shot and thrown into prepared pits.

Individuals who escaped reported that on Friday night, they led the Jews to the killing site. The Jews cried and shouted and waited for the help and salvation that did not arrive. They shouted and commanded those who would live to avenge their blood. This command somehow reached us.

And, indeed, we fulfilled their holy command. We fought in the partisans' ranks against the cruelest enemy of our people that history has ever known.

EXEMPLARY FIGHTERS

Shmaryahu Zafran

One day when we were in the village, working at the threshing floor, Linda, the peasant's wife, came back from the city and told us that the Germans, with the help of the Ukrainian militia, were taking Jews out of their homes and into the street, making them lie face down on the ground, and cruelly beating them. Every now and then trucks would arrive to take the Jews to the "Horses' Graveyard" on the outskirts of the city of Manievich. There they forced the Jews to dig pits, and afterwards, shot them as they stood on the edge of the pit; those slain would fall directly into the pits.

She burst into tears. "Even though I also don't see Jews as people, this is too much already," she said, wiping her nose with her hand, and she made us leave, for fear of the Germans.

We stayed in the woods near the village until the evening. Despite the strict curfew, we succeeded in slipping by the German guards, and we arrived home, where bitter news awaited us: Our father and brother-in-law, along with more than 360 Jews, had been killed.

Upon hearing this terrible news, the idea of revenge crystallized in my consciousness. I hid. I found out that several other youths were in hiding. I went out one evening and talked to Yehuda Melamedik (who later, as a partisan, was killed in a heroic sit-

-102-

uation) about leaving for the woods. The two of us talked to Zev Verba, David Flash, and Shimon Mirochnik. We had only one pistol, which had been repaired by Yehoshua Kanonitz after he found it in a grove. It was clear to us that it was impossible for us to leave as a group, and so we decided that everyone would leave on his own.

We designated the nearby village of Holoziya as our central meeting place. After many hardships, we finally were able to leave the town. David Weinshtein helped me. After awhile, we all met in the woods, everyone sharing a story about how he slipped by the police guard posts.

Before leaving home, my sisters, although not my mother, were opposed to my fleeing. My mother was indeed afraid that, God forbid, I would be killed in the woods, but she immediately stopped crying and wished me well, "Go safely, my son, and avenge the spilled blood of your father, your family, and of all the Jews." And there is no farewell more difficult than this, when you sense very clearly that you will never see your mother again.

Successful Operations

Our division received a directive ordering an operation in the direction of the city of Sarni; one of the objectives was to obtain, along with some others who had crossed the border near Zhitomir, automatic weapons that Commander Kruk had hidden. One partisan, who had been among those who had hidden the weapons, came with us. The journey took place without a mishap. Some of the weapons were found, but most of them were apparently taken by the local peasants.

On the way back, we (two squadrons) blew up a train and a wooden bridge over the railroad tracks, and the third squadron set up an ambush not far from a village in the area. Our central meeting place was in a grove next to the village. The operations were successful above and beyond our expectations. We left without a scratch. We found a hiding place, and it was only the next night that we began to move in the direction of the base.

In one of the villages, lived a contact man for the partisans who was known in our headquarters. We

made a detour to the edge of the village and learned to
our joy that the chief of police of Sarni was staying
overnight in the village with three policemen.

The chief of police had a mistress who lived near
the village, and from time to time he went to visit
her. We were given a briefing on the houses where they
were staying for the night. We divided into several
small groups and simultaneously surrounded the houses
where the Ukrainian policemen, who loyally and diligently served the Nazi regime, were staying. I had the
fortune to be in the group that surrounded the house
where the chief of police was staying. After continuous negotiations, the chief of police surrendered
and came out with his hands raised.

The policemen surrendered long before this. We
confiscated their weapons and quietly, without creating
a disturbance, left the village. Regretfully, as we
were drunk with victory, we forgot the rules of
caution, and our men began robbing the collaborators.
We hitched two wagons to horses, and loaded them with
everything at hand, from food to clothing. We
liquidated the collaborators and left the village two
hours before sunrise, going in the direction of the
woods and swamps of Strashov, where there were Polish
strongholds on the former Polish-Russian border. There
were two Jews in this division, myself ("Veirni") and
another young Jew ("Zaytchik"). In our group there
were several Ukrainians who agitated against the Jews
and caused serious arguments among us on the subject of
the Jews. We stationed ourselves about a kilometer
from the village, on the road leading to another
village. We gave food to the forest watchman's family
to cook for us. We placed a guard on the road leading
to the forest watchman's house, and the fighters lay
down to sleep. I stood guard during the second shift,
at sunrise. At the same time the unit commander awoke
and asked me to go into the forest watchman's house to
see if the food was ready. I explained to him that I
had gotten up to relieve the guard. He saw the company
was fast asleep, and he said, "It would be a shame to
awaken them, they did such a nice job, I'll go myself."
And he got up and went.

Dangerous Missions

I stayed there a little bit longer, as I had five
minutes left. On the way to guard duty, before I

reached the guard, a burst of fire from automatic weapons was suddenly heard, followed by light shelling. We immediately hit the ground. After ten minutes, all was quiet. I ran back to the fighters who were in a state of alert. I told the deputy commander that the commander had gone to see the forest watchman. The deputy asked my friend, the Jew, and another Ukrainian to go and find out the source of the shots. To my shock, the Jew Zaytchik refused to go, pleading a stomachache. The Ukrainian claimed that if the "Zhid's" (this disgraceful nickname was prohibited by law in the U.S.S.R.) stomach hurt, then his legs hurt. I felt an urge to save the Jewish respect, and I volunteered to go. The deputy commander, a Russian from Siberia and anti-Semitic in every bone in his body, embraced me and asked: "Who else besides "Veirni" volunteers?" Silence took hold of everyone. I left. I went toward the watchman's house. At a clearing in the woods, I began crawling, and what do my eyes see?

The commander is hanging, with half of his body on one side, and the other half on the other side of the fence, and about twenty meters away from him, his short rifle is lying on the ground, pointing toward the woods, and his pistol is hanging with the holster over it. I crawled slowly. I took the rifle with me, but I left the pistol there. I didn't want to stand up, because hundreds of Germans were swarming next to the house. Some of them poured something (apparently gasoline) on the house; others were busy lining up families with their faces to the wall; another group of soldiers got ready to take them out to be killed -- and perhaps there were those who were being interrogated with threats. I went back and reported and turned in the rifle. The deputy ordered me to go back and try to remove the pistol as well. He sent a Russian fighter after me to see if I really would try to remove the pistol, or if I would try to slip away.

I crawled. When I reached the hanged commander, I stood up in one motion and removed the pistol, while leaving the belt and the holster, and I crawled back. The Germans didn't sense my presence, as they were busy with the forest watchman's family and were preparing to burn down the house and the entire farm.

At the edge of the woods, I met up with the watchman's son, a youth of twelve, who managed to slip away and escape to the woods. About 150 to 200 meters into the woods, I met the Russian who had been sent to follow me.

The youth told us that an hour after we had left the house, the Germans surrounded the entire yard, took positions, and stayed there, as if they were waiting to ambush the partisans who were about to arrive.

The deputy came to see me, complaining that I hadn't brought back the pistol's holster. He ordered me again to make a round and find a place from which we could escape from the siege. The forest watchman's son helped me, since he was familiar with every path. We found just one exit -- through the swamps. I led the division, with the watchman's son and I walking at the head of the line. When we were in the heart of the swamps, and the rest of the partisans were a ways behind us, the Germans sensed us and opened fire. The shots didn't reach us, as they were directed to the middle and tail end of the group. Miraculously, not one of us was hit. The same day we walked, with the boy's guidance, through swamps and woods until four in the afternoon.

We rested. When it became dark, the boy showed us the route, and he himself turned right toward a village, to his relatives. After two nights of walking we had to cross the Styr river. This time, too, I was sent, along with one other, to carry out a mission: I was to liquidate two guards with a silencer, and blow up the "bodkah" (shack) that was next to the bridge, along with the German soldiers inside. The operation was successful, and we safely returned to the base.

Hand-to-Hand Combat

The first snows were already covering the area. The cold penetrated our bones. And, worst of all, the snow showed our footprints, enabling the Nazi enemy to find us more easily. It was very difficult to be careful, to walk exactly in the footprints of the first person in order to prevent the enemy from assessing the number of fighters. But there was no choice. We were obligated to carry out whatever was imposed on us.

The Chief of Staff, Dadya Petya, ordered an increase in operations, this time in areas that, until then, we had not worked in and were, therefore, unfamiliar to us. The targets were railroad tracks, bridges, and telephone lines that connected the towns of Brest-Litovisk-Pinsk, Kovel-Sarni, and Kovel-Rovno. Several of the best lads joined us, including the Jews Yitzchak

Kuperberg and Zev Verba from Manievich and Hershel Blaustein from Lishnivka. His brother Avraham had been captured by the Germans when he was badly wounded in a special mission and had been tortured to death.

After several successful operations on our part including one battle with the Germans, where we liquidated a great number of them, the commander and some of his fighters dressed up in the slain German's jackets. Treating the rules of caution lightly, we moved at twilight on the King's Road, instead of waiting for complete darkness, drunk from our victories. The commander, in a German jacket, entered a peasant's house next to the village of Holovke. We were there about a half an hour, drinking milk and resting a bit when German soldiers surrounded the house and opened with automatic fire. As the commander ordered us, we threw a few grenades through the windows, jumped outside, and waged hand-to-hand combat.

I don't remember much about that battle: After shooting at the first figure I encountered, I received a blow from behind with a rifle butt and lost consciousness. I awoke with a terrible headache upon hearing from afar Hershel Blaustein's voice calling out in a whisper, "Veirni, Veirni." I recognized Hershel's ("Topoi's") voice, and I tried crawling, since I was badly wounded, in its direction.

The silence of the battle's aftermath prevailed, but Vlodya the Gruzini (the Georgian) (he appeared to me to be a Jew), pulled me back and begged for help. He was badly wounded in the left hand. He had chosen to be my guardian and always helped me. With his guidance I tended to his wound. We tried to remember which direction "Topoi's" voice had come from, as Vlodiya had also heard it, but we couldn't locate it. To this day, his voice echoes in my ears -- those were probably his last moments.

Vlodya told me that he had jumped through the window. When he saw that, with his first burst of fire, a figure had fallen, he came up behind the second figure of a short German -- the one who struck my head with his rifle butt -- and had turned the rifle around in order to stab me with its bayonet. Vlodya immediately filled him with a round of bullets and killed him. And he still had time to see the German that shot him. Vlodya got so excited about his wound that he didn't even check to see if I was still alive. The snow apparently awoke me from my faint.

-107-

We continued on, using the northern star to guide us to the base. We entered the woods after two hours of walking and crawling. Since it was very difficult for Vlodya to walk, we had to lie down and rest once in awhile. Vlodya lost a lot of blood. When we went into the woods, looking for a hiding place, we found three of our fellow partisans. They had reached the same woods before us. We were happy to see them. That night we met up with more of our men unexpectedly. A battle almost broke out between us, but we identified the familiar voices, including those of the Jewish lads. But Hershel was missing. My heart ached for him. We also learned from them that his commander had received a mortal chest wound and had lived another eleven hours before passing away. They, the lads, buried him in the same fearful place in which we had hid the entire previous day.

One of our lads hinted to me that he had almost been shot by our Jewish lad, who thought he was a German. The German jacket he wore was the reason.

After several nights of walking, we got back to the base, weak and depressed from the blow we had received -- that it was due to carelessness on the part of the commander that we had made two precious sacrifices -- Hershel, and the commander himself.

The news that Yehuda Melamedik from Manievich, from Max's (Jozef Sobiezek's) otryad, fell in battle hit us like a thunderbolt on a clear day. He was one of the best young men, a brave and modest fighter. We met him when we were in Manievich and were planning an escape to the woods to fight the Germans and their allies. He was fearless. Once in a while, news of his excellence in battles or in blowing up trains reached us. I met up with him only a few times in the woods, and only by chance; either when his unit was returning from operations or when ours was. We would exchange impressions and information. Our fateful battle was at the village of Krasin.

The mission was to capture the Krasin police force, which was made up of Ukrainian nationalists, enemies of the Jews. They were like bones in our throats. They overlooked a part of the region that we partisans controlled. Melamedik was in a house in the village with only three other fighters and poor weapons, when a strong unit of Ukrainian police surrounded him. Yehuda Melamedik was left on his own in the fighting sector and fought until the last bullet. The enemy's hand grenade downed him. We went to him at nightfall, a crushed partisan fighter. The partisans and his sisters, Rivkah and Luba, stood erectly on his fresh grave.

Little Luba was one of a kind. She was loved by all. Twelve years old, she helped the wounded and sick, washed clothes, cooked, and baked. Wherever help was needed, she was there.

Yehuda's death leaves a deep wound in our hearts to this very day. He was a young and daring fighter. He was eighteen years old when he fell.

The Legendary Image of Raiya Flos

I will briefly tell of a young heroine -- Raiya Flos, the daughter of the pharmacist from Povorsk.

A beautiful girl, she was a fighter who went through the seven fires of hell because of her beauty. She fell in a German ambush. The Germans found her at dawn, while she sat leaning on the wall of a barn with a weapon in her hand, asleep. They alerted their commander, astounded by her beauty. The German commander exclaimed, "A beauty such as this!" The Germans held a military funeral for her and fired shots in her honor by her grave. I heard of what she had been through and her life with the partisans from Moishe Edelstein, her friend, with whom I became friendly. Testimonies of her death and heroism were eliminated from the mouths of peasants, and they were forbidden to talk of her. Even the great Russian writer Ilya Ehrenburg wrote one of his stories about Raiya Flos.

Moishe Edelstein

He died a hero's death in a battle with the Ukrainian Banderovstzy. After we left the woods, he was buried, in a park in Rovna, in the section for the Soviet Union's heroes and received the title, "a Hero of the Soviet Union." I went more than once to his grave in the park to be alone with his memory. There were not many young men like him as a fighter, a human being, a comrade in distress. He had been modest in his actions and quiet. His only desire had been to avenge, for the sake of his parents, his family and for

-109-

his wife whom he had loved and who had loved him. A comrade at arms, a Russian, had tried to steal her from him. She had preferred to die rather than betray her beloved Liba Moishe.

In 1944 I had to go with Moishe to Chernovich to organize an illegal immigration route from the liberated regions to Eretz Israel. He was more suited for this job than any other young man, but he more and more requested to go on "clean up" missions and retaliatory operations against the Bonderovstzy. It was from one of these operations that he didn't return. My trip to Chernovich was postponed for a month because of his death. Yaakov (Eliyusha) Zweibel went with me in his place.

The Tragedy of Kahat Finkel

A fighting figure worthy of mention was Kahat Finkel of Manievich. We, the town's children, knew him and admired him for his brave disposition even before the war, when Polish rioters would attack old Jews and pluck out their beards. Kahat, the simple wagoneer with the warm Jewish heart, dealt them severe blows. The Poles knew that Kahat's hand would get them, and so they became very cautious. Only after the war, was it clear that he had been taken out and killed by the otryad commander, Max; his gentile comrades-at-arms had set a trap for him, because he was brave, honest, and a Jew.

THE HEROIC DEATH OF TWO YOUNG FRIENDS

Zev Rabinovitz

I'm not going to tell about the heroic deeds of the Jewish partisans. I don't want to tell about the number of trains that were destroyed, nor to list, one by one, the bridges that were blown up. In my eyes, it was the millions of Jews who died for Kiddush Hashem (Sanctification of the Holy Name), including the small children, who were the real heroes. And it was they, in their bravery, who brought us to the State of Israel. Anyone who says otherwise doesn't know what he's talking about; nor does he know about the souls of the martyrs.

I would only like to relate what happened to my two dear friends who fell, whose only thoughts, desires, and dreams were for revenge. They wanted revenge for their parents, relatives, and friends who were murdered; they wanted to revive their dreams for a nation among nations, living on their own soil, in our own State of Israel. We were youths then, and it is for our nation's youth and for Israel's youth that I'd like to tell my story.

I don't remember exact dates, as they have all gotten mixed together in my mind. It was around the spring of 1943. German planes flew over our woods and fired into them. The company scattered to find cover, when suddenly Major Mahmed appeared, calling out, "Stay where you are!"

Zev Avruch ("Valovish") and I continued running. "Stop!" the major shouted, "or I'll shoot!" He had a mauzer (a type of rifle) in his hand. We stopped and when the shooting stopped, the major called to us and said, "This afternoon we are going to start an interesting job. I will teach you to look straight into the eyes of death."

The "interesting job" was, after several unsuccessful attempts, setting up a workshop for the extracting of explosive materials from heavy shells that the Red Army had left behind when it retreated. It was necessary to release the "head" of the shell, to heat the shell in a cauldron of boiling water, and to pour the explosive material into molds that each weighed five kilograms (about 11 pounds). The fighting otryad (detachment) brought the shells to its camp.

After we spent a number of days extracting explosive material, Siyomka Biderman, a twelve-year-old youth from Manievich, came to see us, saying: "I've had enough of working with Shimon and of taking care of horses. I'm staying with you. I know that another person is needed, and I will be that person, volunteering out of my own free will!" And so our group of three youths worked. And there was more: Even Nechamka, the cook, treated us with great respect. Siyomka would laugh, "She's giving us better food, because she sees our going to the world to come and she wants us to request a good place for her in the Garden of Eden and to be a "champion in the right" for her before the Master of the Universe."

Eight shells were left, which the major forbade us to touch as they were too dangerous, in his estimation. He was an expert in these matters.

We prepared a new transport. Meanwhile, we were resting in the evening, sitting with the company, when the major arrived. He looked around and called me, as he was accustomed to doing, by my Jewish family name, Rabinovitz. (In the camp, they felt that he was a Jew.)

"What a nice moonlit night -- we need explosive material. Come, and we'll try to release one of the forbidden shells. Go by yourself so that if, heaven forbid, there'll be an accident, there will only be one sacrifice, for the sake of the parents and for the sake of your people." (He always added "for the sake of your people.")

This was Passover eve. After about an hour, I returned and reported that I had in fact succeeded in releasing the "head" from one of the shells. The major was actually radiant from happiness.

"Go to the company, Rabinovitz. Tomorrow you will work and prepare whatever is possible."

The next day he came to visit us. He inspected the shells. He ordered us to put one of them, the rustiest one, aside and not to touch it. "That's an order!" This was on the second day of Passover. Siyomka said to himself "What a shame, we could extract about eight kilograms of explosive material from this shell. It would be possible to blow up an entire train with this, and perhaps also the Germans inside of it. What a shame to leave it. But the order was not to touch it.

The next morning Major Mahmed arrived with Kostin, the partisan commander from headquarters. Siyomka was humming a song. He stopped humming.

"Good morning boys! Siyomka, why did you stop singing?" he asked.

"My stomach hurts," Siyomka replied.

"O.K. I'll bring you a pretty girl!"

And to Kostin, "Look, they say that Jews are cowards. But look at the dangerous work these Jewish boys are doing! Who else would do that?"

And to us,

"And for you, boys, I have news. A revolt broke
out in Warsaw. Courageous Jews rose up and struck at
the Germans. They are standing bravely against many
Germans. That's what they're saying on Moscow radio.
Listen, don't touch this shell! That's an order!"
Mahmed repeated, warning us. The major and Kostin left
our workshop, satisfied. Siyomka again walked around
the shell, mumbling, "Eight kilograms of explosive
material! Aren't we here to take revenge?" he says to
us, a childish smile and serious adult expression
mixing together on his countenance, and he left us.
Not a lot of time had passed, when a loud explosion was
heard. There was fire and smoke. I thought that the
Germans were attacking. But then we heard Siyomka's
voice, "Mama, Volvish. Ratevet." ("Mother, Volvish,
Help me!")

All around, the explosive materials that we had
extracted and were cooling in molds, were burning. The
major came running, and shouted "Flee!" I shouted
"What a waste of material!' "Do what you want," Mahmed
shouted.

Volvish ran to bring help. We removed the explosive material, turning over the cauldron of water we
had used for extracting the material. We quickly
removed the shells from the boiling pot. Only after
this did we put out the fire.

Siyomka was lying on the ground with his guts
spilled out. He was completely torn to bits and his
eyes were blinded. He was just a lump of flesh without
legs or hands. Only his mouth still pleaded, "Save me,
shoot me, take revenge. Sh'ma Yisrael." ("Hear O
Israel.") These were his last words. The major took
out his mauzer and asked Kostin to shoot Siyomka.
Kostin turned his head and shot him. Silence
prevailed. Only his final words still echoed through
the woods and, to this day, in my ears: "Nemt Nikomeh
(take revenge), Shema Yisrael...!"

We brought Siyomka to a burial place in the
afternoon. We, his two friends from work were not
allowed to take part in his funeral. We had to continue working. There was an urgent need for explosive
material.

That same day a group of Jews from Troyanovka
arrived at the camp. The major introduced us to a

-113-

youth who was sixteen years old, tall, and of a strong character. His name was Payskeh. We became friendly. His entire family had been killed. His brother was killed in a battle with Germans and Ukrainian police, and he joined us to avenge their blood.

The major ordered us to move the workshop a distance from the camp, so the spot wouldn't remind us of Siyomka. Volvish was meanwhile transferred to Sokolov's unit, one of the tough and distinguished units.

We were again a threesome. Are'leh would prepare the boxes, and we went on with the shells. Time passed. We acted more carefully and never worked together. We made some improvements in the pouring of the material. The major would visit us every morning. One morning Payskeh was singing some song. When the major appeared, he stopped singing.

"Why did you stop singing, Payskeh?"

"My stomach hurts."

"I'll bring you a pretty girl," said the major.

In the afternoon, Are'leh and I released the heads, and Payskeh transported the material in the wagon hitched to horses. Suddenly, Payskeh appeared without the wagon and horses. There was an alarm, he says, and they took the horses from me. Just at that moment, I was releasing a bomb head.

"Let me. I too want to test my strength. I too have an account with the Germans. I, too am a Jew! They killed m-m-mine, too. All the Jews of Troyanovka and Manievich." Tears welled up in his throat, but he choked them back. No fighting man would cry.

I gave him a shell and moved away from him. Then all of a sudden, there was a thundering explosion! Without a moan or a groan. Silence. There wasn't a trace left of Payskeh. I managed to hear just one word from his mouth: "Revenge!"

Siyomka had been torn apart widthwise, and Payskeh, lengthwise.[20] Together they were length and breadth as it were. The remains were collected and brought to the burial site.

The group continued on with its work. Yisroel-Hirsh Flash, twenty years old, from Manievich, was brought to us. They transferred me to Volvish's unit. I recall that before this, we had tried to remove explosive material from a German shell, and we were nearly poisoned; our faces turned a pale green like a lime, and our tongues turned completely blue. It was only with difficulty that we were saved from this poisoning.

Flash continued to direct the work in the workshop. He lived to see victory and died immediately afterwards from tuberculosis, which he had contracted at his job at the workshop.

I also remember two wonderful Jewish girls, Faygeh Avruch and Chasyah Blaustein, who perished after they had left the woods, when the train the two of them were travelling in to Kiev was bombed by Germans.

The two of them had worked tirelessly in the hospital that was set up in the camp. They would meet us joyfully and warmly when we returned from field operations. They especially gave attention to those youths who were lonely or without family.

And I remember David Blaustein and the slap he gave my cheek when I joined him in my flight to the woods, and I was just a youth. "Go home," he shouted "to father and mother!" And in spite of this, he took me to the woods with him and helped us as much as he could. He was dedicated to us and concerned with us, just like a father.

DEEDS OF A CHILD

Tzvi (Vova) Verba

With the retreat of the Red Army, an atmosphere of uncertainty prevailed. We were living in fear. My father and my five brothers and sisters and I fled and moved in with a Ukrainian peasant acquaintance, in an isolated house outside of a distant village. We had thoughts of fleeing, following the Red Army's retreat (from the German attack). But father was confused and unable to make a decision. We returned home to the town.

-115-

We viewed those first days after the Russian retreat as a great tragedy for the Jews of Manievich. Even I, a boy of nine, sensed that something frightening was happening, and that it was just the beginning of an impending disaster. And, indeed, it happened. My father, my brothers Shikel and Motel, and my brother-in-law were taken, together with another 370 Jews, on the pretext that they were needed for work. But they did not return. (They were all shot.) And so, as the only "man" left, I became the head of the family.

Once I was caught without the yellow patch. They took me to the police station. There were other Jewish children there. An interrogation began, accompanied by blows from the Ukrainian policemen. I was rescued from the blows when a policeman recognized me and released me, saying "I knew your father; he was a decent man."

I recall an incident when the Germans passed through the houses and held searches. They searched my pockets for gold jewelry. A shuddering passed through my body that is now difficult for me to describe.

They began to round up the Jews on "the other side." I said to myself, "They're going to take all of us out and kill us!" I hid in the cowshed of a Ukrainian neighbor, Sovotnik, without his wife knowing about it. At night I would go out to the garden and gather vegetables. I returned home after four days and found all of my relatives from the village.

In the meantime, my three sisters began working in Polska Gora. Every day girls would go out to the town to work and in the evening return in a cargo train, tired but satisfied. A German from a military engineering squadron promised the girls that he would warn them when the situation became critical, and in fact, one day at sundown, he informed my sisters that they should flee at all costs, because the day of liquidation was near.

This information spread quickly, but people were helpless and lacked the desire to flee. And where could they flee? My sister Rivkah and I fled with Hershel Trager and his daughters, Polya and Vitel. Trager decided to go by foot to Rozhishetz. We walked day and night without water, going around villages and eating sugar beets from the fields. I decided to try my luck as a child. I entered a number of houses and

asked for food. In most houses, they gave me a piece
of bread, while shaking their head sympathetically.
But in one house, a peasant came out to meet me and
wanted to "wrap me around his pitchfork." I ran away
with all my strength, and he ran after me. I succeeded
in slipping away and arrived safely at the place where
the Trager family and my sisters were waiting for me.

We reached Rozhishetz and found a city empty of
Jews. They all had been liquidated! We returned to
the Manievich woods. Near the town, we came across the
pits of the Jews of Manievich who were murdered. To be
sure (was this not a bad dream?) we went back and found
that in the pits were Jews shorn of their beards, rob-
bed of their souls. We broke out into bitter crying.
Our group divided up. Trager, who was familiar with the
surroundings, parted from us and went with his
daughters, and I remained with my sister, Rivkah.

The Woman Angel Tanya

I'm returning to a time when we were wandering
about in the vicinity of Manievich. My sister, Rivkah,
and Vitel Trager would go out by themselves to check
the possibilities for obtaining Aryan papers, and to
learn of the fate of the rest of Manievich's people.
Rivkah found out that her sister Tzviya had escaped and
was hiding with a Polish woman, Tanya, along with our
sister Krayndel and her daughter.

My sister Rivkah and Vitel were caught and brought
to Manievich, where hundreds of Jews were concentrated.
These were Jews who had managed to flee but were caught
by the peasants. The Germans spread rumors that no
harm would befall those who were still alive, and so a
number of Jews were persuaded to return voluntarily,
since the conditions in the woods were intolerable.
Among those who returned was my aunt from Tzravecha.

However, and I my sister, her two-year-old daughter remained with the Polish peasant woman, Tanya.
Tanya gave us a hiding place in her home, in a <u>Khutor</u>
(bunker) that was built under two houses. The peasant
from the second house was an enemy of Tanya's aristo-
cratic family (her husband, and their two sons, one
fifteen, and one twenty years old). Tanya laid down
the rules and made the decisions in the home. They
greatly feared that the hostile Polish family would
inform on them, especially since more than once, Ukrainian police and Germans had visited their house.

We hid inside a bunker under the floor. We entered it from a closet; a camouflaged exit was a distance inside the garden. At night Tanya would open the bunker, and we would go out and get a breath of air, then immediately go back into our hiding place.

One day, some people came to Tanya's house, while we were below in the bunker. Suddenly, little Bronya burst out crying; my sister and I tried with all our might to quiet her, pulling our hair out of nervousness and holding onto one another, because we knew that the danger was great, not just for us, but also for Tanya and her family. Tanya decided then to bring us to the woods.

Tanya's sons prepared a bunker for us in the woods, covering its entrance with a decaying log. Tanya continuously supplied us with food. For Tanya, saving us was like a holy mission, which she desired with all her might, to the point of her own self-sacrifice and that of the members of her family. Her attachment to my sister Tzviya, who had stayed there before we arrived, was so strong that she wanted, in this way, to compensate for her loss.

Looking in a mirror of those days, when a man suspected his friend or a son informed on his father, when murders and looting were common occurences, Tanya's behavior was really unusual. To this day, I go over and over again in my mind what her motives could have been for endangering her life and that of her family in order to save us.

Tanya would visit us frequently in the woods and provide us with our food and clothing. This continued for about a year. Later, when the Ukrainians began to abuse and kill the Poles, Tanya fled with members of her family to the town. So we remained alone in the woods and were forced to worry about our survival.

At night we would go out to look for food in the fields. We gathered potatoes, beets, and carrots. We had to accumulate food for the winter. I would light a fire, striking a piece of steel on a stone. Many times, while we were searching for food, we would meet up with Ukrainian murderers who tried to capture us; they also fired shots at us.

We began to become accustomed to life in the woods. I was familiar with every path for a radius of tens of kilometers. I would walk about with my niece. At a number of kilometers from our bunker, railroad tracks crossed the woods. We would hear the noise of the trains, and very frequently we began hearing explosions. We suspected that this was the work of the partisans, and we were right. The partisans were active despite continuous guarding by the Germans and Ukrainians of the railroad tracks.

The railroad tracks formed almost naturally the border between the Banderovsty and the Soviet partisans. It was like an agreed-upon boundary. Our bunker, unfortunately, was on the Bonderovsty side, and it was dangerous to cross the railroad tracks to get to the other side. The partisans refused to receive us in their ranks. (Once partisans visited Tanya, and she urged them to take us, because we were threatened by liquidation. They did not consent, saying that they did not accept anyone without firearms. Also, they did not like the idea of a little girl.)

And so we remained stuck in the middle of an area filled with dangers. Meanwhile disturbances started up against the Poles. Ukrainian nationalists murdered entire families in a most cruel manner, cutting off their heads with axes. I found corpses with wooden stakes stuck in their heads.

I taught the little girl how to be familiar with the paths and the area surrounding the bunker, so that she, on her own, could find the way to it. The girl quickly adapted and acted with the utmost caution in the woods. Hearing a suspicious noise, she would hide among branches or bushes, and it really was difficult to find her. My sister also became very familiar with the woods.

I, the man, nine or ten years old, also went astray once in a great while. Fear grabbed hold of me when even I lost my way to the bunker, coming back from my frequent trips to gather food from the fields the Poles had abandoned or from their homes where I some- times went to look for clothing they had left behind. In the winter of 1943-1944, I would more and more fre- quently meet up with groups of young Ukrainians who came to the Polish villages to loot and take apart the houses, and I would slip away from them. I learned to plan my visits in such a way as not to run into them. My sister would always be afraid when I went out to the villages and often asked to come along with me.

Subsequently we went out together, from time to time, with Bronya on my back, holding onto my neck with her delicate fingers. Tens of kilometers. I walked along in this way, with my niece fastened to my back like a knapsack. We would only go out at sunset, when there was relatively less danger.

One time, as we approached a Polish village, we sensed that there were people around. We began to go back the way we had come. When we crossed the dirt path, we noticed a wagon full of Ukrainians who began shouting at us to stop. They jumped out of the wagon and began chasing us and shooting. As the bullets whistled around us, the girl her fingers wrapped as usual around my neck, stammered, "God, help us..." Apparently her prayer brought us help. We succeeded, fortunately, in reaching the woods, which were thick and impenetratable. The murderers lost track of our footprints. We were saved.

When we were alone in the woods, we dreamt and trusted our dreams. We knew to interpret the dreams as if something was guiding us in our flight. It happened more than once that we dreamed we had to leave the place, because danger awaited us. We would leave, and after a while, when we returned, we found out that indeed there had been uninvited guests there, who took with them all the food we had prepared for the coming of winter.

We began hiding the food in a number of places inside the woods. One time I dreamt that I saw three snakes and that I had to kill them. The next day I found two snakes, and at sundown the same day I found the third snake. To this day, I don't know how to explain this phenomenon. Did the merits of our ancestors stand us in good stead?

It happened that heavy rain soaked the burnt rag which served us for lighting a fire; only after desperate efforts for a full day did I finally succeed in lighting it. There is no describing the great amount of joy I felt. At night we would hear the howling of wolves, and entire packs came near the bunker. We were afraid they might get inside, and so by means of fire, I would, with difficulty, chase them away.

I recall an incident that won't leave my memory. I knew, generally, where birds, squirrels, and all kinds of wild animals built their nests. One time I climbed a tall tree and found inside a nest three fairly large fledglings. I removed them, with difficulty, and prepared a tasty meal that was particularly enjoyable to the girl, who had not tasted a meal fit for kings like that in quite a while. The parents flew about shrieking around the bunker in their search for their fledglings. This went on for a number of days. A deep shuddering took hold of us, for our sin in stealing chicks from their parents. We feared that perhaps we would pay for the theft.

This difficult life, the war for survival, and the struggle for our lives, continued for a year. Somehow, the will to stay alive fixed itself in us -- we wanted to tell what happened to us. It was a desire that stayed with us during all our days of wandering in the woods.

On the Way to the Woods

Spring of 1944 was late in coming. Snow still fell. The Germans retreated from our area. We did not know this, but we sensed something different in the air. We did not hear any more explosions by the railroad tracks, but we were afraid to leave our hiding place. Only a month after the German retreat, a Ukrainian hunter discovered us when his dogs led him to our bunker. On seeing us, he became frightened and began to run away. We called to him, and he told us that the Germans had retreated, but he advised us to still stay in our hiding place until the atmosphere had calmed down a bit in the area. We decided to leave the spot, fearing that perhaps the Ukrainian hunter would decide to liquidate us.

We started to walk in the direction of the town. My sister Krayndel walked with great difficulty, because her feet were swollen and wrapped in rags. On the way we went into a house, where the peasant who received us served us food. We warmed ourselves in his home. I recall how Bronya, three and a half years old, was like a little hunted animal, looking around as they brought food to the table. Her whole being was frightened, as if she had fallen into another planet.

We arrived at the town and did not recognize it. On the entire main street, only a few houses remained. Our houses were not there, not the one on the main

street, not the one on Tiatralen Street, near the
woods. There were only ruins, foundations covered with
thorns and grass. I did not find Jews in Manievich.
We found out from the Ukrainian peasant that only in
the town of Rafalovka were there a number of Jews.

I do not remember how we reached Rafalovka,
whether by train, horse, or foot. Once there, we
entered a house where Jews lived; we were like a
miracle to them. How was it that we survived on our
own, and that only now, more than a month after the
German's retreat, had we left the woods. Truthfully,
the reception was not enthusiastic. Everyone was concerned with himself and his family. In this house we
were given a small corner into which we settled, and my
sister began working as a cook in a kitchen in Rafalovka. I fell into bed. I was sick with typhus fever,
and I was taken to the hospital in Rovna. The Germans
continued to shell Rovna every evening. The shellings
actually helped me. I would go into the kitchen and
gorge myself with anything I could find. I recup-
erated. The resiliency I had acquired in the difficult
conditions in the woods stood me in good stead. During
my illness, no Jews came to visit me. I returned to
Rafalovka, and I found my sister and her daughter relatively healthy.

I was then an experienced man, twelve years old,
and I began to "trade" in all kinds of merchandise in
the train station with the soldiers going to the front.
Once a woman came down from a car, speaking Polish to
me, hugging me, with tears in her eyes, and whispered,
"I had a little brother; you are a brother to me." She
left me a gift as a momento and continued on her way.
I recall her waving to me with her hand as she moved
further away, going toward the front.

We reached Israel through Youth Aliyah in 1947. I
enlisted in the Hagana at the age of sixteen. In
clashes with the Arabs and the British, a number of my
young comrades fell. With the declaration of the State
of Israel, I served in the regular army of the Israeli
Defense Forces (Tzahal), and I participated in the
battle for the liberation of the Galilee in Israel.

I DECIDED TO DEFEND MY LIFE

Asher Mirochnik

At the outbreak of the German-Russian war, we were only children, twelve and thirteen years old. We feared what was coming, and entire days we sought advice about what to do, if ....

The first German columns arrived in the town on motorcycles. Out of the curiosity that accompanies fear, we gathered in groups, we children, around the Germans, in all five or six soldiers. After a short rest, they left the town.

After one or two days, the Ukrainian police began to get itself organized, and a relative quiet prevailed. The townspeople, the youth, began organizing the herds of cattle to go out to graze outside of the town. (Almost all of the town's residents owned a cow or two, which they had to take out to graze.) Generally, we four youths would herd the cattle early in the morning with the falling of the dew and go out to the fields and woods. At nightfall we would return, laden with mushrooms and all kinds of blackberries. This was at the end of the summer, near the beginning of the fall. In fact it is possible to say that the food the women and children gathered in the daytime was the Jews' main sustenance.

There was however plenty of food for the craftsmen, blacksmiths, tailors, shoemakers, carpenters, wagon makers and others, since the peasants paid them with food products. Once, as I went out with a herd of cattle, Zelig Khizhi -- a Hebrew teacher and neighbor accompanied me. Suddenly I saw an S.S. policeman, who had reached the entrance to the town. The Ukrainian and Polish peasants bragged to us that on this day they were about to slaughter all of the Jewish men. On hearing this, I asked Khizhi, the teacher, to stay with the herd of cattle, and I would run to the town, but he would not agree to stay by himself, deciding that he would be the one to return to the town. I asked him to tell my father -- with urgency -- to get out of the town and go to the woods.

The teacher did meet my father and passed on to him the things that I told him. He told my father that I said there were things, it wasn't clear what, that were likely to occur. But his manner of telling this, and even his trustworthiness, did not influence my father, who at that time was working in the smithy of our blacksmith neighbor, Hershel.

My father did not take Khizhi's words seriously, and when I returned home at sundown, my mother told me about the tragedy. Father had been taken out of the blacksmith shop and, along with 370 other Jewish men, was brought out to the fields to the "Horses Graves." This was the first action.

About two months after this, a peasant came by, bringing a letter in my father's handwriting, in which he asked that we send him winter clothes and warm underwear. I urged my mother not to believe what was written in this letter, because it was apparent to me that it had been written under coersion before his murder, but my mother wanted to believe that my father was still alive. I heard stories of the atrocities that had taken place from the Ukrainian shepherd youths (who had heard about the murders from their parents). I recall being told about Binyamin Eizenberg, the blacksmith-locksmith, who was nicknamed Niyoma the hero. He struggled with an S.S. officer, and his head was cut off, and he, Niyoma, a body without a head, continued running for a ways, until he fell.

After the liberation, when we left the woods, I was walking with my friend Zev Avruch to the site of the murder, and there we found skulls with hair lying in the field and uncovered pits with the soil falling into them. About fifty meters from the brothers' grave, we found a huge skeleton without a head, and we knew that this was Niyoma's corpse. No one had even taken the trouble to bury it in the dirt, and it stayed unburied out in the field.

Life had to continue. I recall that the respon-sibility of taking care of the house, which had belonged to my mother and my sister Chaya'leh, became mine, and so I began searching for food.

In spite of the strict prohibition on leaving the town and going to a village, I would go out by myself to the surrounding villages, to peasant acquaintances, collecting anything I could get. There were peasants who remembered my father, who helped out once in a while by giving a loaf of bread, a bit of flour, or potatoes. I would slip back into the town with a sack

on my shoulder. In this way we got through a very difficult winter.

In addition to my wandering through the villages,
I engaged in "vital" work for the German army, which
was in need of sleds. Hershel-Leib, the blacksmith,
was given a quota for the preparation of sleds for the
German army. I filled the place of my father, in
blessed memory, and helped the blacksmith in his work
in exchange for a bit of food. I remember the quotas
that were given to the town's Jews, when they had to
collect fur coats, brass utensils, gold and silver, and
also sums of money. These Jewish policemen worked very
diligently in their search for these things.

The Forester Slovik

With the arrival of spring, news reached us about
partisan units that were conducting raids on police
stations and killing people in them.

At the Manievich police station, they began
building bunkers around the building with double thick
walls made out of logs. The peasants, as well as the
Jews, worked at this task (the few men that were still
alive). A group of about fourteen youths, twelve to
thirteen years old was organized to remove the outer
layer of the logs. Every day we went out to the woods,
accompanied by Senkah Melamedik -- he was our group
leader, as he had worked before the war as a tree
sorting expert.

We went by foot six or seven kilometers to the
Koninsk woods. We received a quarter of a kilogram of
bread in exchange for this work, but our main profit
was in the mushrooms that we gathered in the woods.

When we went out to work, we sometimes met with
Jews who had fled from the surrounding towns: Kolki,
Melnitza, and others. They told horror stories about
the total liquidation and destruction of the towns'
Jews.

We began to contrive plans of escape, and we prepared bunkers as hiding places. In order to camouflage
our work in preparing bunkers, one or two people would
withdraw from the group and prepare the bunker while we
tried to fill their quota. The preparations continued
for a long time. I personally prepared a bunker in our

house underneath the floor. I decided to myself that I would defend my life at all costs.

I knew that the youths who were eighteen to twenty years old were organizing themselves in order to leave for the woods, but it was impossible to join them. It was known that a group of adults had attempted to leave in organized form and had failed. The police apparently knew about their plan of escape and began shooting as they left for the woods. A number of the company were killed, and the rest returned to the town.

The hangman's noose began to tighten more and more around the town's Jews, who were concentrated in one section. The Jews living on the other side were brought over to us on a Friday and were settled in the Jews' homes.

The day before this happened, they forbade the group to go out to work in the woods. On Friday night, a Ukrainian policeman, an acquaintance of my father, in blessed memory, who was grateful for past acts of kindness, knocked on our door and begged my mother to leave the town in any way possible. My mother felt helpless, saying, where could she flee? To the woods? Who and what awaited them there? My sister Chaya, sixteen years old, resigned herself to her fate and did not want to be separated from my mother. She said that, apparently, her fate had been decided, and she had to accept it.

Helplessness and despair enveloped us, and we spent a sleepless night. When morning broke, I peered through the window and saw that they were beginning to take people out of the houses on one side of the street. The street was filled with the crying and wailing of women and children, along with the shouting of policemen who brandished rifles and, mercilessly and indiscriminantly, dealt blows, as they hurried the women and children along. I opened the bunker that I had set up and begged my mother and sister to go down into it. My mother complied with my request. She was prepared to join me, but my sister, who for some reason -- maybe because she had resigned herself to her fate -- was set in the opinion that if it had been decided for her to go, then she would go and not resist. It was difficult for me to comprehend those personal motives which prevented her from going into the bunker. But by taking this stance, she influenced my mother to remain with her and not leave her by herself to Fate, from which she saw no escape. I pleaded with them, and with all the people who were in our home at that time, to go into the bunker, but in vain! The only one who joined me was Simah Guz's daughter, who was seven years old, but she immediately came up out of the bunker, saying it was stifling inside. Avraham Gorodetzer went down into the bunker with his three daughters: Zelda-Zavit, sixteen years old; Yaffa, twelve years old, and the youngest one, nine years old, who immediately came out of the bunker, when she could no longer tolerate the oppressiveness inside.

Upon seeing the police approach our home, I jumped into the camouflaged bunker and closed it over me. I heard them take out my mother, my sister, and all the rest of the people who were in the house. During the entire day, searches were conducted in the house, and we, inside the stifling bunker, heard the shouts and curses of the Ukrainian policemen, who took great pains to find people in hiding.

We passed that difficult day of the slaughter in the bunker. At midnight I was the first to leave. I looked for and found a bit of food, and I put it into a sack and called to those in the bunker to come outside. We began running toward the woods. Every road and path between the houses and yards was familiar to me, and so I led the group, which numbered forty people, including myself. My intention was to get to the same bunker in the woods, which my young men friends had set previously.

As we were crossing the railroad tracks that were close to ponds and marshes, we met up with Tzvi Kuperberg, his wife, Chava, their daughter, Elkah, and Dvorah Sherman. According to them, they were heading for Slovik, the forester's, woods. We continued in the direction of the bunker.

At two in the morning, on Saturday night, we --Avraham Gorodetzer, his two daughters, and myself -- reached the bunker in the woods. When we went inside it, I realized that some of the young men had been there before me.

We stayed all day Sunday in the bunker. Its entrance was quite far away, through a channel we had dug during the time we had worked in the woods. It was ten meters long.

The entrance to the channel was underneath the trunk of a very old tree. The bunker itself was a pit, which we covered with tree stumps, branches, and dirt. Grass grew on top of it, so it couldn't be distinguished from its surroundings. Air came in through the channel. The bunker could accommodate the fourteen youths working in the group.

A utensil with water was set up in the bunker, and we brought a bit of food with us which we had gathered when we fled from the house. During the entire first day of our stay, we heard the herds of cattle and the conversations of the shepherds, as they walked on top of the bunker.

That same night, we decided that we would go out at dawn and look for Jews who had managed to escape and join up with them. We also decided to go see Slovik, the forester. Slovik got frightened when he saw us, fearing that we had been seen coming to his house. He asked us to go into the nearby woods, promising that he would come to see us. After a while, he came. We suspected that he would alert the police. He calmed us down, promising to bring us a group of Jews who were staying in the woods. Supposedly, they all passed by Slovik's house, and it was he who brought them into the depths of the woods.

Slovik walked in front, and I was about one hundred meters behind him, for the sake of security. We did this in case there was to be trouble, and we'd have to flee. We still weren't free of the suspicion that he possibly wanted to hand us over to the Germans.

In the morning hours, we arrived at a plowed up field of fodder. The area was open. Slovik crossed the field and entered the bordering woods, while we stayed at the edge of the other woods. (The field, about one hundred meters long, divided up the two woods.) From afar, we saw Moshe Rosenfeld going out to meet Slovik, and our fear dissipated.

We joined Moshe Rosenfeld -- a sixty-year-old Jew, after Slovik instructed him to take us to the group of Jews. I am sorry to note that Moshe Rosenfeld hesitated to bring us to the group and started to argue with Slovik. Rosenfeld, of course, gave in in the end and did not stop us from going on.

Despite Moshe Rosenfeld's opposition, (which may have been due to hunger, the threatening conditions, and the danger of death), we energetically continued on according to Slovik's directions, and two kilometers away, we found a group of Jews. There were about seventy people, including four to five of the friends we had worked with in the woods. They told us that the previous night, on Sabbath eve, they had managed to flee from the town, along with Senkah Melamedik, who was shot as he climbed over the fence at Porotzki's farm; the son of Elka and Mordecai from Novoroda was also shot.

Our arrival caused arguments and anger over whether we were entitled to join the group. Sensing we had food with us, the men took it from us, sat down, and finished it. This was like a bribe to stay with them. The group had been living without food, or means of livelihood, with no contact with the outside world, with the exception of Slovik's son, Kazik, who would come by to transport the group from one place to another. Sometimes he would also bring a bit of food, but not one bit of this reached the small, weak ones in the group.

After we had been in the woods for a number of days, I organized the five youths in the group. They were, Yehuda Melamedik, Senka's son, Yehuda'leh Lorber, and others whose names I don't remember anymore. We decided to go out to the village of Volchetz to ask for food from the peasants.

When the five of us went out on the dirt road leading to the village, a Ukrainian forest guard caught us and wanted to take us to the police. At that time it was being publicized that, for every Jew captured, dead or alive, they would pay in salt, which was a precious commodity.

At first it wasn't clear where he was leading us, but on the way the Ukrainian bragged to me that he would receive eight sacks of salt for us; it was then that I understood his intentions. I managed to communicate to my friends with signals that we had to get away at the first opportunity and not allow ourselves to be taken to the police.

When we came into a tangled grove, I gave the signal, and every one of us fled in a different direction. The guard got flustered, because he hadn't expected that we children would dare run away. He fired two shots, and we fled while the breath of life was still in us. I reached the group in the woods first and related what had happened. After waiting for a day, we went to look for my four friends, but with no luck. It was only after two days that all four of my friends returned to the group, each one coming separately, with a story to tell of his hardships from the escape.

We stayed for about a week and had to get organized again to find any kind of food. We left at night and arrived at the village at midnight. We knocked on the doors of the cottages and asked for food. Sometimes the door would open, and a peasant man or woman would take pity on us and give us a piece of bread or some potatoes; other times those who saw us slammed the door while uttering curses and insults.

In spite of setbacks, there was a lot of booty. Every one of us carried away half a sack of precious food. In the meantime, family camps began to get organized and take care of themselves.

One night most of the people left, and Avraham Gorodetzer and his daughters and I stayed by ourselves in the woods. During this time, I began to become very familiar with the surrounding area. I became very well oriented to the woods and developed a kind of sixth sense and was able to find the Jews who were scattered about in a short amount of time and join them. This happened many times. I regret having to recount an embarrassing incident. I was struck by one of the men, because I had dared to join the group, and the situation became threatening, but then, in time, the adults came to see that they could derive benefit from my being so familiar in the woods, and they began using me as a guide.

Once I took Michal and Zisel Brat and their son Moshe to the village of Sarchov, where they gave their valuables to peasant-acquaintances. In exchange, they received food and then they returned to the camp. I also received for my trouble something to refresh myself. I became well known as an outstanding guide. I also served as guide for Avraham and Chava Puchtik and others.

The winter drew near. We got ready for it by digging a "winter palace." Those who had relatives in the fighting unit began moving with their family to the family camp, which had started to be organized by Max's

-130-

and Kruk's fighting units. In the end, I remained alone in the woods, next to the farm of the Sorma brothers, who were Polish blacksmiths from Koninsk.

I was helped by them. They always warned me in good time of peasants that were wandering by, of the appearance of policemen, and more. One day, during this same period, I met up in the woods with Rachel, the widow, and her two small daughters who had succeeded in hiding and escaping. I invited them to stay with me.

The Long Road to the Citizen's Camp

At the first snowfall, I decided to leave for the town and to ask the Pole living in our house for the clothing and valuables that we had left with him for safekeeping. I dressed as a villager in a coarse woolen jacket and shoes made out of tree bark and went "home." Except that in the interim, his place of residence had been moved to another house, to one of the "choice" houses. I found him. He had moved to Dr. Stokalski's house, on the other side of the town, near the Ukrainian police station that had located in the house of Geler, the dentist. I arrived there in the afternoon. They were startled to see me and urged me to leave the house immediately and come back at night. I went to a grove, and hid there in the bushes until nightfall.

Walking at night inside the town, or outside of it, was an activity laden with mortal danger. At dusk a curfew went into effect, and those who violated it were shot without warning. The main difficulty was in crossing the railroad tracks, where Germans and Ukrainian police stood guard. I finally succeeded in taking advantage of the sentry moving away, and I went over the crossing. The town's paths and yards were lit up well, and so I safely reached the Pole's house. With all of this, they gave me a guest's reception. They served me a warm meal. They returned some clothing to me -- mostly rags that could hardly be used any more. "This is all we have left." they said. I managed to return to my hiding place in the woods and gave the clothing to the Sorma family. They told me that the Germans had issued a directive to the villagers, forbidding them to walk in the woods with its accumulation of three consecutive days of snow. They didn't want them to cover the footprints of the partisans and Jews hiding in the woods.

Rachel went into the Sorma's house, the girls stayed outside by the campfire, and I went into our hut. I was exhausted and fell asleep.

When I woke up, I saw four armed men in front of me, pointing their rifles at me. But they told me not to be afraid of Red partisan-comrades. They told me that when they came into the woods, they saw a woman from afar who began to run away when she saw them, toward the hut. They chased after the woman, because they had had a bad experience with a peasant woman from the village of Chrovcha when they were going out to a sabotage operation on the railroad tracks. The peasant woman had alerted the police, and the partisans had been forced to retreat until they came to the Koninsk area.

I offered them roasted potatoes that were in the hut. They said that they belonged to the partisan unit under the command of Naseikin, and they were involved with mining railroad tracks. In the meantime, Rachel and her daughters returned to the hut.

The partisans proposed that I serve as their guide and bring them to the railroad tracks. I happily consented to their request. I was ordered to prepare knives from strips of metal, in order to dig into the frozen ground.

I asked the Sorma brothers for metal strips to be used for making these knives, needed to dig potatoes. I knew that they had such things. Sorma gave me a number of knives. The same night, I led the partisans to the railroad tracks, where peasants stood guard, 250 to 300 meters away from one another. A campfire marked their presence. One of the partisans strangled one of the guards, and another partisan and I moved quickly to plant the mine. At first I was ordered to plant the mine on my own, but one of the partisans objected to sending a youth to do a job that was dangerous and unfamiliar. At any rate, I set up the mine so that the long cord was attached to it, in order to activate it.

I planted the mine with the partisan's guidance and stretched the cord to the entrance of the woods, a distance of about 200 meters. We managed, with difficulty, to reach the woods as the train approached. The partisan and I stayed at the entrance to the woods with the cord, while the remaining three retreated to the depths of the woods.

I pulled the cord when the locomotive was on the mine. A loud explosion was heard, and the locomotive and eight cars filled with soldiers were hurled into the air. I wanted to run and grab a gun, but the partisan reprimanded me and ordered me to run quickly after him to the woods. This was the first act of sabotage that was carried out in the Manievich region. And later on I would be proud of that.

We returned to our hut, and the partisans promised me that they would report my participation in the blowing up of the train to headquarters. After several weeks, a few partisans from Kruk's unit came to see me with an order to have me join the partisan unit. To this day, I don't recall if Rachel and her daughters were taken into the family camp.

In Kruk's camp, I was told essentially what had happened. At Naseikin's headquarters, charges were made against Kruk that his unit wasn't carrying out enough sabotage operations, while a single youth, hiding in a hut in the Koninsk woods, had blown up a train with his own hands. Apparently, it was then that it was remembered that I was staying by myself in the hut, and they came to take me to the unit. The news about the first bombing spread quickly through the partisan units. I was then fourteen years old, and I was taken to the family camp. I joined up with the guard unit of the camp.

Once, while I was on guard duty on the road leading to the family camp I saw from afar two partisans from Naseikin's unit approach. I saw hands waving about as if they were arguing. The two partisans saw me and began to come over to me. I knew one of them, Ostrikov, who had been with me during the blowing up of the train. He recognized me and began talking with me, asking how I was and if I would show him my sawed-off rifle. I didn't mistrust him and handed him the rifle, when suddenly he said, seriously, "We are Germans dressed up as partisans. You are under arrest!" He hit me over the head with the rifle butt and brought me over to the guard of the fighting unit. I saw that blood was dripping all over the guard, and that he didn't have any weapon. They had, through deceit, taken away his rifle too.

This was Fayvel Zafran from Lishnivka. They made us kneel one behind the other, with me in front and Zafran behind me. Suddenly, as I turned my head around, I saw one of the partisans loading his rifle. They simply wanted to kill the two of us in one shot. Two shots would alert the partisans in the camp. When I realized what was happening, I jumped up and ran quickly into the woods, in order to reach the camp and inform the Jewish partisans about the two murderers. Just as I arrived, one shot was heard, and I knew that Fayvel had been killed. And in fact, a Jewish partisan was murdered by the Russian partisans. One of them was a Jew from Odessa, by the name of Bezikin, who had concealed his Jewishness, by actively taking part in the murder of Jews. One day he was murdered by Banderovtzy, who were conducting business with a group of partisans. The Ukrainians among them were released and he, the deceitful Jew, paid with his life.

A New Life

Life began anew. The fighters among us went out once in a while on sabotage operations, and while the groups changed, there almost always was a fighter squad in the area.

It was decided to set up a frontal guard unit with patrols, next to the sezanka. I was assigned to be in the patrolling and guarding unit and I stayed there until the second hunt, at the end of 1943.

During the second hunt, I left our base. All of the conscripts joined the liberation campaign of the city of Rovna's partisans. When the town of Manievich was liberated, I moved there where I joined the Lorber family ("Malenka"). I lived with them until I was conscripted into the anti-Banderovstzy unit.

I left the town, and after continuous hardships, I reached Israel. I took part as a combat soldier in the War of Liberation, the Sinai Campaign, the Six-Day War, and the Yom Kippur War.

A COMMANDER PRACTICES WHAT HE PREACHES

Asher Mirochnik

Life in the family camp was conducted according to schedules set by the military camp; there was a division of labor, with order and discipline.

One day we learned that the Germans, surely with the help of the Ukrainians, were planning a hunt in our area of the woods. And it was then that something happened that I am unable to forget. Yankeleh Wolper, who was twelve or thirteen years old and a relative of the three Wolper siblings, asked if he could join the fighting unit, which was beginning to retreat.

It was said in the camp that everyone was responsible for his own skin, according to his familiarity with the forests. If he knew the dangers of the forests, he could survive.

Yankeleh approached commander Kruk and asked for permission to join the partisans. I heard with my own ears Kruk ordering him to leave, warning him that if he tried to ask him one more time, he would shoot him. And indeed, when Yankeleh approached him again, pleading with him to let him join his relatives, Kruk shot him without hesitation with his automatic rifle. Yankeleh was left lying on the snow, lifeless, one hand under his head, and one leg raised. When we returned to the base after the hunt, we found the boy's corpse in the same position, covered with snow -- Only his eyes had been gouged out by crows. This incident shook many of us to the core, and I am unable to forget the sight to this very day.

A HUNGRY BOY

Asher Flash

Chanukah 1942, the beginning of the winter. The first snow has fallen. It is the start of our organizing in the woods, with Kruk as the leader of the group. The youths only had a few weapons. There was still no division between the fighters and the non-fighters. It was simply a camp of refugees who were afraid to leave the woods and made do with the little food that Kruk, whom they had appointed as commander, and the Jewish youths brought them.

We also had with us a group of youths and children who had managed to slip out of the surrounding towns and escape to the woods. Among them was a ten-year-old boy, Yideleh (Jack) Melamedik, Senka's son from Manievich. With no one to take care of him, he suffered greatly from hunger and didn't have the strength to endure it. Suddenly, Yideleh began disappearing from the camp. Once, twice, three times. Once in a while he returned with a bit of food in his sack. It became apparent that he was going out to the village of Holoziya, where his father and grandfather had been born, and finding peasants who still remembered past acts of kindness from his grandfather, Avraham, and his father Senka. These people fed him and once in a while gave him some provisions for the road.

Kruk found out about this. He was horrified to hear that a small Jewish boy was going out alone to beg for food, fearing that he would be caught and would tell the police the location of the camp, or, that they would follow his footprints.

As one of the adults in the camp, he summoned me and told me that it was necessary to frighten the boy so that he would no longer dare to leave the woods; if he didn't obey, he would have no choice but to shoot him.

On Kruk's orders, I took the boy and led him to the outskirts of the camp. There I ordered him, with my help, to dig a pit. When the pit was dug, I told him to get inside of it and lie down. Yideleh, in his innocence, went into it and said to me "Reb Asher, How can I lie down, I'm cold...."

I told him to come out, and I warned him that this time I was only frightening him, as Kruk had ordered, so that he would stop going out on visits to Holoziya. But if he slipped away one more time from the woods and ran to the village, Kruk would kill him and bury him in that very pit.

This incident affected Yideleh, and he no longer went out on independent missions to the village. Yideleh (Jack Melamedik) stayed alive for many years, and is today living in Montreal, Canada.

FROM A PARTISAN'S NOTEBOOK

Dov (Berl) Bronstein

For many hours we held council. What should we do? Escape? Where to? With whom? And we didn't have even one weapon. One of the obstacles that hindered an early and organized escape from Manievich was the danger to the families. The Germans and the Ukrainians distributed warning notices saying that an entire family would be held responsible for one person's escape. Fear began to enter our hearts. Hints from the Ukrainians about liquidating the Jews increased.

Klimtziak, the old Ukrainian, and his son lived many years amidst the Manievich Jews. They acted decently toward us, and at times were very helpful. Jews brought some of their possessions to the Klimtziaks for safekeeping. Most of the possessions stayed with them, for most of the Jews were liquidated, but there was never a time when Jews who had been hiding in the woods or in villages would come to them for the return of property, and they would not comply. They sent me personally a message by means of a peasant, saying that they wanted to send me all of my belongings.

Before the second "action," the elder Klimtziak came to me and suggested strongly that I flee to the woods and hide there for several months, until the war's end. It became clear that I was not the only one who received this advice from him.

He visited most of his Jewish acquaintances and advised them in the same way. The Klimtziaks truly acted despite a great deal of personal danger; they were even endangered by their son Androyshe, who was in the German's service and, later, an officer with the Bonderovstzy.

The atmosphere that prevailed in Manievich was one of depression, and people were wary of one another. We were meeting frequently and consulting on the issue of fleeing to the woods. Encouragement to flee came, in fact, from the head of the "Tudnikim" group, a German who was living in Yeshayahu Zweibel's house during the years 1941-1942. He extended friendship and help toward us, although he did so in a disguised manner. The German did not agree with what was about to happen, but he was forced to take part in the Germans' and Ukrainians' program of annihilation. But he immediately passed on a communique about it to Yeshayahu Zweibel and Pinchas Tina, in blessed memory, who worked near him in the woods, preparing trees for transport. He, the "Tudnik," did not know enough to specify an exact date, but he warned that the event was likely to happen in the upcoming days. The news was passed on. The Zweibel family (Yeshayahu, Sarah, Esther, and Ida) and the Singel family (Aryeh, Malkeh), as well as Pinchas Tinah were the first who fled.

I worked then at a saw mill in Butznitza making oak wood brackets and loading wooden sockets for railroad tracks, along with my brother Zev, Chaim Sherman, and Shmaryahu Guz. And then my sister-in-law, Ethel Finkel, arrived with her baby in her arms on the 19 Elul, 5701 (1942) and shouted that the city was surrounded by police and the Gestapo and some people were shot while trying to escape by way of Porotzki's fence. We tried to flee in the direction of the old church, through the old graveyard, but were fired upon. We went back. We tried again to cross through the Liyodova road, but here too, we were heavily fired upon. We walked the entire length of the Tragova Road. Here a Ukrainian policeman tried to stop us by directing us to our workplace. We gladly went, because from there, we began to escape to the woods in the direction of Koninsk, to Yazenty Slovik's house.

Slovik was known as a religious man, well-liked, with a decent attitude toward the Jews. His house was near the section of woods that belonged to him. His son Casimir was a forester during the German period and behaved as his father did, endangering his own life for the sake of saving Jews. Consequently, all those who fled sensed instinctively, without speaking to one another, that refuge was to be found with Slovik. And it was not surprising that nearly a hundred people were concentrated in the woods near his house during the first days after the slaughter, and that those who reached his home survived and later got organized into a family camp or who joined the fighting unit later. I stayed with Slovik only one day; he received us pleasantly, fed us, and told us about a number of Jews who were hiding in different parts of the woods.

The same evening, we four men departed in the direction of the Usdenikim in Lisabo. We reached the home of the Sorma family, seven brothers, the oldest of

them being Frank. Frank fed us until we were full and
presented us with a revolver and fifteen bullets, in
spite of the fact that Shmaryahu Guz, who was one of
our foursome, had not acted well toward him in the
past. Shmaryahu removed his wedding ring and gave it
to Frank. The latter refused to take it, but Shmaryahu
insisted.

We went to see the Polish shoemaker, Putchvoski,
in Jukova. We asked him to help us in getting Jews out
of Manievich. This was on Wednesday, 20 Elul. (On the
23rd of Elul, 1942, the slaughter was carried out.) The
shoemaker agreed to this, and even revealed to us that
two Jewish sisters, D'vorah and Dinah Zilbershtein,
were hiding with him. They immediately joined us, and
we returned to Slovik's forest. Slovik went to check
on the possibility of saving more Jews, and, indeed, he
brought, in a wagon covered with hay, Raizel Guz,
Shmaryahu's wife, and their two children, Itkah and
Yakov. They had been hiding with Klimtziak, and Slovik
got them with his help.

The Power of Arms

The means for survival in the struggle against the
murderers of the Jews was arms; it is impossible to
underestimate the importance of the Jews having weapons
during the Holocaust period. The wretched Jew stood
condemned to death -- but with weapons in his hand, he
stood erect and saved face -- his own and that of his
people.

My group had a pistol and a Polish rifle. With
these loaded weapons, we arrived at the village of
Sovietin, in order to obtain food. We knocked on a
peasant's door, and several Ukrainians, with axes in
their hands, appeared in front of us. When they saw
weapons in our hands, they lowered the axes, claiming
they had thought us to be Jews. These gentiles were
not able to imagine Jews with weapons. We looked like
Ukrainians in every way. "And what would you have
done, if Jews had shown up here?" we asked. And the
reply was, the same that had been done to the Brill
family with its three members. "Three Ukrainians
handed them over to the police and, in exchange, received thirty kilograms of salt!" We took the gentiles
outside, took the axes away from them, and, using our
weapons as a threat, got from them the addresses of
those who had exchanged Jews for salt. We ordered them

to dig a pit, and they were shot and thrown into it. With great effort, we also caught those who had received the salt, and they too were shot. We set fire to the house of one of them, the fire spread through the village, and the church bells were rung. The news spread quickly: "Jews are avenging their brothers' blood!" And, therefore, our operations deterred the "Jew Hunters."

We had Polish friends who were clearly antiGerman. Young Ukrainians also joined up with them. We met with a few of them and explained to them that at the present time, the Germans with the Slav's help, were liquidating the Jews, but after the Jews, they would subjugate and liquidate the Slavs as well. The common enemy was spoken of here -- the cursed Germans and their followers.

We convinced them and received a Polish rifle and thirty bullets. I practiced with the rifle and felt ready to use it. The first opportunity came immediately; about ten Ukrainian policemen, under the command of a German sergeant, occupied an area at the crossroads between Polskeh-Goreh and Koninsk. We passed through the area and then we heard "Halt! Don't move!" The company fled, and I stayed behind with the loaded rifle, hidden away. I shot the policeman, Vaskeh Zaruk, whom I had known for a long time. He was hit in the knee and shouted, "Save me!" The police left the area and got a horse and wagon in order to transport the wounded for medical treatment. (His children survived the Holocaust.)

In a Snow Pit

A refugee family from the occupied territory of Poland, two brothers and two sisters, lived with my uncle Yosef Merin in Manievich. At the time of the first action, they caught the oldest brother, Tzvi, and beat him until he spat up blood. Fortunately for him, they let him go. During the second action, Tzvi managed to escape to the woods. Tzvi's sister Chanakeh, was already standing naked in a pit, ready to be shot; but at the last second, the German told her to run away. She snatched up a dress from the pile and fled. She crossed over the railroad tracks and got as far as Lisova-Usadvah.

As she wandered about, there in the bushes, she noticed a man's shadow. They played "hide and seek,"

-140-

she and the shadow. Chanakeh would alternately emerge and hide until she decided to look at the "shadow," close up. And then they met. Shouts of joy shook the surrounding silence. It was her brother, Tzvi.

At night they found shelter with the Poles. After several days, the two met up with another Jew from the Kovel area by the name of Mundek. The Poles somehow hid them from the Germans and their allies. Until one day, Max (a partisan leader) happened to meet them and they, these Poles, entreated him to take the Jews from them, to save them from German atrocities. The Germans had one penalty in those days for both the Jew and those who hid him: death.

Mundek had arms. Like the Polish residents, he too, cooperated with the partisans in everything asked of him. Among the things we needed were batteries for flashlights, and equipment for radio communication with Moscow. One time the Stazlatzy commander, Narovski from Manievich, brought us these items. He got them from the pharmacist, Bilinski, in exchange for meat. We arranged that on one Sunday evening, we would come and get the items we had asked for. Narovski was late in arriving. We waited for him. Having nothing to do, I went through the rooms, and I suddenly saw a woman quickly get into bed and cover herself. When I asked who she was, the woman of the house replied, "My daughter." We sat down at the table to eat and in front of me was a hole-ridden curtain covering the doorway of the room where the woman was lying down. She turned away from the bed, looked at me, and seemed to recognize me. After I finished eating and was already outside, Narovski came out and said to me, "Someone wants to see you." For a second, a trembling passed through me. Maybe it was someone from my family.

I went back into the house, and suddenly I saw Chanakeh Goldberg. "Why did you hide in the bed?" I asked. "I thought you were German policemen." "And where are the two boys who were with you?" "Not far from here," she said and burst into tears, begging us to take them from there and save them from certain death.

At that moment, Narovski came in and added, "This is an opportunity for them to go with you. We very much fear a surprise visit by the Germans. If they suddenly show up, they will kill all of us."

I instructed my friends to go to see Frank Sorma, and I went out with Chanakeh to bring the two boys. After we had gone quite a distance on foot, I asked Chanakeh, "Is it much further?" "No," she answered, and burst into tears. "And why are you crying?" "God knows if they are still alive," she said. "It's already two weeks that food hasn't touched their mouths, since the first snow fall, and I have been unable to go see them." "And who provided them with food before the snow fall?" "Kalish," she said. I was startled to hear his name. The same Kalish appeared on our blacklist for liquidation. Only the previous week, our men had liquidated one of his sons, and then I heard that Kalish made a hut on top of a pit for them and equipped them with a saw and an axe -- vital things for forest dwellers -- in addition to eating utensils. "I myself," says Chanakeh, "sew, and two weeks ago, I went out to sew for the Poles in a village and stayed with them." "Is it much further?" I asked her. "No, very near," she replied.

That night I wore a long fur coat. I had a rifle and a satchel with bullets. I was already drenched with sweat, and I did not see the place where the boys were to be found. At last, we reached the woods. Chanakeh began shouting, "Tzvi, don't be afraid. Berl is here." I looked. The size of the hiding place was perhaps the size of a small table, and snow was piled on it, at least half a meter thick. The boys tried to get out, but they were not successful. I decided to go to Kalish's house, a distance of several kilometers. I awoke him from his sleep. He hitched two horses and took two shovels with him. We quickly removed the snow from the "Shlash" and brought out the two frozen boys.

It was hard to say whether they were alive or dead. I seated them in a sleigh, and we went to the Surma family. In the house, a wave of warmth engulfed them, which they so much needed. The mistress of the house put a large bowl on the table with cheese in sour cream and a loaf of bread. All of this was devoured in an instant. I refused them additional portions because of their health. After they had sufficiently warmed themselves, I transferred them in the sleigh to a more secure location, where we were staying temporarily. Food was not scarce then. Meat and bread were hanging on the trees.

After ten days, I transferred them to Kochov, where we were more established. We had orderly trenches, makeshift showers, and almost an abundance of food -- really the "comfortable life." After several days of rest and intensive bathing in our showers, they were transferred to a citizen's camp, where they stayed until the end of the war. The two of them emigrated to South America. Chanakeh married Shaiya Flash. They, too, emigrated to South America, and during their visit in Israel, they also visited me.

Blood Revenge Operation

Here a few memories about the first of the Ukrainian partisans, the founders of the Partizankeh in our vicinity.

In 1933, the young people of several villages got together in the area and requested a permit from the Polish government to demonstrate on the first of May. The permit was not granted, but the Ukrainians demonstrated anyway. Police from Kraskin and Manievich were summoned, and a special train of police arrived from Kovel. Tempers flared, and one of the demonstrators threw a rock at the face of the Karsin chief of police. He was hit, and some of his teeth fell out. He shot and hit one of the demonstrators. The commotion grew. Arrests and quick trials began. Many of the demonstrators were sentenced to three, four, five and ten years' imprisonment.

After some years, with the changeover of power in 1939, all the prisoners returned home. The government was now in the hands of the Soviets. Property owners' lands were confiscated by force in accordance with local orders.

Kolchozes and agricultural communes were established. The May 1st demonstrators from earlier years got jobs as directors of the kolchozes, food warehouses, and other things of that nature.

In 1941, with the outbreak of the German-Russian war, the Russian army retreated; the local directors and pro-Soviet workers of the city of Kharkov followed it. There they all received instructions to go back to their home towns and to organize a partisan movement.

One day, four residents of the village of Manievich returned home. But on that same night, they were arrested by their friends, the demonstrators and prisoners of May 1, 1933, who decided to collaborate with the Germans. The four were transferred to the prison in Kovel, and there awaited their turn to be taken out to be killed, as was the custom of the Germans in those days.

During their time in prison, the four became acquainted with two other young people from the Kovel area. In prison, they also met Sohar, who advised them to escape as their end was approaching. He promised them he would turn a blind eye to their escape. The next night, they sawed through the grid, wove a rope from their clothing and, one by one, lowered themselves to the bottom; from there they crossed the fence and fled to their two friends.

On the same day, they obtained two semi-automatic rifles with ammunition, and all six arrived at our regiment. Another four were equipped with arms, and together they began functioning. In the beginning, they operated on a small scale but consistently. They liquidated informers, Ukrainian police, and plunderers of Jewish property. For a while, the Pole, Max (Sobiesek), myself, and several other Jews joined them. The small, restricted unit grew. We went over to the localities of Kochov and the Suzankeh, where already the first units of Polkovnik (colonel) Brinsky (Dadya Petya) which later became the central command, and Kruk's unit, were located.

The pressure on Dadya Petya from the partisans in Max's unit for retaliatory missions increased to the point of agitation. And then, one day, Max returned from the high command with the news of Dadya's agreement to the hoped-for campaign. Immediately we thirteen fighters went out to the road. From Kruk's camp, another three Jewish fighters joined us: David Blaushtein, Zev Avruch, and Yosef Tanenbaum. Still that same night, we got not too far away from the village of Manievich. We hid there until sunset the next day, maintaining a position where we could see, but not be seen. I was responsible for the execution of the operation. But when the zero hour arrived, I didn't know where to begin.

After I had thought it over, I went to the nearest house and ordered the mistress of the house to go and call the village leader. But she came back, claiming that the leader was not home. I ordered her to go a second time and not to return without him. When the two of them appeared, I sent out two men to secure the road leading to the village from the town of Manievich, in case Germans or the German police would come and surprise us. The order was to shoot at the Germans and retreat. I sent three of our men to the church at the crossroads in the center of the village. I divided the rest of the men into two groups, one under David Blaushtein's command, and the second under my command.

I arrived with my men at the first house and removed my sheepskin. Then Sirkov came up to me and said, "You'll be cold. Wear something else that's lighter." I remember my heart was beating loudly. My hands shook. The depressing thought did not leave me: How is it possible to enter this house and kill for no reason? Suppose I know the people. But the moment the murderer of Jews, who was reknowned, appeared before my eyes, even I became a wild man and shot him.

We went on from there to the village leader, who was collaborating with the Germans and we liquidated him. The leader's wife, Marya, managed to escape through a window. Shaiya Flash was on guard outside and he shot at her, but he did not hit her. At the same moment, our group arrived, bringing with them the leader's daughter and her husband. We were thrown into a moment of uncertainty. We deliberated. The husband was my neighbor from the town of Manievich. He fell at my feet and begged for his life. I still did not touch him. Meanwhile, his wife too pleaded that we let him live. Acccording to the information we had received about her, she too deserved to be killed. Her husband became hysterical. I pitied them and warned them not to leave the house.

We continued on to another Gentile, known as an arch executioner of Jews. His friends were there also. We shot them, one by one. From there, we went to several more houses in the "blood revenge" operation. At the end of the campaign, we met up with the second group.

In summary, we liquidated at that time forty-one German collaborators and all those who were with them. The rest fled. The next stage in that operation was confiscation of their property, property that had been stolen from Jews. We also took oxen, cows, and horses that were hitched to wagons and were there for the taking. The convoy continued for a distance of three kilometers. The next day at dawn, we arrived at head-quarters to report to Dadya Petya.

-145-

The young men who were among the founders of the Partizankeh were largely involved in this operation. It was these same young men who, in his time, conducted conversations with the Ukrainian police commander, Slivtziak, who had, with his own hands, murdered partisan families.

Nadia the Cook

We left Slovik's woods and found Kruk with his partisans. We situated ourselves not far from him and went to work.

My house in the town and Yakov Bergman's house were close to one another. I knew that in his house there was a cook by the name of Nadia. She was originally from Russia, and she had connections with the Ukrainian police, for whom she was cooking. One day we went to see Vasil Baron in Manievich. We asked his wife to put us in contact with Nadia. We set up a specific day and hour for this meeting.

We arrived, five partisans, at the agreed upon location. Two of us secured the location on the road, outside the house, and I waited with two others outside. The meeting in the village of Jokov was brief and to the point. We proposed to her that at the next meeting, she come with several Germans, if this was possible.

Eight of us arrived at the next meeting, at eight o'clock in the evening. We waited until ten-thirty. We looked through binoculars and saw about twenty-five Germans approaching. We immediately left the area.

We contacted her again, and she began to shout about how we had not come to the meeting. Of course, we apologized and let it pass. We set up another meeting next to the brick factory that was near Manievich. This time she came with ten Germans.

A third meeting was agreed upon. This time, we advised her to obtain a bit of poison and put it in the food of the Ukrainian police. She agreed to carry this mission out, on the condition that if she would have to run away as a result of this deed and would reach the woods and there meet up with the Jews, she would want to blow them up with a grenade, even if she were to die with them. I wanted to kill her at once, but my

Gentile friends would not let me. Because of this transgression, I was transferred to another location.

Nadia took the poison with her and the word spread that at a sawmill in Tcheruvkah, she had poisoned twenty-five Germans and afterwards fled, along with two Cossacks, in the direction of Moshchitzki Buglovoki's farm. There she met the staff patrol, and they took her to the woods.

The person responsible for the kitchen in those days was Ostshenko Moriniak and his son Koliah. After a few days, when she had become familiar with the surroundings and was slightly known by the partisans, they made her responsible for the cooking. And then suddenly, she was caught red-handed with the same poison in her hand, intending to put it in a pot of milk. She was immediately taken to a special unit -- Base 5 -- under the command of Major Mahmad (Melamed). In spite of the strict guard that was placed on her, she managed to steal a rifle and escape.

That same night, I went off with Shaiya Flash. We were travelling in two wagons with sacks of flour from the village Cholozia to Base 5, when our horses suddenly became alarmed. I jumped out of the wagon -- and saw Nadia in front of me. When I asked, "Where to?" she pointed her rifle at me.

I did not get flustered. I grabbed her rifle with one hand and with the other, pulled her hair. I told my friend Shaiya to inform headquarters of the incident. Immediately, Machmad appeared from the other direction and, without much delay, drew his pistol and shot her. At that moment, the commander of the special unit, Vasilinko, also arrived. On seeing what had occurred, he turned around and caught the two Cossacks, Nadia's friends. He found them sleeping, took them outside, and shot them.

The Wedding Operation

During operations at railroads in the town of Manievich, a train with salt, a vital commodity in those days, was among those damaged. This enabled the villagers to steal considerable amounts of salt.

After this operation, we learned that in the adjacent village, Vilkah, there was to be a wedding on

Saturday night where a Ukrainian policeman was to be present. I reported this to the captain, and he ordered that we kill the policeman. Toward this end, we obtained two horses, which we returned after a few days. The informant, a policeman, hid at his brother-in-law's home (Sak), because he refused to cooperate with the Germans. I urged him to cooperate with us, the partisans, and he agreed. When Jews walked about the woods and villages, knocking on the doors of villagers for a piece of bread, a potato, or any kind of food to satisfy their hunger, he would give them something and even ordered his younger brother to transport Jews behind the village and send them to the woods. When I showed up at their house, I was warmly received, despite the fact that the first time he saw me, he was completely shaken. I calmed him down and assured him that humane deeds were rewarded. The members of the household began to hug me and kiss me with great emotion. They set a table fit for a king, given the conditons of those days, and eventually, with great difficulty, I was able to take my friend out of the house.

We went out on the road in the direction of Vilkah. In the middle of the road, we saw from afar a flashing light. We decided to find out the explanation for the light. When we reached the site, we saw one of our liaisons boiling whiskey. He urged us to drink with him. And so we finished a full liter of liquor. Dead-drunk, my Russian friends arrived at Vilkah, and there was no one to go with me to the "wedding." I situated myself at the village elder's home. I put my Russian friends to bed. I assigned Yitzhak Segal to guard duty. I left my rifle in the house and took one of my drunken friends' submachine guns. Shaiya Flash and I went out to the school in the village, where the wedding was being held. When I called out, asking if the policeman was among those present, they answered that this man did not exist. But next to one of the tables, I noticed unusual movement among the people. I called out his name a second time and fired into the air. I approached; it became apparent that the people were trying to hide the policeman under the table. I ordered him to throw down his arms. Shaiya Flash grabbed his rifle, and the policeman crawled outside. We tied his hands with rope and moved from there to the elder's house.

On the way, we received 11,500 gold rubles from him. I joined my company, and before dawn, we reached Szankah, where the commander Chunek Wolper was staying.

-148-

There, we took him out of the wagon into the bushes and shot him, according to Dadya Petya's orders.

The Eighteen Fat Cows

We were informed that a herd of cattle that belonged to the Germans was grazing in the village of Holoziya. Eight of us went and waited not far from Manievich's church, until the shepherds returned from lunch. Upon their arrival, we immediately surrounded the herd. The shepherds quickly scattered in every direction, but we managed to catch a few of them. We picked out eighteen cows. I gestured to a young boy shepherd who was about fifteen, and asked him, "You know me; what's my name?" "Yes," he answered, "your name is Burku." "And do you know my friend?" "Yes, Segal," he replied. "And now, go and tell people that Yitzhak and Burku confiscated the cattle."

The shepherds informed the Germans about the deed in the meadow. The Germans immediately sent forces next to the small wooden bridge on the road leading to Holoziya to block the partisans retreat. I succeeded in outwitting the Germans. Instead of sending the cattle to Holoziya, as the Germans imagined I would, I sent them to the Hoptovah woods; and then I, with two others, arrived at the cemetery of the village of Holoziya and ambushed the Germans. When they reached the small wooden bridge, which had been burned down for a while and was not passable for vehicles, we opened fire on them. Upon hearing shots, a reinforcement arrived from the village, from the flour mill that was run by one of our men, Avraham Puchtik. After this, an advance unit from a frontal position joined us, from the village of Sarchov.

The Germans were forced to retreat. We maintained eighteen fat cattle for quite a while. We held a feast for kings.

The Jewish Partisans and the Local Population

The Jewish boys from Kruk's unit excelled at forcibly entering homes of villagers and confiscating clothing, food, and the like, which was the most natural thing for them. As Jews from the area, they knew about this or that peasant's role in plundering, or in the murder of Jews. They essentially returned Jewish

-149-

property that had been stolen for the good of the citizens' camp. But headquarters did not view this kind of behavior favorably, and tragic events occurred. Complaints were made to Kruk about his Jewish fighters, and he took severe measures against them. Melinka (Dov Lorber) was once stood up at a formation, and his commander and friend Kruk slapped him in front of everyone. Melinka was forced to restrain himself, because he knew that opposition would lead to severe consequences, for him and for others.

Once a Jewish fighter from the unit took a pair of boots from a peasant from the village of Horodok. This matter was brought to the attention of Kruk. The fighter denied it, but his things were searched, and the boots were, in fact, found. Kruk, seething with anger, drew his pistol, and was about to shoot the Jewish man.

With great difficulty, Yosef Zweibel succeeded in convincing him, for his sake, to not shoot the fighter. Afterwards, Kruk apologized to him, speaking as a close friend, saying that all of the slander was coming from his Jewish comrades, and so he had no choice but to react as he did.

Once, a peasant by the name of Dimitry, who served as a liaison in our unit, made a complaint to me. This peasant had a warm relationship with the camp's Jews. He and his sons would take the children from the camp to their homes, giving showers and feeding them. In those days, a lot of significance was attached to such things.

He complained about a partisan from Kruk's unit who had confiscated a sewing machine, a pair of oxen, and a wagon from him, pointing out that he wasn't angry about this and wasn't asking that the things be returned to him, because the matter could cause reactions and retaliations.

I knew that I was obligated to act in a quiet manner, so that the matter would not reach headquarters and Dadya Petya, who closely watched over the integrity of the partisans toward the village population. I consulted with Kruk, and he ordered that the confiscated items be quietly returned to their owner.

And there was another incident. I was ordered, as head of a group of fifteen partisans, to confiscate all the belongings in a distant house in the middle of the woods, that were to be used for a wedding there.

We arrived in three sleighs, after a three-hour trip. We found many goods -- boots, clothing, coats, and a lot of food that was prepared for the wedding.

Everything was loaded onto the sleighs, and we got ready to leave. Suddenly the peasant remarked that "if only Nikolai (Kruk) knew, they wouldn't be doing this to him." And the peasant told me about a battle between four partisan-paratroopers from the great army and one hundred police and Germans. They all fell, except one wounded man who reached the peasant's home, and he, the peasant, hid him in the attic and gave him medical treatment. I knew that he was telling the truth, and I ordered that the things we had confiscated be returned, but the peasant asked that we divide them up, fifty-fifty. And so we did. Then he pointed out a place not far from there where they made "smogon" (a liquor). We supplied ourselves with twenty-five liters, and with great difficulty, I prevented the partisans from getting drunk. I had to threaten them with my weapons to prevent this. In the past, tragic incidents had occurred when a company got drunk and fell into the hands of the Bonderovsty. When I reported this to the commander, Captain Unishtchenko (Dadya Sasha), he came up to me to kiss me on the head. "You acted in a manner worthy of a Soviet partisan."

A Ukrainian partisan slandered a peasant, because he was courting the peasant's daughter, and she didn't return his love. Disappointed, he decided to take revenge in this base manner.

Once, while on reconnaissance with the objective of attacking the Krasin police, we passed by Zmoshtziya and went on to the road leading to the Polish forester, Tvolski. The latter sensed us coming and, thinking we were Ukrainian police, jumped out of the window and fled. The next day, about twenty of us paid a visit to the forester, with an order to confiscate all of his property. We didn't find him, only a woman, whom we thought to be his wife. We loaded up everything, and one of the partisans, Yeshayahu Shalosh, called to me in Yiddish, "Berl, lomir gayen..." Upon hearing this, the woman was jolted and shouted, "Are you Jews? Please don't do this for the sake of the Pole who rescued me. I am a Jewess from Lotsk."

We returned the things and later established very friendly relations with Tvolski, who served as a liaison. He greatly excelled at this job.

Germans Following Max's Blood

When we found out about the German hunt in the woods that was to occur at the beginning of the frost and snow season, we immediately got in touch with Kazik (Casimir) Slovik, and he contacted the former school lprincipal in Manievich who had been a forest watchman during the German rule. The two of them contaced Sliptchiak, the Ukrainian chief of police.

Sliptchiak was willing to meet with us, the partisans. We agreed upon a location not far from the town. From the partisan side, three Ukrainian youths, Max and I appeared. On the way to the meeting, a youth from the village of Grivoz who served in the Ukranian police force came out to meet us. He was also said to be participating in the upcoming hunt, and he told us its approximate date (February 2, 1943).

The policeman took a hat with a particular sign on it from the sleigh and asked that, during the hunt, we wouldn't fire at him and then he too would not fire on us. He also advised us to leave the area for awhile until things calmed down. The meeting with the chief of police took place in a tense atmosphere, because it was the same chief of police who, thirty days previously, had ordered the murder of partisan families and Jews, including the families of the three partisans sitting there with us. These three requested that we liquidate him, but the order that Max received from Dadya Petya was unequivocally, "Don't harm him." The three left after many pleas and words of persuasion. When we returned to the woods after reports and clarifications, it was decided that we leave the woods and station ourselves in the village of Svaritzvitz, which was under the command of Feodorov-Rovnae.

The retreat from the woods took place on Saturday night, the 10th of January, 1943, at midnight, north of the village of Kochov. We stationed ourselves for a few days in a local school in the village of Svaritzvitz. Shaiya Flash, Yitzchak Segal, and I were sent out to secure the road leading to Dovrovitch. Meanwhile, it was decided at our headquarters to send out patrols in the vicinity of our base, which we had left only a number of days earlier.

-152-

The mission was assigned to Max, who already held the rank of captain. He joined up with me and two other partisans, and we went out to the road, which was full of surprises. The first of them occurred when we crossed the Styr River, which was icy and slippery. One of the horses slipped and was torn in half. He was shot on the spot. I tied ragged sacks onto the second horse's feet, and in this way, we crossed the river. Further along the road, we confiscated a peasant's horse that we chanced upon on our route. The same night, in the freezing cold of 32° Celsius, we travelled 120 kilometers to the village of Bialskah-Valeh. We entered one of the houses, whose owner (Yosef) was a foodseller for the German government. He complained to us that a while ago, partisans had burned 3,000 tons of kernels. We tried to clarify among us whose unsuccessful operation this had been, and reached the conclusion that this had been one of Kruk's unit's operations. We were hungry and frozen, tired from the journey and from lack of sleep. Yosef put a bottle of vodka on the table, which emitted a burnt odor.

I ordered him to bring spirits and dessert at once. After the meal, we continued on to the sawmill in the village that belonged to a Jew by the name of Mikolitch (He is today in Israel). Near the sawmill were wooden shacks that were the workers' quarters. Max set up a resting place for us there for the day. I pointed out to him that it was not a suitable place for resting, but he did not heed my warning. We unharnessed the horses and went to rest. Everyone went. One of the two partisans urged me to also go and rest so that I'd be able top continue on, but I was unable to fall asleep and went outside. I sensed that imminent danger awaited us.

While standing outside, I heard a loud racket coming from the center of town. I asked the first man I met on the road what the noise was, and he said, "To tell you the truth, I don't know if those are Germans over there, or partisans."

I weighed these words carefully; I did not want to lose the good reputation I had won in a short time as a fighter and an implementor in the young partisan movement. I thought that maybe they were in fact partisans. But very quickly I realized that other partisans besides us could not be here in the area at that time, and that I must quickly and immediately wake up my comrades. I followed the Germans' movements and saw them dividing up into two groups. In one there were seven Germans heading toward the village of Sarchov, and in the other were five Germans going in the direction of the village of Vilkah. It was clear to me that we were surrounded. Just at that moment, a young girl from the household burst into the house shouting, "Holy Mary, we are surrounded!" Partisans burst out of the house, including Max who was barefoot, and this was in -32 degree cold. He fired from his automatic rifle to the right flank and ordered me to strike at the left side. We waged a battle in this way for twenty minutes.

And then I sensed that the ammunition had run out, that the bullets in my satchel had been used up -- and so I gave the command to retreat in the direction of the grove. Completely exhausted, we reached a tree that had been uprooted in one of the storms and, as a result, blocked the road. A lot of blood dripped from Max's legs, and the Germans pursued us following the blood stains. Max removed his shirt and tore it to pieces, in order to bandage his legs, and we went to a clearing in the woods. A pile of hay was there. I took two grenades from my satchel, and we decided to prepare for the final battle. We observed from afar that the Germans were getting closer and closer to the uprooted tree -- and when they didn't see the bloody footprints, they turned around and retraced their steps.

We continued on toward one of the houses, where we ended up the day, and at night we went on in the direction of the Village of Sarchov. We stayed with a Pole by the name of Dikneski, and he told us about the Germans, who, during their retreat from the woods at the time of the hunt, captured a Jew from Chelm by the name of Chaim. The Pole also told us about the battle we had waged the previous day in the village of Bialskah-Vola. We went on from there in a sleigh, which we had confiscated for our use, and reached the village of Koninsk. The next night, we travelled to headquarters to report to Polkovnik Brinsky (Dadya Petya). I received an order to take ten of the best young men and to try to find out who had informed on us in the village of Bialskah-Vola. And if the investigation were successful, we would liquidate the informers and confiscate their property. Anything that could not be taken, we would burn.

The road was a good one. We arrived quickly and immediately began the investigation, but we came up against a stone wall. No one talked. We arrived at the house where we had recently been, but we were unable to single out anyone. The members of the household received us nicely, returning a blanket and fur to me. I urged them to tell me what they knew, but in vain.

We returned to the sawmill and to the families where we had originally been. We searched the houses and every type of potential hiding place. We discovered some things, mainly precious strips of leather that really had been stolen by the "tenants." I returned to report to Polkovnik Brinsky. He smiled and said, "Next time they will kill you, because you didn't kill all of them."

Fifty-Six German Casualties

During the war, great importance was attached by both of the fighting armies -- but especially by the Germans -- to transportation. The Germans transported most of their equipment and manpower to the front by means of the railroad. Because of this, emphasis was placed in the partisan movement on disrupting the transportation system whenever possible.

Two men were assigned to this task from each unit. We stationed ourselves in the Holoziya woods, with the purpose of making sudden attacks, mining the railroad tracks, and carrying out acts of sabotage. We would visit the tracks every other night, or when we had early information about German soldiers being rushed to the front. The information was leaked to us by Ukrainian and Polish workers, the signallers who had worked during the Polish and Russian rule until 1941. In this way, we received information about a train with German army officers, making its way to the front. Nine of us men went out for the mining operation. We sat near the tracks for three consecutive days. At the estimated time of the train's arrival -- at ten at night -- we went up on the tracks with a large mine, set up to be pulled by a cord. It weighed seventy kilograms. When we finished setting up the mine, the patrols signalled us that a guard unit was approaching to check the tracks. We didn't know whether to remove the mine or leave it, as it could be discovered. The danger was great. I suggested that we leave it, because a few weeks earlier, a partisan from Kruk's unit had been killed in a similar operation.

-155-

We were still discussing this matter when the train approached. We pulled hard on the cord, and a powerful explosion, whose echo was heard over a forty kilometer radius, shook the air. The entire train was turned over on its side. Only from the last cars, shots were heard, fired wildly. We went off in the opposite direction in order to mislead them, so that they wouldn't follow our path of retreat. The next day, we learned there had been hundreds of casualties and many wounded. This was March 23, 1943.

We returned to headquarters. I was sick, my whole body was covered with wounds, and I was forbidden to leave the woods. They set up a bed for me behind the trenches, in the bushes, and there I received medical treatment from Dr. Melchior. Once, while I was lying down, half awake, half asleep, I heard someone coming. I quickly opened my eyes, and Polkovnik Brinsky was standing in front of me. He calmed me down, asked how I was, and we began talking. I said, "What brought you to see me, Comrade Polkovnik?" And he told me not very good news. "Headquarters' patrols brought word that tomorrow the Germans plan to confiscate 300 head of cattle in the villages of Krasin and Zmistey; I'd like to stop them from doing this," Polkovnik said.

"You are putting this on my shoulders, Comrade Polkovnik?"

"I'm not happy about disturbing you when you're sick, but there is no other way. Take a mine from headquarters, get a shell from Kruk, and at the village of Holoziya pick out whichever men you choose -- and go safely!"

I did as I was commanded. I equipped myself with a mine, asked my older brother, Velvel, to hitch a good horse to a wagon for me, got the shell from Kruk and went out my myself to Holoziya. On the way, I made all sorts of calculations about how to carry out the operation in the best possible way. I got an idea. I figured that some of our comrades must have lived there, after they had escaped from prison but before joining the partisans. And I was right. I met eight of them in one of the houses, sitting around the table eating and drinking. I joined them, and we began to work out a plan of action.

At dawn, when we were ready to go, it rained, and there was a flood. But we continued on. The mine, as well as the shell, got wet. I sent a local youth out to the road leading from the village of Manievich to Krasin, telling him that the minute he saw the Germans, he should quickly run back and tell us. Our messenger met a peasant who was returning from Manievich, and he told him that the village was full of Germans and Ukrainian police, and that they were said to be heading for Krasin. We acted according to this information, opening fire with every weapon we had.

In the villages, panic ensued. The Germans fled back to the city, and the villagers in Krasin led the cattle to the central location, as they thought that it was Germans who were firing the shots.

The villagers, some delighted and others disappointed, stood openmouthed when they saw us. The village leader, who had brought his two oxen, was shot on the spot, and we confiscated his oxen. We picked out fifty-five cows and set the rest free. Some of the villagers asked us to kill their cows, so that the Germans wouldn't take them and eat their meat. We fulfilled their request.

A Chapter of Events on Passover

Passover eve, 1943. Two Poles from Stepneska-Hota came to us, and asked Max, our commander, for help in setting up a Polish partisan movement. Max consented. He chose twenty men and went out with them to the road, a distance of about 120 kilometers. In Stepneska-Hota, it became clear that the situation was not improving. The local residents, the Poles, either were unable or did not want to defend themselves with their own resources. Many Poles also lived in the town who had fled their hometowns and Polish villages and settlements that had been established during the Polish rule were found there. In these people's neighborhoods, there were also Ukrainian villagers who were notorious for their hatred of the Poles, no less than that of the Jews. These Ukrainians were persuaded by the Germans to make names for themselves among the Poles, after committing murderous deeds against the Jews. The Ukrainians would torture the Polish men and make them die unusual and unnatural deaths. They would throw Poles upside-down into wells of water and do other brutal acts.

The Ukrainians' cruel actions spread alarm and fear amidst their Polish neighbors, and the Poles fled to the city. The overcrowding in the houses increased. There were about fifty people crowded together in every house -- women, children, and babies. The pandemonium was great.

Max called together the city dignitaries and tried to talk with them. Taking into account the existing conditions, he tried to incorporate them into the partisan network. We suggested that there be a cooperative guard duty over the town, day and night (a suggestion that Polkovnik Brinsky did not agree to). In the end, it was decided to send a different unit, under the command of Porotchnik (a lieutenant in the Polish army), who was a native of Stepneska-Hota. Twenty of us went with him. We crossed rivers and railroad tracks that were closely guarded by the Germans. After we safely crossed the railroad tracks and arrived at Hals, the Shtalitzim (similar to the Gadna youth corps in Israel) reached a commander who supplied us with wagons and horses, -- and we went on to Stepneska-Hota. Together with the Polish fighters' commander, we outlined a plan of action. There was an explicit and severe order given not to fire unnecessarily, because all of the residents knew that an open fire was a signal for them to defend themselves and ward off any kind of an attack, whether it be by Ukrainians or Germans.

With our appearance, the Poles' sense of security increased tenfold. They led counterattacks on the Ukrainians, who imposed fear on the area.

We found out that in the Hota vicinity, two Ukrainians were moving about, one of them more than two meters tall, that they were armed with machine guns and were assigned to an area extending over a square kilometer. Quite a lot of murderous acts were credited to them. We immediately investigated their security techniques. It became clear that they were very simple. The two of them regularly left the center, each one going in the opposite direction, and then they returned to the center. We divided up into two groups and lay an ambush for them.

When they came near the edge of the section, we surprised them in such a way that they had no time to activate their weapons. We tied their hands from behind and, bound, we brought them to Hota, to the former post office. There we imprisoned them in one of the rooms and posted a guard over them. We went out to

eat. To be on the safe side, Yitzchok Melnitzer and I
went back and tied their hands and feet with wires.

The post office serviced the Polish headquarters,
so it buzzed with people all hours of the day, but
during that day, it did even more so. The Poles wanted
to punish the two murderers by "lynching" them, and
when we returned, the two looked like corpses. The
next day we brought them to Salonay-Baluta, salty water
spa, where we buried them alive.

Once when I returned to the center of town, near
the church where a meeting of the local Polish high
command was taking place, presided over by the
Comissar, I suddenly heard six shots from the direction
of the village of Virka. One of our fighters was
hospitalized in this village. I suspected that he had
been liquidated. I burst into the church and reported
the shots to Porotchnik. He sent a Pole with me and a
pair of horses hitched to a wagon, and we went off in
the direction of the shots. I broke into the house,
where I found Vanke and a young woman with him who made
a strange impression on me. I observed her closely,
and I had no doubt in my heart as to her origins.

When I asked her who she was, she burst into
tears. I calmed her down. I asked her if she lacked
anything, but she insisted, "I don't lack anything
except freedom." She also told me that she had been
with the Kasiyondaz (Polish priest). I thanked her for
the help she had extended to the wounded man, and I
extended my hand in a parting gesture, when she again
broke into tears and begged me to take her with me,
pleading that I should not leave her there. I said to
Vanke, "I'm taking you home." He started to cry, "How
am I going to be able to make it through a long and
very dangerous route such as this?" We had to cross
over railroad tracks and the Styr River.

I calmed him down. I told him that I had another
sick person, Dadya Malishov, and also two wounded
people from our woods. I took leave of those who were
in the house, and we went with the Pole to the road
leading back. When we arrived at Salonay-Baluta, I saw
many people gathered together, blocking the road. We
had to walk around in order to get over to them. There
we met about twenty Polish youths, armed with automatic
weapons and several hundred citizens surrounding the
two youths, who it became apparent, were partisans.
When I asked them why they had fired, they answered

-159-

that they were testing out their weapons. I interrogated the two of them as to who they were and what they were doing, and it became clear that they were partisans from Suborov's unit. I suggested to Yitschak Segal that we take action against them, that is, take their weapons from them. I wanted to show them what Jews were capable of doing.

In a matter of seconds we had their submachine guns, and I made them sit in the wagon. We had just started moving, when we saw from afar their commander approaching. They reported to him and pointed to us. Their commander asked me what had happened. I answered, "I don't know you, either. Come back with me to our commander, Vanke Danilchenko." After some brief clarifications their weapons were returned, and they were set free, in the midst of warm handshakes. They, the Sovorovtzy, were impressed by our actions, especially when Vanke told them that Yitzchak Segal and I were Jews. He also told them that, when they were in a village staying with peasants, after the disintegration of the Red Army, they had established ties with Jews, who were always desirable candidates for the partisan movement.

This was during Passover. We were coming into the village, when two youths come up to me and asked me if I'd like to see how Jews conduct the Passover-night seder. We went to the edge of the village, Yitschak Segal and I, and went into a barn. The people were startled. I immediately calmed them down, "Don't be afraid. We are Jews too. Continue?" It pained me to see their fear, and my eyes filled with tears. Silence prevailed. Old people, men and women, held a "seder." I asked them if they needed help. "Only Haribono Shel Olam (The Almighty God) can help us through all of this in peace." they said. We wished them a good holiday and parted from them with tears in our eyes.

After two days, I left the place. I received an order to transfer the sick ones to headquarters, which was, so to speak, home. I brought with me one of my Ukrainian fighter friends, Lazar Kadek. Three more wounded people from another unit joined us, among them a young woman who was slightly wounded. They had gone out, ten of them, on an operation and come up against Ukrainian nationals. Seven fell during a battle with them. Those who remained asked to go to Stepneska-Hota, which was in the direction we were going. I received under my command twenty Poles, who were to help us cross over the railroad tracks. I divided the Poles up into two groups. The first one posted itself on one side of the tracks, and the second on the other side, across from the bunker's entrance. Kadek and I crossed over to the second side and took a position across from the bunker. The wounded young woman appeared to help us, with a submachine gun in her hand. The wagons with the wounded and sick safely crossed the railroad tracks.

Before we were done with one obstacle, we had to face a second danger. The nationalistic village, Jalotzk, stretched out before us. I stopped the caravan of wagons and, with my friends, slipped into the village to check out the situation. We immediately noticed two villagers moving about, with sticks in their hands. We took them to the wagon with us and tied their hands from behind. We learned from them that their job was to go to the church and ring the bells if partisans appeared in the vicinity of the village, and then the weapon-owners would organize themselves and fire at the partisans. Fortunately for us, this plan was frustrated. We made the prisoners go up on the wagons and slipped out of that place, in the direction of the village of Bavka. There, in one of the homes, I obtained a pitcher of milk and a loaf of bread. I threw the two prisoners out of the wagon and continued on to Stepneska-Hota, where the young woman had stayed with her two wounded comrades.

From Stepneska-Hota, we continued on to Karimna. There we had a frontal position with four men. From the large amount of information we received, it was clear that a German unit that had left the town of Rafalovka was pursuing us. Very quickly, we approached the Styr River and went up on the bridge, which was temporary and small, and apt to move and get closer to the edge of the river which we wanted. Our men from the frontal position, under cover, brought the sick down to the shore, to the bushes, and we camouflaged them. The Germans got as far as the river, stayed there a bit, and retraced their footsteps.

With the Germans' retreat, I freed the Poles on their wagons and horses. I took, in place of them, two wagons and horses from our unit. I gathered the sick together and travelled to headquarters, to report to Dadya Petya. In spite of the late hour -- two in the morning -- he listened patiently to the report, asked questions, and advised me to sleep at headquarters and

not go "home." He even gave an unequivocal order not
to wake me in the morning. When I got up, he invited
me to eat breakfast at his company. Meanwhile, the
doctor visited the sick, and he, too, reported on their
condition. One of the sick was in critical condition
(He later died.). Vanke was out of danger and remained
alive.

I went "home" to the mother-unit under Max's
command. They held a nice reception for me. I also
reported to Max about his Polish brothers. He made
many endless comments, but generally received
everything in a good and sympathetic manner.

During that time rumors circulated, saying that
there were those who wanted to poison the captain, that
is, Max. Max was invited to celebrate the Polish
holiday, Pascha, that was coming up at that time, to
stay with Tzivolski, in the village of Krasin. Max
informed me of this and added that he would not go
without me, because I was responsible for him and would
not cause him any harm. We arrived at Tzivolski's
house. I couldn't stare long enough at the abundance
of food that was laid out on the table. In the midst
of eating and drinking, our host told us that in the
town of Manievich there were close to 20,000 Germans.
It wasn't clear what they were planning to do -- attack
us or attack the Ukrainian nationalists in the vicinity
of Kolki.

After the meal, despite the fact that Max was in
Gilopin, we headed for Koninsk, to our friend, a Pole
by the name of Casimir Slovik. We were sure that he
already knew about the German's plan. Slovik was
already waiting for us, impatiently. He had been sure
that someone would come in light of the situation.

He knew that the Germans were going to Kolki. I
was relieved. It was difficult to speak with Max, as
he was dead drunk and in a deep sleep. I politely
postponed the invitation to have breakfast, saying, "I
must report to headquarters, and I have a thirty-five
kilometer journey ahead of me." Without rest or sleep,
I reached headquarters the next day at eight o'clock in
the morning and reported to Dadya Petya about what was
going on in the region. That was the end of my operations during Passover.

Another incident occurred earlier, when we were
staying with Slovik in the woods. We once returned

-162-

late at night, after an intensive operation, and we were very thirsty. When we passed by Lisova-Usdava, I knew that there was a spring of water among the bushes. I put my gun down, stretched out on the ground, and scooped up water from the spring with my palms. My friends did as I did. Suddenly in the quiet of the night, I heard a moan and then a groan. My sharp sense of hearing, which had developed during that time, led me in the direction of the groans. With my rifle extended, I advanced a few more steps. I was stunned. On the ground lay two dying men. I immediately recognized them. They were Yosef Tanenbaum and Dr. Melchior, the two refugees who had fled the German occupation of Poland and had come to us in 1939.

I lay them down in the wagon and brought them close to the partisans' central meeting place. I told them how we had found two Jews, one of them a doctor, but they adamantly refused to receive them in their ranks. The reason was this: when the partisans were getting organized, one of the fighters, "Lozvoi," was hit badly in the stomach. They sent a messenger to the city and requested that this same doctor come to treat the wounded man; he refused. Because of this, they were not willing to receive him now. (By the way, the wounded man recovered and prepared a rifle for me, with bullets, during the time he was still in the ghetto.) I argued with them and raised many different points and reasons for taking the two in. I argued that if the doctor had really left the town at that time, it was likely that he wouldn't have had enough time to reach them, and the Germans would have killed him on the road; secondly, our struggle with the Germans was still our chief concern, and we still needed a doctor. One of them shouted in an angry voice, "If you feel that we must receive him -- go and bring both of them!" I quickly ran and brought them.

Later on, when we moved to Kruk's area, where there were also Russian partisans, Dr. Melchior served as the brigade's doctor and lived with us, the fighters. When I once brought him a piece of soap, he was delighted. In 1944, with the entry of the Red Army, Dr. Melchior left the woods and moved to the city of Rovno. I, along with a number of other Jews, had to go across the Boi River, that was under German control. And so, we reached the Boi River that was then a line of battle.

In 1945 I arrived in Lublin and worked there with "Antek" Zuckerman in the Breicha[21] movement. Later on, at the end of 1946, I was in Israel. Once, in Jaffa, in the milk factory, T'nuvah, a man passed by me like a shadow and disappeared. I asked one of the workers at the place if that was not a doctor by the name of Melchior. At that instant, she called out, "Mr. Melchior, someone's looking for you!" He came up to me, brought me coffee and cake, and told me, in answer to my question, that his brother the doctor had been looking for me for a long time. He had even been at Kibbutz Yagur, looking for me there.

One day I met with the doctor. He could not control his emotions and burst out crying. We sat, together with his wife and brother, and talked at length about those days and the problems of that time. One day he later passed away. May his soul be bound up in the bond of everlasting life.

An Evening of Dancing and A Hunt for Murderers

On one spring day in 1943, Dadya Petya came to see us. He advised Max to take on the command of the advanced position in the village of Sarchov. Max, on his part, appointed me local commander. He placed under my authority fifteen men, including two Jews. The villagers of Sarchov were among the worst in the area due to their long-time hostility toward the Polish government. The residents were also distinguished for their cruel hatred of the Soviet government and, particularly, of the Jews. When we reached the place, I chose a house close to the woods, next to a Pole.

With Anshichenki's visit, the reason for the gang of murderers, the Banderovsty's hasty disappearance became clear to me. Using the weight of my position as local commander, I ordered that a general meeting convene in the school on Saturday night. The school was filled from wall to wall, but the wanted murderers did not show up. On the spot, I announced that the next day, on Sunday, an evening of dancing, accompanied by an orchestra would be held in the same place. I warned them that whoever didn't come today and also didn't come the next day would be punished.

The next day, four men from the Bonderovsty arrived. Also, some musicians came. I immediately sent out patrols to the village to set up the situation. When Manchi from Povorosk arrived, we went into the school. I instructed the musicians to play energetically, to make merry and make noise. My instructions to the comrades were, for each of them to go up to one of the wanted men and arrest him. During a break in the music, I went up on the stage and announced, "In the name of the Soviet government, and by orders of the partisan movement -- the Bonderovsty are under arrest!" Our men stood paired up with each of the wanted men, and the order was given, "Hands behind your back!" They were tied up right away. The large crowd began to escape through the doors and windows. At the entrance to the house, two wagons were waiting, and we loaded them, two by two, onto the wagon.

We brought them to an advanced position in Holoziya, where Vaske Bodko was the commander. He was one of the young men I had brought to the woods. We ate supper there. Vaske advised me to rest a bit after the capturing mission. I put off his advice, expressing the desire to spend the night in the company of the murderers. He cleared a house of its inhabitants, and there we "hosted" the murderers -- the enthusiastic German collaborators. Among them, was one by the name of Ritz Sopol, a blatant sadist and murderer of many Jews. He dealt murderous blows to my cousin's husband during the first action. I got a wooden stake from the yard and went inside to settle an account with him.

I started to strike him. I struck him one blow after the other, "This is for Niyoma." "This is for Jid Ploni." It was a long list, because he had killed many a Jew with his own hands. After this, I moved on to the other one. Yoachim was his name, and I continued in the same manner. "Tell me," I asked him, "How many Russian soldiers did you kill?" "I didn't count," he replied, "maybe fifty." I shot him on the spot and threw his body outside, into the bushes. The next morning, Max arrived. We loaded the three of them onto the wagons and went to the woods by way of Sarchov. Some of Sarchov's residents were Poles. Max wanted to show them his deeds, as a Pole -- that one of the murderers has been killed, and the other three awaited a similar end. Upon our arrival in the woods, the three were sent to bases, where they were tied to trees with ropes. As was later found out, one of the three, Ritz Sopol, asked the partisan guard assigned to him to loosen his rope a bit. He did the rest of the work himself. (By the way, the aforementioned partisan guard was a former soldier in Vlasov's unit and had served in the German police force.) We found out that the escaped murderer was walking about, armed. I was

warned about this. We continuously laid ambushes for
him in every possible location, but with no results.
Once he sent his cousin to me, asking that I stop
looking for him, "for the good of both of us."

In the meantime, an order from Dadya Petya
arrived. He wanted us to bring back alive one of
Kaplatz's two sons, who was operating as a nationalist
and the other, whose name was Shashka. Four of us went
out to lay an ambush next to Kaplatz's house. We sat
in the bushes from nine o'clock in the morning until
late at night, with no results. The next day my
comrades asked if they could leave the spot, saying
that they were hungry. I urged them to stay a bit
longer, and I would take care of the food. I moved a
few hundred meters away, into the bushes and came to a
clearing in the woods, enclosed by a wooden fence.
This spot was used as a plant nursery by its owner.
From a distance, I could see the murderer moving about
inside of it. I quickly retraced my steps and reported
to my friends that he was definitely armed with a
submachine gun. I cautioned them not to act hastily.
We had to close in on him from every side and fire in
such a way as to not hit one another.

When we got close to the fence, the first one to
jump inside was Pavkoi (Pavel) Mitkalik, a seventeen-
year-old boy, our friend "Solovay's" son. Pavel
advanced a few steps and shouted to him, "Hands up!"
while pointing his gun at him. He, the murderer, came
out instead under the bundles of grain that were piled
up in the nursery and jumped Pavel, grabbing his
throat. On seeing this, I shot him from behind and
fired a few more rounds into the air. The murderer
fell, rolling in his own blood. On hearing the shots,
his wife, and daughter came running, and they began to
wail. I advised my friends to go back and set an
ambush for the two sons. But they suggested, in
contrast to this, that we take a break and rest a bit.

We returned to our command post and began planning
the liquidation of Shashka. One evening we went to his
house and told his wife that we wanted to meet with him
and have him join the partisans and be like "one of the
guys." His job with us would be to take care of the
horses, to feed and water them -- In short, a job that
was not difficult. The next evening we met at the
designated spot, at the home of Vanke Vavluk's father,
who I had once brought out from Stepneska-Hota when
Vanke had been sick. Andrei Shashka was pleased with

my offer. We filled up two large sacks with straw and loaded them on our wagon, hitched two horses, and left for the woods with the murderer. On the road, I exchanged a few words with my friend Vanke, as to which one of us would liquidate him. Vanke proposed that I do it. I, in contrast to this, offered the task to Vanke. And going on like this we came to a point not far from our command post, Szanka, which was under the command of Chunek Wolper. This was an area where, from then on, firing shots was absolutely prohibited. Sitting in the wagon next to this murderer, Shaska, I pushed my rifle barrel under his arm and shot him. Wounded, he managed to jump out of the wagon, and got a few hundred meters away. We chased after him and overtook him. And thus came the end of yet another wanted murderer.

I reported to Dadya Petya that we hadn't succeeded in bringing Kaplatz back alive, because the moment contact was made with him, he tried to assault us with an axe. For that reason we had to shoot him. "That's good, too", the Polkovnik replied. "And what about the other one, Shashka?" "He, too, is dead." I told him. "You are a 'moloditz' (a clever guy)", she said, "Come on, let's drink something." From there, I went to report to Max as well.

The next day, as I passed the Szanka, I saw that they had buried Shashka, and a cross was waving about over his grave. I kicked it over and sent the cross flying. We learned that, not far from the Szanka, in Lifnik, Shashka's brother lived. With the cease-fire, this brother came out to see what had gone on, and he discovered the corpse of his dead brother. He buried him and notified the man's wife about it. She, upon seeing me in the village, began to wail and shriek. I wasn't able to pass through the village, and I was forced to imprison her in one of the houses. She escaped at night and threw herself into a well.

In the woods and at the command posts in the village, there was one set procedure in regard to guard duty. We never sat in a house without a guard outside. One time we were sitting down to eat, and we heard our comrade's voice outside, "Stop. Who's there?" I hurried outside to see what had happened. Despite the darkness, I could make out several horsemen. I shouted to them, "Who are you?" "Feodorovtzy!" "And who are you?" asked their commander. "From Dadya Petya's otryad (fighting unit)," I replied. The commander came up to me and dismounted; we shook hands. We clarified some details and he presented me with two letters from headquarters that were intended for me, in which I was requested to help them obtain food. They were five partisan fighters, patrols from a large unit of 4500 fighters, armed with the best weapons for partisan warfare. Their purpose was to become familiar with the rear line of the German army and to incessantly harass it. With the break down of resistance on the eastern front and its disintegration, we were ordered by the military command to leave our base in the Briansk woods. I took several men from my command post, and we went with these partisans, the Feodorovtzy to the village. There we confiscated several sacks of potatoes and a few wagons for them. They thanked us warmly and left.

The next day the patrols came back, along with another two hundred men and with two more letters from headquarters. This time I was asked to assist them in a sabotage operation at the railroad tracks by my own home town, Manievich. I received a saddled horse from them, and we left for the village of Holoziya. There at the command post, we had thirty of our men. Also, our flour mill operated there, supervised by Abraham Putchtik.

Before the war, he had owned the mill. There we found all the comrades sitting at the tables and eating breakfast. Someone welcomed me loudly, "Good morning, Burko!" I recognized him. He was a Ukrainian, the police chief of the town of Krasin and was on our blacklist. His actions of chasing after Jews were numerous and reached the Trochenbrod woods. By chance he joined up with the partisans, during one of their encounters with the Ukrainian police. He was captured by our comrades, by the brick factory near Manievich. I called the Feodorovtzy[22] commander outside and told him about the Ukrainian policeman. The commander ordered that he be brought inside the stable. There we put him on the ground, and two partisans beat him with sticks until he breathed his last.

Outside, a young woman by the name of Pasha, from the village of Vilka, passed by. She had worked in the town of Manievich for many years. And whenever partisans appeared in the village, she would report to the Germans. This young woman received heavy blows, and was warned not to chatter anymore.

-168-

We left Holoziya and went towards Koninsk, to the woods. We set up huts there. For several days I slept in the same hut as the comissar. This spot served as a temporary base for sabotage operations on the railroad tracks. Night after night I went out with a different detachment, each one numbering thirty men, on sabotage operations. One Sunday morning Max turned to me, asking me to get him a liter of vodka from Slovik. I had one of the Feodorovtzy come with me, and we went to the address. The owner of the house received us warmly, inviting us for breakfast -- after all, it was Sunday. We left with two liters of vodka.

We left Slovik and went to see Frank Branovski with the same request. And again, there was the same refrain, "It's Sunday!" We ate and drank there, too. We finished off a bottle and went on our way. We returned -- and I was shocked at what I saw. About forty fighters and nurse-medics in wagons hitched to horses were preparing to leave for an operation. I reported to the captain, presenting him with the vodka he had requested. He thanked me and added matter-of-factly, "The time has come for you to take the blood-revenge that you have desired so much. You will be able to settle your accounts with those who, one time at night, when you came by chance into their village in search of food, ran to take your weapons from you and hand you over to the Germans," and he handed me the "blacklist."

I pondered over how to reach our destination, Polska-Gora. There were several possibilities. One of them was to go from the Manievich side, but it was possible that the Germans would ambush us there in an area of the graveyard. I chose a roundabout path. We went along a marked route through parts of the forest and reached the village from the other side. From a distance I saw a campfire between the bushes. We quickly and cautiously approached the spot and met an old peasant grazing four horses. I immediately recognized two of them. They were the horses of Hazenkor, whose name was on the blacklist. I asked the old man what was going on in the village. He said that if partisans appeared, he must immediately notify the village. We confiscated the horses and took the old man with us.

The first one we went to see was Hazenkor. When we appeared, the men began to flee. I signalled to the patrol-commander to open fire, and he immediately hit the Batzukim leader of those who were fleeing. We entered his house, and I saw through the window that he was only wounded. I saw him gasping and trying to run away. "Pavel Pavlovitch," I shouted, "Here he is!" He rushed outside, mounted his horse, and chased after him -- he rode over him on his own horse and trampled him. We took one of his sons with us and two other suspects. One, who was on our list but whose name for some reason wasn't written clearly, slipped away from us. This was the very man who had plotted to steal my gun, during my stay in the village with my brother Zev. The luck of a Gentile.

When we went outside, we ran into an acquaintance, Chavador Kolev. "You didn't stop the main organizer, the most dangerous of the murderers -- Stach," he said to me. "But he already escaped to Polska-Gora, to the Germans." It was too late to chase after him by foot or by vehicle because of the tangled growth on the road.

We left with the three murderers. I looked behind us and saw our prisoners' wives walking along. I stopped at the edge of the woods. "What do you want?" "Our husbands," they said. "O.K.," I said, "You will get them if you bring us vodka." They agreed. We waited for them. We got the vodka from them, and told them that we would set them free after an interrogation.

We changed our direction and passed through the Polish village of Optova. A heavy rain accompanied us to the entrance of the village. The sun set, and the shepherds brought their flocks home. When the shephards saw us, they began to run away, thinking us to be Ukrainian nationalists. I recognized among those running away a girl whose father was a forest guard. He had hidden several Jewish children, until they were taken by us. I called the girl by her name so that she wouldn't run away. She turned her head and shouted, "Matke-Boska, I didn't recognize you!"

We were about fifty men. We stationed ourselves at the village school. We immediately assembled all of the village's residents. I was asked, among other things, if we would spend the night at the village. When we agreed to this, they began bringing us food and drink. Later on, about forty men offered to stand guard around the village. Our comissar and the captain were getting worried about us, as they didn't know our whereabouts. When at last we appeared, the joy was great. We set tables and got ready for breakfast. I personally submitted complaints about inaccuracy and vagueness, in relation to the fifth murderer, who had slipped away from us. I handed over our prisoners to Davidenko, from the special unit. He interogated them, and later killed them.

With Commander Kostin

I was with the Fiodorovtzy for two months. I was credited with the blowing up of twelve cargo trains carrying military equipment that were on their way to the eastern front. They transferred Max to another location, and a lieutenant by the name of Kostin took his place. People who knew him, from Kartuchin's unit, said that Max's men were lost. He, Kostin, was a professionally military man and not well suited for the living conditions and the fighting in the woods. I took advantage of Max's absence and went to the village of Sarchov, where a Pole lived who was involved in pillaging and plundering in the town of Manievich. Two Feodorovtzy called him outside. I made him sit in the wagon, and we went to the woods. There we took him and tied a rope around his neck. As it says, "Who by strangulation and who by stoning."[23]

The new commander, Kostin, sent Shaiya Flash with an order for me to return to the unit. I was standing talking to the commissar of the Feodorovtzy at the same moment that Shaiya gave me the message by heart and in Yiddish. The commissar was amazed "We slept in the same tent together for two months, and I didn't know that you were a Jew. I'm also a Jew," he said. "Send your weapons back to your unit, and stay here with us." "I was one of the unit's founders, " I told him, "and so, I'd like to remain with it." I returned, then, to the unit and stood before Kostin. "I'm here, as you ordered!" I said to him. "Bravo, very good!" He warmly shook my hands.

I had known Kostin since 1942. I met him at one of Kruk's meetings, where we became acquainted and together became familiar with routes for operations in and outside of the forest. Among those invited, were Captain Kartuchin, who sat with Lipa (a Jew) and Kostin, Max, myself, a few others from our unit, the Polkovnik Brinsky, and several assistants. As we sipped a healthy amount of vodka, we began talking.

-171-

Kartuchin said, "I personally wouldn't take twenty Russians partisans in exchange for one Lipa." Max said, "I wouldn't take twenty Russians partisans in exchange for one Barku." The last of the speakers was the Polkovnik, whose words were brief and matter-of-fact. Among other things he said, "From now on, Berl Lorber and Bardu (Berl Bronstein) are entitled to come with Kruk and Max, respectively, to the main headquarters at any time. The Russians had often complained, generally, that Jews were cowards. If they were captured by the Germans, they said, they would give out information about the partisans. At two o'clock in the morning, the meeting ended, and I brought the Polkovnik home to headquarters.

Kostin read out his orders to a formation in order to become familiar with them, despite the fact that he was familiar with most of them from before. We had with us some of the thirty soldiers from the Red Army who had escaped from prison with him. There was also a group of Jews, more or less unified, that could not adjust to the way he ran the unit. A delegation visited his trench and in an unambiguous manner, he said to him, "If you want to succeed in your job, leave the Jews alone, because otherwise they'll go over to the Feodorovtzy, and without them you can't do anything." He freed me from all other duties I had, and I would accompany him just about everywhere. We frequently went to Brigade headquarters, and to Feodorovtzy headquarters. One time he wanted to make a detour and visit Kruk's civilian family camp.

Yeshayahu Zweibel, the one in charge of the camp, welcomed us. He spoke with Kostin about the conditions in the camp, the daily schedule, the employment of the people, the diet and the future of the orphaned children, widows, and old people. Friends from bygone days surrounded me, as well as Jews who just wanted to see me and hear from me what was new. Kostin asked me what the people in the family camp wanted. I replied to him, that they didn't believe that "the residents of the camp under your command live better than they do." He looked at me in a kind of amazement and said, "So, then, let's go visit our civilians' camp while we're in the neighborhood!"

Immediately we went up to the road leading to the camp. I introduced him to Zisla Brat, and they talked among themselves. I, as much as I could, spoke to those standing around me, and hinted to them that now was a chance to improve their situation. Immediately a request was raised to Kostin that he put in an order for meat and salt. Kostin turned around and pointed at me "He is guilty! Aren't there enough calves in the woods -- slaughter them and eat them and he'll soon bring you salt!"

The visit came to an end. We returned to our camp, and I related the details of the visit to Mitka, who was in charge of the food. His family also lived in our civilian camp. It was decided between us, that after supper we would bring two sacks of salt to the civilian camp. Kostin himself wanted to make sure the salt was delivered to his satisfaction.

In the meantime, events occurred one after the other in the woods. The Germans did not accept their defeat on the Stalingrad front and tried, from time to time, to pursue the partisans and liquidate them. We learned that the German sent out from the front an antitank division, that numbered about 18,000 soldiers, and they were getting ready to lay a siege on our woods. I got in touch with Major-General Feodorov to hear his opinion on the subject.

It was decided that we stay where we were and go to battle with the Germans. The surrounding outposts in other places were strengthed and reinforced as much as possible -- and we waited for whomever would come. At one of the outposts, a battle took place, a few against many, with little ammunition. We were forced to retreat, but first two squadrons were sent in an attempt to ward off the invaders, mainly to stall for time so the sick and wounded could be transported to a secure place. The only path for retreat was in the direction of the Styr River where, on the other side, Germans swarmed with Ukrainian nationalists all waiting for us. As we neared the river, they opened fire on us. We retreated about a kilometer in order to assess the situation.

A peasant came up to us. I brought him to the commander immediately. Under interrogation, he said that he was from the surrounding area. But I knew his place of residence. The commander, Nikolai Buzruk, hit his face with a whip and ordered that he be liquidated, because it had become clear that he had joined those retreating into the village of Uzritz and had informed the Ukrainian nationalists of our actions.

We approached the Styr a second time, with intensified strength, and laid out a bridge using logs. We arrived at Svarotzvich, where we had encamped during the first siege. Our situation was now much worse. The Germans destroyed everything in the woods -- trenches, living quarters, food, and they poisoned the water, set fires in the woods, and threw oil barrels from planes to increase the burning.

In spite of all of this, we returned "home". Our trenches were completely burnt. So we temporarily lived in lodgings at headquarters. The overcrowding was great, and I slept in a wagon. The nights were cold, autumn nights. Rain and snow were common. One night, after strenuous activity, I fell asleep as usual. I felt a strange heat, but I continued sleeping. That same night, snow fell and completely covered me, and if Captain Anishchenko hadn't happened to be going by and wakened me to tell me good news from the front, I would have slept like that until the morning and maybe would not have gotten up at all. The next day I got a place to sleep inside a bunker, like everyone else.

One night they woke me up at two in the morning, with an order to present myself immediately at headquarters. On the way there, I saw six horses tied up in a strange manner; the saddles were also not in line with our standards. In any case, I went on. I stood before Captain Malin and received instructions to bring back six Feodorovtzy patrols, who had gone off their path to call for help for those under attack and now couldn't find their way back to their base. About 3,000 Ukrainian nationalists attacked the partisan camp, "Vaneda Vasilevska," in the village of Charvishetz. I jumped onto one of the good horses, at the head of the patrols. "Forward, after me!" The distance from where we were to Feodorov was about ten kilometers, and then night was dark and dismal. I couldn't see the horse I was riding on, nor, for that matter, the road. After we had gone about six kilometers, the patrols recognized the road; but I reached Feodorov's headquarters long before them, despite the fact that I was stopped several times by sentries. In the end, I appeared before the General-Major. After a short report, General Feodorov ordered that tea be prepared. In the meantime, the six arrived, and he couln't control himself and burst out shouting. "With patrols like you, the nationalists will eat us alive! They'll reach the woods before we have time to move!"

And to the liaisons, who stayed permanently next to headquarters, he said, "Battalion 5 and 9 -- go fight the nationalists!" To me he said, "Finish your tea and you're permitted to leave! And tell your officers to set up ambushes on the side roads, in order to obstruct the path of undesirable Ukrainian nationalist elements."

Despite all of our preparation to forestall the danger, the nationalists succeeded in penetrating our frontal outpost in the village of Lishnivka. Our forces retreated. Our second destination was the village of Krasin. They also made a breach there, and our forces retreated from there as well. From Krasin, they continued to Sarchov. This outpost was controlled by the Feodorovtzy. In time, they reinforced and drilled their troops and waited for the arrival of the nationalist force -- and then, the Feodorovtzy opened fire with machine guns and light artillery. The attackers withdrew and retreated. They didn't expect such a strong reaction. A reinforcement of about eighty men was sent from headquarters; their objective was to obstruct the path leading to Holoziya. And that is what happened. When the nationalist attackers met up with heavy fire at the Krasin outpost, they were forced to retreat in the direction of Holoziya. I knew the roads were uncrossable swamps on both side and, in the middle, a bridge made out of logs. We lay down on the sides of the road, and when the nationalists approached, we shot them in a crossfire. We took just six of them prisoners. They claimed that they were Russians, former soldiers from the Red Army, and that they had no idea what Ukrainian nationalists were.

During one of the battles with the Germans in the area of Lovoshov, the partisans took a woman doctor and a girl prisoner,and brought them to headquarters in Krasin. With the approach of the second siege on the woods, Sashka Voronov, who was in charge of that station asked Kostin what to do with them. Without much thought, Kostin ordered that they be liquidated. And so they were. They took them out to be killed next to the lake, in the Zemistya area. When the battles against the Germans and Ukrainian nationalists had scaled down, our operations and those of the Feodorovtzy were resumed -- and then two bodies were discovered -- those of the woman doctor and her daughter.

During the Feodorovtzy's investigation, the blame was placed on commander Kostin, and he was arrested by the special unit. During the preparations for the citizens New Year, 1944, I packed a parcel with food and vodka and sent it to the division commander, Kovlov, for the imprisioned Kostin, but he sent it back to me. I took the parcel a second time and went to the General-Major Feodorov. I strongly requested that he allow me to bring the parcel to Kostin. He hesitated, and said, "This time I'll let you, but don't go to see him anymore. You're permitted to come to see me whenever you want, even after midnight." I sat with the general, and we talked a bit, drank, and were all feeling pleased, but the one who was the most pleased was Kostin's love, Katherina Gargureyvna. Kostin's life was saved, thanks to Polkovnik Briansky, who at that time was in Moscow, where they asked him for his opinion. Kostin was freed, given a hundred men under his command, and went across the Bug River to establish a partisan movement in the center of Poland.

The Partisans Ward Off Attacks and Capture

Kostin's position was filled by the former commander of the special unit, Vasilenko. During those days, we were supposed to receive supplies from Moscow by air. The problem was how to parachute them down. The woods were virgin forests. There were many ponds and swamps, and also there was the population, but we were mainly anxious about the Germans. We went out to locate a site according to Moscow's directives, but it became clear that the distance was great, and we were afraid that we wouldn't be able to arrive on time. We contacted Kruk, who was settled deep in the woods, and together we located a clearing in the woods not far from the Sazanke. Following agreed-upon signals from the ground, the pilot dropped the "goods." We got ammunition, arms, medicine, and clothing and also radio technicians and officers. We received such consignments several times.

One night a captain was parachuted to us with new equipment. When we entered the base, there were three of us: The commander Vasilenko, the captain who had parachuted, and myself. The two officers talked among themselves about every subject under the sun. I listened, but did not take part in the conversation as long as it did not concern me. Vasilenko said to the captain-paratrooer, among other things, "You see, this is an outstanding partisan, and what a pity that he's a Jew." I didn't remain quiet, and I said, "Comrade Com-

-176-

mander, don't be sorry. I was born a Jew, and I'll die a Jew!" "You see." Vasilenko said to the captain, "A Jew - and proud of it."

With the collapse of the front at the Moscow-Stalingrad lines, the Germans tried, without much success, to present themselves as a power that was still able to stand up under the pressure of the Red Army at the front and the partisans in the rear. In fact the situation was just the opposite. While the Red Army forged on at the front, the partisans tried, successfully, to occupy key points along the length of important, almost exclusive, railroad tracks.

One night it became known to us that our division, which numbered more than thirty men in the Rafalovka area, had succeeded in repelling the Germans and taking back the town. On hearing this news, the staff commanders, including my commander, Vasilenko, went out to the place. Among those going to Rafalovka was the chief of staff, Provishka, a captain who had served in the Bog region until the outbreak of the war. With the deterioration of the front, he was imprisioned by the Germans, but had managed to escape, and he joined up with the partisans. In Rafalovka he learned that the unit he had served in was a distance of eight kilometers from there, and that his good friend from his days of military service was there. He decided to meet with him at any cost. The meeting of the two friends was emotional. Tables were set. Afterwards, the regular army captain took us into the supply depot and equipped us with some arms. In a discussion with the regular army captain, he expressed annoyance about the actions of the partisans in the area of the civilian population. "There's too much taking people out to be killed," he complained, " and too little training." We asked him to be more tolerant, and said that in time it would be decided who was right.

We went to Rafalovka to see a film about the life of Vanadeh Vasilevska. The movie hall was filled with soldiers from the captain's unit, and, by his request, the soldiers gave their seats to the partisans. We concluded the day's events with a good sleep at the division where the conquerors of Rafalovka were staying.

The next day the general-major from the city of Sarni came by and addressed us. Among other things, he said that Stalin had ordered that assistance be offered to partisan units in need of it, and that the partisans held 50 percent of the credit for the victory over the Nazis. On account of the assistance that he had to offer us, he requested meat from us, saying he would pay us in tobacco, salt, and other -- "good things." We got cattle ready for him, and I was responsible for bringing it to a designated place. I went with the cattle into villages that were under our control and under the Red Army's control. In one of the villages I again met with the captain from the "regular army." The conversation again turned to the hostile civilian population. Now he agreed with me. The captain's being in agreement about the Ukrainian population's hostility was not incidental. A truck with soliders passed by Vladimicitz and met with fire from an ambush. Some of the soldiers were killed, and the wounded were burned along with the truck.

After a number of days I went out with some of the men to patrol the Povorsk area, to gather information about the Germans -- if they were still in the town, what their conditions were, etc. We had just approached the village of Chirsk, when everything became clear to us. We changed our direction, and went to Manievich, my town. This was my first visit in two years. The house I had lived in and had built with the sweat of my brow, the home where I knew happiness, still stood in its place, but it was all in ruins, with the doors and windows broken into and wide open. I didn't go inside. My heart ached. I pulled out a hand grenade that was with me, but my commander prevented me from doing this. I looked all around at the nearby houses and saw smoke rising from the chimney of one house, where a Polish policeman had formerly lived. I approached it, and a Pole, Stephan, who in our time had helped us a bit, came out to greet me. He asked that I allow him to live with me in the house. I agreed. I arranged a few more visits before we went on to the village of Manievich, and the next morning we returned to the base, to the woods.

Upon coming into the base, I saw unusual movement. My commander, Vasilenko, had received an order to find a hundred men and go with them across the Bug River. He had wanted me to go along, but the staff captain, Anishchenko, opposed this. And so I stayed temporarily.

With the liberation of Rafalovka the mainland communication with Moscow was renewed, although with limited dimensions. In any case, people came, mainly by train. They transported the wounded to hospitals in the Russian rear lines, children were transported and partisan commanders went. Stalin had invited the commanders for consultations about the continuation of the campaign. Our commander, Dadya Petya (Briansky) was also invited, and I was the only Jew among the escorts to the train in Rafalovka. I parted from them in friendship. I suspected that Briansky was a Jew. He stayed with me, and the two of us returned to the woods.

The woods were in turmoil. The traffic was like that in a beehive. In every place, people were packing; they were rushing about and whispering secretly. The family camp's residents had received instructions to be ready to leave the woods and to go in the direction of Rafalovka. Young men, especially Jews, were released from the fighting units and were attached to the family camps. Some of the Jews stayed to guard the camps, in case we'd have to return. They divided up and organized the young fighting men into new units; they prepared plenty of food, arms, and ammunition, for the trip across the Bug River.

On March 23, 1944, we left for our destination. The men were among the best, and most of them had secondary duties in addition to fighting. There were a few Jews, myself and my nephew Yaakov Bronstein among them. The road was difficult, the snow that had fallen in the last few days had melted, and so there was mud. Progress was slow. Worse than this were the Red Army's regular units conditions. The weapons were silenced, standing in the street corners without shells; trucks got stuck in mud up to the axles, and couldn't move. Rifle cartridges were dropped from single-engine planes that flew almost as low as the treetops. Once in a while, these planes -- "Kokoroznkim" -- were shelled by the Germans. Also we, who were in a convoy about a kilometer long, were harassed by German planes. Through all of this, we reached the vicinity of Ratena. Despite the shortage of ammunition, and means of transportation, and food, the Red Army soldiers succeeded in capturing Ratena, but the general in charge of this section of the front ordered an evacuation of the area, fearing German raids. And indeed, the Russians had just evacuated the town, when a squad of German bombers appeared, turning the city into a heap of ruins.

Our objective was to cross the front which wasn't solid nor cleared of Germans, in the opinion of many in the Russian high command. Even more severe was the situation across the Bug River, where our patrols returned from. (Because of this we made rounds close by the front.) During the nights, against the background of the sky, we clearly saw the firings of rockets that bombed the German centers. In return, the Germans shelled the Russians with heavy mortar from the air. The Germans tried to recover from their defeat the entire length of the front and took advantage of the Red Army's supply hardships.

We reached the vicinity of the city of Kovel. The Polkovnik Nazarov, who had been parachuted to us while we still were in the Kochov woods, was with us. Nazarov met with a general from the Red Army in one of the houses in the village. I and another, Vanke Tratiakov, went out to get food for the horses. The villagers in the vicinity of the front left their homes, especially the men. The villages themselves were ghost towns. We gathered barley, oats, etc. At one of the houses, a little girl opened the door. I asked her, "Are any of our men here?" "Yes," she answered, "They're sitting over there with Russian soldiers, playing cards." We went back and reported to Polkovnik Nazarov. Immediately, a squad went out and brought them to headquarters, with their hands tied. After I related to the captain the content of our conversation, he ordered that we kill them. We stayed for several days in that place.

Not such good news reached us about the partisans under the leadership of Kovpak, who had suffered heavy losses in the Carpathian Mountains. An order from Moscow was issued to transfer all the partisan units that were close to the front to the army command, in order to reinforce and fill in the thining columns. They left us alone in the meantime, because we were thought to be a military unit. Captain Brigada approached me, and in a friendly manner asked me if I wanted to go home. I replied to him, "Your decision is final." His answer was "Go home!" In the afternoon the secretary, Kolia Tzitzel, called him and ordered him to make up official papers for us. We were three Jews. We received arms and ammunition for self defense. Each one had a rifle with bullets. After a walk of several kilometers, we met up with the Red Army's guard. We were interrogated; they read our papers; and afterwards released us. And so we went on to Libovna. The next morning we continued in the direction of Povorsk. There was only three of us when we arrived at the town in the evening. Right at that time, a train was about to leave for Manievich, our destination. The cars were all full; there wasn't even room for a pin. And suddenly I heard someone calling me, "Bronstein! Bronstein!" -- and who do I see but the natchalnik Maneko, who had served from 1939 in our town, Manievich. He asked me where I was coming from and where I was going. "Don't you see the arms," I said. "You're a clever guy if you could stay alive! You want to go home?" "Yes" I answered. He went up to one of the sets of steps of the car, removed a few villagers from there, and put my nephew Yaakov and me on the steps.

In Manievich I entered Leib Singel's house. I met several Jews there. The next morning I went to see my house. It was difficult for me to go inside, to cross the threshold and I turned toward Shimon Blaushtein's house. Finally I went over to my house. One morning I went out to the street, and heard that Tzigenski, my father's neighbor, was arrested by the N.K.V.D. I stood before the police, presented the three documents I had with me to the commander and said, "I am a local resident." He looked over the documents. One was from our unit, written in Russian, the second was from General-Major Feodorov, also written in Russian, and the third was written in Polish, from Greenvald's unit, under Max's leadership. The chief of police, Grichenko, took out thirty rubles and handed them to me. Very politely, I pushed away the money and said to him that it wasn't for that that I had come to see him. "With your permission," I said "there's a man here in prison who is one of the city's righteous men, and it is my wish -- with your approval, of course -- that you release him despite the 'sin' that he committed, as it were, when his son fled with the Germans. This man Tzigenski deserves freedom for his deeds and for the information he passed on to us, the Jews, during the occupation." "If so" he said to me "come with me to the prison house," and Grichenko opened the door for me.

Tzigenski's property extended over half of the town and was surrounded by a high wooden fence, which was almost uncrossable. He had a spacious garden of fruit trees. In the shade of trees the Jews found a hiding place fortified for them, and there they found a loaf of bread to break their hunger. He had served as the town's leader during the Polish rule. "At the request of your good friend, I am releasing you!" the chief said to him. Tzigenski hugged me tightly and the two of us went straight to his home. He and his family did not live in their own house, but with their housekeeper, Yaldoviska, not far from the flour mill. When his wife saw us from afar, she ran to meet us, falling on my neck and bursting into tears. "I'm crying from joy and grief" she said. "If it weren't for you, who knows if he would have stayed alive. God is repaying us for our helping the Jews."

I Avenge The Enemy, And Illegally Immigrate To Israel

I found out that Olek Schchevski was working as a telephone operator. I immediately informed the N.K.V.D. and he was arrested. Later on, one of Domrovski's sons was arrested. Both of them were strong collaborators with the Germans. On my third day in Manievich, I invited several Jews to go to our relatives' graves. At the first ditch, a terrifying picture of the martyrs was revealed to us. We cried a lot and said Kaddish.[24] When we turned to go, several Red Army soldiers appeared and asked what had happened. I told them. They looked, and their eyes filled with tears.

I received permission to use the horses. We removed some cement blocks from Feyvel's (Olinik) house and brought them to our relative' graves, and Feyvel, who was a builder, built two gravestones with our help.

I received an order to present myself at the recruiting station. I attended to the order in order to stay -- as indispensable -- at the place. But I found no rest. Men, Jew-murderers were moving about freely. I contacted the N.K.V.D. and put Simon in prison. His crime was very great and serious, at least in regard to the Jews. Among other things, he handed Itka Ferdman over to the Germans. I was called to Rovno to testify against him and succeeded in getting the better of him. I had just returned when a N.K.V.D. man informed me that Olek Sokhachevski had managed to escape and was working in Kovel in a workshop repairing railroad cars and locomotives. I turned to the N.K.V.D. commander on this matter, and we brought Sokhachevski to Manievich. When his mother found out, she began looking for people who would testify, because she said her son Olek didn't do harm to anyone, and it was all a complete and utter lie. And in fact, a woman was found who testified. The N.K.V.D. commander told me, that apparently she received a pay-off from his mother. Olek was sent to prison in Lutzk.

During the time I was working on the railroad, I developed a strong desire for revenge. This was natural. I was the voice and prosecutor against those who were guilty. One night, a Gentile town resident approached me, one of those who had signed a petition for the Germans to carry out the first action, in which three hundred and seventy men were killed. His name was Yaakov Jalotzki, and I immediately recognized him. He asked me different questions and invited himself over for breakfast. I was quiet and then immediately informed the N.K.V.D., and, on his way home, he was arrested. He was released on account of his wife, who worked as a cook in the kitchen there; she had good relations, in bed, with the officer's corps. I didn't let up on them. I reproached the army corps for their weakness, and I mocked them for being able to sell their homeland for the sake of a woman. My words apparently influenced them, and I was called to testify. To begin with I was briefed by the deputy commander of the N.K.V.D. Afterwards, they brought in Jalotzki. His face became white as plaster when he saw me. The commander came in after him. He reprimanded his deputy for leaving the submachine gun near the accused man. Before he was interrogated Jalotzki said, "Even if you hung the submachine gun on my nose, I wouldn't know what to do with." "Quiet!" the commander reproached him. He was transferred to the Lukzk prison. After several weeks I was called upon to testify against him at a military court. At first he tried to be evasive, unintelligible, and later he began to be unruly, trying to deny any connection to his deeds. The judge became irritated and sentenced him to the maximum penalty for a crime against humanity: death.

The Germans meanwhile resigned themselves to defeat. They tried, even before the death throes of the Third Reich to confound the Red Army's victory. They incessantly bombed the railroad tracks, the supply trains, the anti-aircraft artillery batteries and, for the hell of it, the peaceful population. And there were many who were hit. Then, too, the constant struggle to stay alive continued, as it had before, during the time in the woods.

Once I was called to the city of Kovel, to stand before the officer in charge of manpower. After presenting my documents, the deputy to the officer in charge turned to me, "You can speak Yiddish with him," and added, "I can't believe, and no one will believe, that a Jew did everything that's said about you in the documents."

One day, a committee was established consisting of Polish citizens who wanted to live in Poland, under the leadership of Tziganski, the same Tziganski that we had freed. I had a word with him, and we agreed, that if there were problems in releasing me, he would act accordingly. My officer-in-charge was not opposed to this, but my release had to come from Kovel, from the same Jew in charge of manpower. When I appeared before him a second time, he started shouting at me. I calmed him down and told him, "The Polish committee was established by the Soviet government which is your government." I appeared before the Polish committee and received a letter from them. I brought the letter to the officer in charge of manpower in Kovel, and I left the room, slamming the door. He sent his secretary after me, to ask me to sit down, and a smile came onto his frozen features. He apologized to me. "I know that where you are headed is not Poland, but rather, Palestine. I wish you a successful journey and much happiness in your work and in your life. It's my wish and request, that you leave your documents with me. It would be a pity if they got lost." "These documents are more precious to me than gold," I replied. "They tell of my readiness to die for freedom more than once." I shook the hands of all those present in the room and left for my journey. He accompanied me a few hundred meters. With his hand still grasping mine, he again wished me well. In the end, tears welled up in his eyes. "I am a Jew," he said.

I returned to my workplace, because I had to make up for a few days of work. Once, I met a woman who was by herself. She quickened her steps toward me and asked me directly, "Are you a Jew?" "Yes, and what do you want?" -- "I am a partisan," she said, "and it is my wish to reach Poland. Please, help me!" I directed her to "Sil-Sveet," where Berl Lorber (Malinka) worked, and I gave her several thousand rubles. She spread the word about my "Jewish heart," and caused masses of Jews to come to me. They, the few who remained after all the different hardships and annihilations, were searching and searching. There were those who were searching for a relative who was still alive, for a survivor of a family split apart, for a next of kin, for a road, a path, for any kind of crack -- "so long as we get to Eretz Yisrael (the land of Israel)."

We sent a man to a certain address in Warsaw. He knocked hard on the door. For some reason he became disappointed and left in despair, but the man who was inside went after him on the steps, and when he caught up to him, he asked him who he was looking for. The unknown man introduced himself as a Jew, despite his Aryan appearance. "You found the man you were looking for," he said "I am Yitzchak Zukerman, and my alias is 'Antek.' Return to Lublin, and prepare the people. I'll come in a week!"

On the designated day, a crowd of several thousand Jews assembled for a meeting, in which one of the main items was the election of an action committee. From out of the crowd, came cries of "Bronstein! Bronstein!" I tried to slip away and exit through the back door. Nothing helped. I was elected to the committee along with Berl Lorber (Malenka) and a rabbi from Pinsk.

Our first undertaking was to prepare a list of names. Using a password that we received from Antek, a group of Jews was sent to Krackow, and from there, via Czechoslovakia, Hungary, and Romania -- to Israel. Another time I received an order to organize a group of partisans and assume its leadership. We went out, about eighty men, and came to the Hungarian-Austrian border. After a short rest, we approached the road heading in the direction of Austria. But there was a roadblock in front of us, and next to it were armed Russian soldiers. We retraced our steps. All of a sudden, two Russian officers appeared, and asked us for two watches and a pair of boots. Two Jews from Lithuania contributed the watches, and the boots were donated by Shimon Wolper. The Russian guards removed the roadblock between the Alafim mountains and pointed out the road where we could go. They left --and three other soldiers appeared. They asked us for three watches. After some bargaining, they received what they asked for, and left us alone. We walked a bit of a way, until we reached a small train station, and from there we travelled by train and reached the city of Gratz; we went to the hotel Weitzer, where once Hitler, may his name be blotted out, stayed. After a short rest in the hotel, we went to a camp that was under British rule.[25]

We had just managed to get a bit organized when there was a search. They were looking for weapons and were preventing the organizing for immigration to Eretz Yisrael. Antek from Poland arrived at this camp, and in front of a meeting that numbered about 2,800 people, he introduced me as a partisan, as a fighter against the Nazis, and as one who was worthy to lead the first group immigrating to Eretz Yisrael under the revered name of the commander of the Warsaw Ghetto uprising, Mordechai Anielewicz, of blessed memory.

The stream of refugees who left Eastern Europe was increasing, and there was an urgent need to organize and direct all of those people, who were so different from one another, but were unified by one desire -- to leave the European soil which was saturated with the blood of Jews. A considerable portion of these operations are to be credited to the soldiers from the Jewish (Palestine) Brigade, emissaries from the Yishuv[26], and to anonymous individuals who did their job tirelessly, through the day and through the night. Many Brigade officers endangered their positions, and perhaps their lives, in their search for Jewish orphans and those baptized into Christianity. Among those, I especially want to make note of Mordechai Sorkis, who did a lot of work in this area. He set up for our use two covered trucks, after we were forced to leave a train, when we were later in Italian territory, in the Alafim mountains. We arrived at Mastero, where a Jew from England worked as director of the train station, and he arranged for two railroad cars with a locomotive to transport us to Aquacento, in Italy. At this place, there were already forty people. I knew some of them from before.

One day I met with Dov Karpuski, a man from Kibbutz Ein Harod, who came as an emissary from the Yishuv to organize people for illegal immigration. His objective was to take out of the camp, which numbered about eight hundred people, only one hundred selected individuals who would be able to endure the hardships of the journey. The response was beyond all expectation. About two hundred people signed up. One evening we left in the Brigade's truck for a deserted coast in Italy. at a certain distance from the shore, a "boat" as it were, came to anchor, where nine rooms of couches were set up, to sleep, and we lay down on these. On January 12, 1946 we moved out of that place, on our way to the final destination, Eretz Yisrael.

The journey to the island of Crete was tolerable, but later on, the sea raged and our boat was about to descend into an abyss. We were given over to the mercy of heaven. Food and drink were at a minimum. They forbade us from going up on deck. The oppressiveness was unbearable. The resentment grew, but for the most part, the people gritted their teeth and suffered in silence. The main thing was to get there!

The small ship approached the city of Haifa. The city's lights glittered. The distance was now only about sixty kilometers.

At night we would have to go down to the shore. And then, suddenly, we were surrounded by warships of the British Navy. For twenty-four hours, negotiations were held between the Jewish Agency and the British Mandate government. We were taken to the Atlit camp, where we were imprisoned behind a barbed wire fence for three weeks. Upon our release we went, forty people, to Kibbutz Yagur. We were finally at home in our own land.

MY LIFE UNDER THE UKRAINIAN-GERMAN OCCUPATION

Dov Lorber (Malenka)

On the 22nd of July, 1941, Hitler's Germany ordered its troops to march into Russia without declaring war and on the same day, Russia declared a full mobilization of her armed forces.

I left my post at the Karl Marx arsenal in Gereyvara, a village near Manievich, and joined the mobilization point in Manievich, Ukraine.

Almost every youth from Manievich, as well as from the surrounding villages, gathered there and waited impatiently for the command to tell us where we would be transported.

Hitler's troops easily passed through the Russian borders and quickly forged deep into Russian territories, destroying massive Russian forces. The situation was very chaotic.

The next morning, we were loaded onto trains and sent to the Russian-German border which at that time was established at the River Bug, between Poland and Russia. Arriving in Kovel we were stopped. There was no road further up the line because the German forces had forged ahead without stopping. Our leaders decided to transport us deeper into Russia and on the 24th of July, 1942, we were already in Sarni.

The atmosphere in Sarni was hectic. Thousands of people were wandering the streets, not knowing where they were. Everyone was asking each other what they were doing and what they were going to do. Many decided to go on further and others decided to go back and see their family, or to take their belongings and escape deeper into Russia. I joined a group of peasants from our area who decided to go back to their homes to see their families and in a few days, I was back in Manievich.

Arriving in Manievich, I met the Russians but they were ready to leave. The panic was great and the Jewish population was very frightened, not knowing what was awaiting us.

At that time, I was staying with my cousin Gittel Pliatch and I told her that I was planning to leave the village with the Russians and go deeper into Russia. Her opinion was that regardless of how bad the situation would become in Manievich, one would still be in one place and she didn't believe Hitler would kill us all for nothing. She talked this into me to such an extent that I changed my mind and remained in Manievich.

In a few days, the Russians left the village. It became anarchic. Since there was no legitimate power, the Poles and Ukrainians declared themselves leaders and established a militia. Their reigning decree was that the town would now become a free for all, and that everyone could do what they wanted with the Jews. All of the peasants from the surrounding villages came pouring into Manievich, robbing what was possible, accompanied with beating and threats.

For three days this wild ecstacy of rape, robbery and murder continued and on the fourth day, it was quiet. While many of the Manievicher residents remained without a shirt on their backs, the same occurred in the surrounding towns. Degraded and humili--ated by this fine piece of work, we sat and waited for our murderous rescuers, the Hitlerites (Germans), to come and bring order.

In a few weeks, a few dozen Hitlerites came. They supported the existence of the Polish-Ukrainian militia and gave them instructions as to what kind of evil decrees they could enforce against the Jews.

Then began the bitter persecution against us Manievicher Jews. Through the Ukrainian-Polish leaders, and with instructions from the Hitler murderers up to the liquidation of our dear friends and families who were killed for the sanctity of the name of God, our conscience will always haunt and hate these murderous Ukrainians, Poles, and Germans.

January 28, 1959

* * * * *

Life Under Occupation During The First Liquidation In Manievich

Under the reign of terror and persecution, day-to-day living was very difficult. Every day there arrived new evil decrees against the Jewish community. One lived with the hope that perhaps a miracle would occur and Hitler would be crushed. Unfortunately, the miracle came too late. Various rumors were spread how the Germans were persecuting Jews in the surrounding cities and towns. The news came that the Germans were recruiting all the men from the surrounding small towns to work, and the town of Manievich was also included.

On a beautiful early morning, the murderous Germans attacked our village and began capturing all the men, disturbing each house and corner. The Ukrainian police helped them. They caught about three hundred men, loaded them in trucks, and took them away to the next village, Gereyvara -- driving them to the <u>Ferdishe Mogiles</u>, the horses' graves, a field outside the village, where three ditches were prepared. The men were unloaded from the trucks, undressed naked, and sadistically beaten. Many of them, while still alive, even had slices of skin cut out of them. They were then systematically put to death.

The Germans filled up two ditches with bodies which were still alive -- twenty people to a layer, one layer on top of the other, shooting them in the head as they were lying. This was done in such a manner so that no one in the village could hear any shooting. The last ditch, they covered with the remaining earth, and any earth left over they took in trucks with them.

I believe I was the first to have discovered the details of this horrible murder carried out by the Ukrainian police and the Germans.

Before the Germans came into Manievich, while riding through the village of Gereyvara, they took with them a group of peasants with shovels. They dropped the peasants off outside the village and ordered them to dig the ditches. These same peasants witnessed the cruel scene, and they were also the last ones to cover the graves with earth.

Because I knew these peasants well, I had a chance to find out the details even though the Germans threatened them to remain silent. Finding out what happened sent a shiver through my soul.

Returning to Manievich, I told my relatives about this but they did not believe it. Why? They heard no shooting.

My aunt, Pearl Pliatch, talked me into going with her to see the ditches and learn the truth. Her two sons, my cousins Shlomo and Yehuda, both died in the action and I remember that it was a Saturday dawn, how we snuck away and went to see where the murder took place. It was terrible. The earth was split, and the blood poured from the surface like a well.

My aunt fainted. I revived her. Broken hearted we turned back, assured that our sons and fathers and relatives were no longer alive.

Although we didn't keep the tragedy a secret and told everyone about this, many didn't believe us and lived on with the hope that their husbands, sons and fathers were still alive somewhere.

The Germans used to send Jewish spies to the Judenrat, a group of Jewish leaders in the surrounding towns, with lies and stories about how they saw their relatives working in factories or on the railroad tracks. They suggested that everyone send packages of food and clothing, and more than one family believed this and really did send things back with the Germans. The reason the Germans did this was to calm the com-

munity and keep the people from organizing any
resistance. And this is how it was. The whole village
was murdered by the Germans and their graves can be
found outside the village of Manievich. We will never
forget how our friends and families were barbarously
killed.

February 1, 1951

* * * * *

The Liquidation Of The Jews In The Villages
Around Manievich And Our Escape Into The Woods

The inhuman treatment by the Ukrainian police made
life unbearable in Manievich.

I had planned to escape to the underground
together with the Chairman of the village of Gereyvara,
however I lost contact with him and he was killed by
the Germans as a Russian spy. Because of this, I
decided to leave Manievich and go to the village of
Lishnifka where my family lived.

Life there was esier because one didn't come into
daily contact with the police, but the situation was
still bad. The police from the nearby village of
Karasin often came to terrorize Jewish families.

Lishnifka was a small town where, before the First
World War, nearly 200 Jews lived. After the war, the
Jews from Lishnifka settled in the surrounding towns,
however six families came back.

Their livelihood came from stores, free enter-
prise, and anything else they could trade. A few families made a living spinning wool and another family was
in the blacksmith trade. All of them had children who
totalled about forty. There was also a teacher with
whom the children studied. On Shabbos and weekdays,
there was always a Minyan (quorum) and the shul (syna-
gogue) was located at the home of Yaakov Aryeh Gold who
was a pious Jew. He was also a Torah reader and a
moyil (circumcizer).

The Jews from the villages would come here for the
High Holidays. The relationship between them and the
peasants was friendly until Hitler's occupation; then

-191-

the situation quickly changed for the worse. The peasants waited impatiently for the day when their Jewish neighbors would be annihilated.

Two weeks before Rosh Hashannah, 1943, on a lovely summer day, the news came that the Germans were taking Jews from the nearby village of Karasin. Knowing that after this, came us, I and the other youth in Lishnifka scattered into the surrounding woods. There were twenty-one of us ranging in age from fifteen to thirty years old.

After spending the day in the woods, we returned to the village in the evening to find out what happened to the rest of our families. We discovered that the Germans did not come to Lishnifka that day, and we found our parents and the small children of the village waiting for their destiny, knowing that tomorrow it would surely come.

We decided to return to the woods and while lying in a silo, waiting for dawn, the door suddenly opened and my name was called. I recognized the voice of Shimon (Chunek) Wolper. I answered him and he told me that he was looking for me and wanted to tell me a secret. He said that Joseph Zweibel from the neigh-boring village of Griva came to him with a peasant and wanted us to join the partisans. He didn't know what to do and wanted me to meet with them and come to a decision. After meeting with them, it became clear that the peasant was the former mayor of Griva who was in the underground all along and with whom Joseph Zweibel had a secret contact.

Having decided to go underground with them, we immediately left to find the others and take them along. The blacksmith and his family didn't join us because the Ukrainian peasants in the village needed him there and promised to explain this to the Germans.

Joseph Zweibel suggested that since we had no food nor clothing, we should remain until the next day to confiscate what we could from the peasants and thus a group of us, under my leadership, remained hidden in the silo. I sent another group into the woods to cap-ture whatever goods they could.

On the second night, we decided to meet at a cer-tain spot outside of Lishnifka but the Germans had already been there. They took all the Jews and seeing that more than half were missing, they threatened to kill everyone on the spot unless the rest were found. They eventually took everyone with them to Manievich, leaving the blacksmith and his family and giving him twenty-four hours to find those who were missing and to bring them to the police who waited in the village for us.

A peasant working near the silo where we were hidden noticed that someone was inside. He opened the door and shouted for us to come out of the hay. Having no choice, we came out. He warned us against hiding there and told us that we were sentenced to die. I denied this, saying that the Germans were merely concentrating us in one place in Manievich, begging him to let us stay until nighttime when we would go to Manievich ourselves. He ordered us to leave the silo and we started running through the woods and the open fields. Luckily, the Germans and the police didn't notice us, and we hid in the bushes until dark when we were to meet with Joseph Zweibel and the mayor of Griva, Nikolai Konishchuk, alias Kruk.

When night came, we went to the designated meeting place and along the way we stopped to see a peasant to learn what happened to our families. He told us that Abraham Meyer, the blacksmith, came to see him and if any of us should appear, he would like to see us. I sent two of our men to him. They came right back with the blacksmith's son who warned us to go back. He said that the Germans were taking Jews from surrounding villages to Manievich and if we didn't return they would kill our families. He also said that the police were waiting for us.

In the meantime, we met with Kruk who came to get us. A discussion started as to what we should do now -- to return to Manievich or go into the woods. In a few hours, we divided into two groups. One decided to return; the second decided to go into the woods. I, my three brothers, the widow Mechamke Glupstein with her two sons and two daughters went into the woods. The blacksmith's family, the Zafran family, and my father decided to return to Manievich. We agreed that when the situation became very serious and they had to escape, they should come back here to the spot where we said good-bye and where we would return every night. We told the group that was returning to Manievich that they should tell everyone that we would be in the woods near Griva and Lishnifka.

We said goodbye and departed with the hope that
shortly we would see each other alive again. We all
knew in advance that the gathering of the Jews in one
place was simply a prelude to killing them.

March 4, 1959

* * * * *

My Impressions And Experiences With Kruk

Nikolai Konishchuk was a peasant, born in the
village of Griva, in the Kamin-Kashirsk district. He
came from a wealthy family and had a wife and children,
but had barely finished a few classes in elementary
school. He had been active in the underground
Communist Party of Poland.

In 1939, when Russia occupied the section of
Ukraine that belonged to Poland, he became chairman or
mayor of the village of Griva. In 1941, when Germany
occupied the area, he escaped deep into Russia. In
Kiev, Kruk and all of the leaders of the surrounding
area were mobilized by the Soviets. They were taught
methods of sabotage against the Germans and were sent
back to their districts to organize partisan groups.
Kruk had to filter back through the German lines, often
meeting difficult ordeals with SS troops and with
Poles.

Almost all of these underground leaders fell in
battle and only a few survived long enough to return
home.

Kruk could not return to Griva because the people
there hated the Russians as much as the Germans, and he
remained hidden, only having contact with his family.

Among Kruk's few good friends was Joseph Zweibel
who came from the same village. Kruk used to meet
often with him and if the situation became critical,
Zweibel and his family planned to flee into the woods
with Kruk.

This is what happened. Seeing that the situation
in Manievich was becoming serious, Zweibel ran away and
met with Kruk in Griva. Both of them came to us and
asked us to come with them to the woods.

-194-

Kruk knew the area in the surrounding woods amazingly well. He was a sensitive person with a sense of humor and a smile on his face. He liked wearing a military uniform with a gun at his side and although he never served in the army, killing came very easily to him.

At the start of our co-existence in the woods, he was very humble about himself and once even proposed that I should take over the leadership, but I refused. However, toward the end of the partisanship, he became more egotistical and aggressive against his aides and comrades. He once even killed a twelve-year-old boy who was found in a civilian camp during a siege and who wanted to be in the infantry. Kruk also reprimanded a fellow from Kamin-Kashirsk for hiding some bread which he shared with some civilian friends. He once had an argument with me over a potato which one of the gentile partisans said I tried to steal. Kruk shot at me but I somehow avoided getting hit, and Miriam Blaustein, who lived with him as his mistress, finally calmed him down. She feared the same thing would happen to her brother who was once a foreman in my factory because he was also accused of this crime together with me.

There was a time when the commander of the Nasiekin partisan unit, who was a Jew-hater and killed many Jews in White Russia, tried to influence Kruk to kill all of the Jewish partisans but Kruk refused. The Nasiekin commander, however, did not give up on the idea, and we were constantly in danger of an attack by him. By a miracle, General Dadya Petya came from the main headquarters for an inspection, and the plans of the Nasiekin commander were foiled. General Petya found out about this plan and removed the Nasiekin commander and sent him to the Soviet Central Bureau in White Russia. There were rumors that the commander was tried and received a death sentence, but this was never confirmed.

A few leaders of the main headquarters could not tolerate Kruk. They did not think he was qualified as a military leader, and he was virtually ignored on the field. He was always criticized for not disciplining his men and because his men were unruly with the people in the surrounding villages. Most of all, the leaders disliked the fact that Kruk had a civilian unit. He was often referred to as the "Jewish Messiah."

There was once a complaint lodged against me at headquarters, saying that I disapproved of Communism

and this endangered my life. Kruk defended me saying
that this was not so and that I was a dedicated
partisan. Kruk told me that the squealers were Yitzhak
Segal, Mordechai Hersh's son, and Shaya Pliatch. Until
today, I never knew why they did this. I had no misun-
derstandings with them though I knew they were once in
the Jewish police force of the Judenrat, and they never
repeated the charge again.

The reason that Kruk kept close to the Jews was
well understood. With us, he was commander of a unit
where everyone respected him. Without us, he would
have been an ordinary partisan and would have gotten no
credit for his initiative to organize a unit which had
such a just cause to fight against the Nazis.

Though Kruk had his good and bad moments with the
Jews in his unit, we must be thankful to him for his
determination to take every Jew into the unit, and they
respected him for that.

February 9, 1959

* * * * *

The Approach Of The Partisans

The first group of us who went into the woods consisted of eleven men and women: Kruk, Joseph Zweibel,
Dov Lorber (Reb Malenka), David, Abraham, and Yehezkel
Blaustein, Nechamke, Miriam, and Bailke, and the
children Joseph and Melech.

Kruk took us deep into the woods to a small island
in the mud which was covered with twisted bushes.
Having been disappointed and depressed and finding it
hard to survive, each of us lay down under a tree
trunk. We lay lifeless and didn't speak to each other,
thinking about how slim our hopes were of surviving
here in the woods. Finally, Kruk began comforting us
and told us that we would find a way out. He said we
would have to obtain weapons, and he knew many peasants
who had them and would be happy to exchange them for
any goods that we might be able to steal. If this
would not do, we would find other means of arming
ourselves.

The first week, Kruk acquainted us with the area,
showing us all the side roads and how to reach the

surrounding villages. We used to steal food from the fields and gardens. We also made contacts with friendly peasants, having had close ties with at least one prelate in each village.

Because it was hard for everyone to go out each night, we decided, during the second week, to split into two groups and each night we alternated. Kruk went out with one group, and I with the other. We managed to steal two rifles from a few villages and Kruk carried one with him. The rest of us wore sticks tied with rope.

During the second week, after completing our work, we blew up our food supplies, taking only necessities like salt and sugar and destroying the remainder of our products so that no one else could use them. We felt that we were gaining ground and each day we became more aggressive and eager to take revenge on our enemies.

Remaining in the woods another two weeks, we learned that most of our families were dead. A gloom befell us and there were tears running down our faces. Each of us wondered why we were still living when everyone else had perished.

Eventually, we calmed down, and Joseph Blaustein and I went to the place where we were supposed to meet with our Lishnifker friends to see if any of them survived. When we arrived, we met no one there. Going further toward Lishnifka, we met a group of people outside the village who were walking in a row. Because they looked suspicious, we lay down and commanded them to remain standing, shooting into the air. I thought they were peasants coming from work, so I decided to go farther toward the village. As I passed them, I heard one of them call my name and realized that they were the first group of our friends to escape from Manievich. Among them, whom I remember were: Itzhak Kuperberg, Zev (Vova) Verba, David Blaustein, Asher Pliatch, my father, Kononitz, Chunek Wolper and his wife Blumeh, and others.

I had agreed with Kruk earlier that if we were to meet any people we knew, we would not bring them to our hiding place but settle them elsewhere. This was done in case the Germans should attack, we would not be together but scattered in different places.

I hid these people in the woods outside Lishnifka and told them that tomorrow night, Kruk and I would come and settle them in a safe place. I took my father and Blumeh Wolper with me and on the second night, Kruk and I and the rest of my group came back and settled them in another hiding place between Lishnifka and Nabruska. We supplied them with food and told them not to go anywhere until we returned the following week.

The night before the liquidation of the Manievich ghetto, many people escaped into the surrounding woods. Others ran to look for us around Lishnifka, knowing that we were located there. Every night, new people arrived including Joseph Zweibel's family and most of the other Lishnifker folks. In a few days, we counted about eighty people. We settled them near us.

On one hand, Kruk was happy that more people were coming, but on the other hand, he was concerned because it would be hard to support so many unarmed people.

The time came for us to go meet the first group of friends, whom we settled outside the village of Nabruska. On our arrival, we learned that the Germans were planning a raid. The reason for that was that they didn't listen to our orders and went into Nabruska to steal several things from the peasants. The peasants recognized that they were Jews and told the Germans where they were located.

We immediately took this group away and transferred them to a second area near our base and when the Germans came, they found no one. Thus, we saved them from sure death.

February 12, 1959

* * * * *

The Organization of Kruk's Unit

After the liquidation of the Manievich ghetto, new survivors came to us every day. All of them knew where we were located and after a few weeks we counted more than 100 people.

The first group, headed by Kruk, decided to divide up everyone and send them to three separate places. Thus, the Germans would not find us in one spot. This situation was also more suitable since we had no weapons and could not defend ourselves.

We nominated Kruk as commander and I was his representative. Our hiding place became the chief headquarters where the orders were given to all three groups.

In time, we took several guns and other goods from the peasants. We also carried out acts of revenge against those peasants who had collaborated with the Germans. We killed them.

The peasants in the surrounding areas were afraid because they heard that a large army of partisans were nearby. They told this to the Germans, seeking their protection, but the Germans didn't move from their spot but barricaded themselves with tight security. They feared Jews with guns.

We also intercepted many goods that the peasants were giving to the Germans for protection, and they complained bitterly about this to the Germans.

We also began collecting food and material for the winter so that when the snow began, we would not have to go out and leave any signs of where we were. We captured a few horses and wagons to help us carry the goods.

After staying underground for about six weeks, we came out to meet with the other group of partisans who were located near us and about whom we knew nothing.

This meeting occurred on the way back from a mission where we killed a peasant who aided the Germans and confiscated his fortune. Arriving back at our base, I noticed a group coming toward me. I slipped under a tree, ready to shoot and noticed that their guide was a peasant who recognized me. He came to me and explained that the group consisted of partisans, Jews who escaped from the Germans, and they wanted to talk to me. They explained who they were and wanted to work with us. I immediately called Kruk and after a short discussion, we asked them to our base.

Fearing that they were lost, Kruk showed them where they were on a map, and then Kruk and I took them back to their base.

Their base was not far from ours and their commander's name was Nasiekin. They also had a radio station and contact with Moscow. We explained our situation to them and told of our shortage of weapons. The commander connected us to the Central Bureau in White Russia and told us that he would get us weapons.

Since we knew the area better then they did, our group and their group of about thirty men decided to work together.

Their main task was to destroy the trains which were used to bring weapons, soldiers, and material to the battlefront. They had explosive material which they put under the train tracks and when the train came, it would explode. We also learned that a second group of these partisans, under the command of Kartuchin, was located, near the village of Povorsk and many of our Povorsk friends joined the group.

We agreed with Commander Naseikin that on the following week, a group of us together with a group of their men would go to Griva and carry out a raid to take goods, since their group had almost none.

When the time, one Sunday evening, a group of our unit, together with a group from Nasiekins' unit went to Griva. Arriving there, we learned that the commander and the police from neighboring areas were there. They were drinking in a certain house, surrounded it, and broke in. [I remember like today that the Nasiekin commander put everyone up against the wall and shot them all -- about thirty people. Only a small child was left and the commander asked who wanted to kill him. Near me stood Joseph Blaustein, who was about fifteen years old. He appealed to me to let him do so, so he killed the child.] The rest of the night, we badgered the peasants, gathering about twenty wagonloads of goods and stealing three guns.

February 14, 1959

* * * * *

Survival in the Partisans

Our leader Kruk was in danger of falling into Naseikin's unit. Their commander wanted Kurk to join his unit because he thought Jews were not useful in the partisans, and he felt they should be done away with. Kruk didn't accept his plan and refused to leave. Kruk told me of this; he was concerned that Nasiekin would attack us. Though we were not well-armed, I felt that we had nowhere to run and should stand up to this attack. I strengthened the guard around the base and we waited for the attack. Luckily, in a few days, Dadya Petya came for an inspection. He was sent by chief headquarters, and his appearance saved us from attack. General Petya found out about this scheme and Commander Naseikin was sent to main headquarters where he was tried and sentenced to death.

Dadya Petya remained with us for four months. He helped organize the fighters with instructions from Moscow. He installed military discipline. Because of our poor weapons supply and because we had people of various ages, we split the unit, making a civilian section for those who couldn't fight. We also had a number of girls who did domestic work and who occasionally accompanied us. The chief headquarters didn't like this, but we proved their usefulness and they remained with us.

I knew Dadya Petya quite well and often met with him. He was interested in Jews, and some thought he was Jewish himself though he never admitted it. His aides, however, did not like Jews, often made fun of us, and told lies about us. Dadya called me to verify those lies, i.e., that we abused peasants. I didn't understand where these rumors came from because the military police often checked out the peasants, and they had no complaints against us.

Dadya Petya decided the rumors were started by one of the other units and after this, he had a high regard for my work.

With winter coming, the Germans organized the Ukranian police for a raid against us. We decided that all the partisans should leave the area and return after a few weeks. We went to the Sirnik woods and stayed in a village there. During this time we carried out acts of sabotage and ultimately acquired our first mine with orders to blow up a train. We learned where to place the mines, and Kruk and I and a group went to carry out the orders. We chose the area between Gereyvara and Manievich.

Because of the snow, we had to place the mine on the tracks just before the train came. The tracks were guarded by the Germans and by peasants with two-way

radios. The peasants also made fires near the tracks
to keep them warm.

On the first night we couldn't get close enough to
the tracks. The second night, we waited and when we
heard the train coming, I and one of the Zweibel
brothers wired up the mine. Concerned that the train
was too close, he was careless about hooking up the
wire and the mine blew up and he died. The train
remained standing and although shaken, I got up and ran
back to the group. Ashamed and saddened by this, we
returned to our base having to report this unhappy
event to chief headquarters.

February 15, 1959

* * * * *

Experiences in the Partisans

Because of this event, chief headquarters didn't
want to give us any more explosives. Every piece of
dynamite was as precious as gold.

Things came hard. We had to send people and arms
to White Russia to main headquarters, and the roads
were dangerous. It often took four to six weeks to do
this because we had to carry everything on our
shoulders.

One time, my group and I went to shoot up a train
bringing men to the battle field near Manievich. We
blew it up and killed eleven men. The next time, we
ambushed some guards who were watching a railroad
track. Most of them escaped except one who seemed
dead. I suggested shooting him in the head to see if
he was really dead. Upon hearing this, he jumped up
and claimed to be a Russian who was our friend. We
shot him anyway.

With the arrival of some Ukranians and Russians in
our unit, various new functions were created. There
were also other Russians that didn't like having a Jew
as their commander and once, while returning from a
mission, they told Kruk that I tried to sabotage it.
Kruk removed me as commander, and I was replaced by a
friend of his from Griva.

A few weeks later, Kruk received orders to reinstate me so that our unit would be completely Jewish. I still kept a few gentiles so that I could send them on missions where Jews couldn't go.

My aides were: Joseph Blaustein, Molitruk Zvoda, Yitzchak Kuperberg, and Zev (Vova) Verba as representative.

My first area of operation was between Vibner and Kamin-Kashirsk. The Ukrainian police and the Germans rode back and forth daily. I placed mines along the road and once blew up a car containing a German general. His aide and a few people were killed, and he was wounded.

I was then given orders to go to Kamin-Kashirsk and destroy the viaduct. It was very risky and many tried to dissuade me but I felt that as a Jew, I was responsible for my brothers in the unit and wanted to go.

Nearing the village where the viaduct was located, I sent a messenger to inform me where the guard was, how strong it was, and who was guarding it. The next day, he returned and told us that the police held guard but the Germans controlled it. Two men guarded the building and every two hours they changed. He told me not to go ahead, but I decided to risk it. Late at night, my group reached the main road which led from Kamin-Kashirsk to Kovel. The viaduct was about one mile away.

I left my group there with some explosives in case they had to defend themselves. I took with me Yitschak Kuperberg, two others, and some explosives.

We approached the entrance of the viaduct and looked for an opening. We found one in the fence. We went to the door but it was locked so we knocked on the window, posing as police and asked the viaduct janitor for the key. He gave it to us and once inside, we placed the explosives under the machinery. We quickly escaped, taking the janitor with us, and the viaduct exploded. The Germans immediately began shooting at us but we safely ran away. Thus was destroyed the viaduct between Kovel and Kamin-Kashirsk.

February 19, 1959

* * * * *

After finishing with the Jews, the Germans started killing Ukrainians, whose names were given to them by other Ukrainians. They were labelled as Communists, and they and their families were taken from their homes and killed. We partisans did the same to the Ukrainian peasants who helped the Germans. We killed many in such villages as Lishnifka, Manievich, Griva, and Nova Ruda.

In the meantime, the Russian army was driving the Germans back and our task of blowing up trains became even more important.

In time, there came to our unit a Russian named Captain Mahmed. He solved our problem of explosives shortage by showing us that in the woods there were many used explosives that could be re-used. Our unit had the task of collecting these and by boiling them we could use them again. This process was very dangerous because many of the bombs were highly explosive, and people like Volfich, Avruch and Siama were wounded, one of them seriously.

After a few months operating in the Kamin-Kashirsk area, our job was done and we moved to another place between Brisk and Pinsk. This was the main connection to White Russia and the Germans transferred men and ammunition there. It took us two weeks to get there and we found many sympathizers and Russian partisans. It was, however, hard to hide since there were no woods.

The Germans guarded well the railroad tracks there; nevertheless, our first few missions were successful. We blew up about fifteen trains loaded with heavy weapons. Because of this, the Germans stopped using those tracks at night and guarded them more heavily. We kept tearing up the tracks and they kept fixing them and eventually, their position was weakened.

That summer, the Germans began retreating and our acts of sabotage helped the Russians. We partisans waited for our final victory even though we had no family left. We knew that Jewish life was dead, and we understood that with freedom came pain. However, we fought with pride and defended our honor and we will never forget this.

February 25, 1959

* * * * *

In 1943, we saw freedom approaching. The Russians were driving the Germans from the occupied territories. Orders came from Moscow that Kruk's unit be abolished, and that we should join Max's unit which operated in Poland.

Kruk was against this and persuaded Dadya Petya to leave him one unit. He selected the best men, including me, but I escaped to Max's unit. Max assured me that he would never return me to Kruk.

A few days later, Max's unit was ordered to Rovno to help free the city. When Kruk found this out, he wanted to have me delivered as a deserter, but this didn't happen.

In Max's unit, the conditions were bad. We had to fight Germans and also bomb airplanes.

In 1944, we entered Rovno and were re-united with other partisans who worked together with us. Upon entering Rovno, I gave orders to free the prisoners and then I returned to Manievich to meet with any survivors. I met Lisenko, the former Secretary of the Communist Party. He asked me to take a party position but I refused. I returned to Rovno where I discovered that the N.K.V.D. unit of the Russian army had arrested my outfit. When I asked my commander why, he knew nothing about it, but I knew that the anti-Semites did not want Jews in the city.

Eventually, orders came that all partisans should join the Russian army. I was offered the rank of Lieutenant and was bestowed the Lenin medal and the Red Star. Being considered a hero, they paid me and sent me to their headquarters. After all of this, I decided that I had nothing more to fight for and took a train to Sarni.

In Sarni, I was detained and searched. They kept me for four days and accused me of spying, and I was given over to the police. I somehow proved to them that I was not a spy, and they offered me a post. I promised to consult about this with the Secretary of the Communist Party. Instead, I jumped aboard a freight train and the next moring, I was back in Manievich.

March 2, 1959

* * * * *

(Dov Lorber eventually left Russia and came to America. He resides in Seattle, Washington with his family.)

Translated from the Yiddish by Esther Ritchie.

AT THEIR DEATH THEY ORDERED US TO TAKE REVENGE

Dov Lorber

The relations between the non-Jewish fighters and the Jewish fighters were, so to speak, decent, but it is worthwhile to emphasize that this was only out of fear of the Moscow command, because there were many non-Jews who were willing to kill Jews who were their comrades at arms.

In particular they made charges and attacks on the fact that we set up the civilian camp. It was mainly made up of old men, women, and children, who were unable to actively participate with arms in our battle against the Germans and their allies.

This issue gave them (the non-Jewish partisans) no rest and they grumbled about it incessantly. But the Jewish partisans did not lag behind the non-Jewish partisans in ability and initiative; sometimes they even were superior to them, and the anti-Semitic partisans were forced then to take them into account.

The beginning of Partizankeh was not easy for us. With the help of mock wooden rifles we had to persuade the local peasants that we Jews were a deterrent fighting force and were not to be disregarded.

With the mock rifles, we forced them to supply us with food, guns, and pistols. We burned down the "cooperatives" that the Germans had set up for their

-206-

food supply, and the German produce designated for the Germans was taken. Also in battles in the village centers, we destroyed transports on the way to urban centers. The local population at first lived in fear of us, but after a short time they cooperated, for the most part, with us against the conquerors.

Our _otryad_ unit, along with some of the men from Max's _otryad_, was successful in an expulsion campaign of German and Ukrainian police from the large village of Krasin, that was near the town of Manievich. During the operation we burned down the police station that was built like a fortress. In this operation a number of policemen were killed.

We conducted a battle the entire night with the policemen of the village of Vivzer. The police station was built out of bricks, and with the light arms that we had, we could not easily take control of it. We were forced to end the battle, and we called on them to surrender. Their answer was that they would not surrender to Jews. The emphasis was on Jews, because in that entire area most of the partisans were Jews, and they very much feared falling into the hands of Jews "who knew no mercy."

Although we did not succeed in taking the police station, we spent the entire night in the village. We destroyed a lot of food and clothing, collected the medical supplies from the single pharmacy in the village, and destroyed anything that we could not take with us from the German estate that at one time had belonged to a Polish landlord.

We took advantage of every opportunity to settle personal accounts with the Ukrainian murderers from the local villages. Scores of peasants paid with their lives for collaborating with the Germans in the murder of the Jews. We carried out the first operation in "Kuterim" (isolated households) in the village of Ziravah, where the head of the town council lived. He had been found to have extensively participated in the liquidation of the local Jews, especially in Kamin Kashirsk.

We were a group of ten, armed with two rifles and a pistol and rifle-shaped sticks. We reached his house before evening. Kruk and I went inside and found the village's head official, his wife and another peasant eating at the table. We ordered them to hold up their

-207-

hands, and I ordered the official to go outside. We
tied him up and made him lie on the ground. We
demanded that he hand over his weapons, but he insisted
that he did not have any weapons. We dealt him hard
blows. After hours of torture, we shot him, without
succeeding in getting him to say where he was hiding
the arms. We were certain that he had a lot of arms,
which we desperately needed. I was shaken by this
retaliatory operation, because it was the first time I
had taken part in killing a human being; but I knew
that this "human being" had murdered my parents,
brothers, and defenseless children in cold blood. We
took the Jewish belongings that we found in his house
and returned to our home in the woods.

We carried out another retaliatory operation after
a short time in the village of Griva. The decision was
made to liquidate not only a collaborator but also his
wife and two children. At dawn several men from my
group went to where he was staying. We knocked on the
door of the peasant's house. He opened the door. We
ordered him to get up on the bed that was by the stove.
I ordered Yisroel Puchtik (Zalonka) to shoot him, but
Yisrael was so nervous he was unable to fire. Someone
else volunteered and shot the peasant and his wife.
The two children, on seeing this, started to run.
Outside, we took pity on the children, and I ordered
that no one hurt them. I wondered, would their father
have behaved in this way, he who was an organizer of
the murderers of so many Jews?

Meanwhile we made plans to capture a peasant in
the village of Sarchov. The peasants in this village
were notorious. They had taken part in the murder of
the Jews of Manievich and the surrounding area. We
knew that one peasant owned many weapons. We burst
into his house suddenly, with the intention of
surprising him. He was truly surprised. "How can this
be? Are there really still some Jews left? And they
even dare to break into my home! Jewish impudence!" We
tried nicely to get him to talk and to develop a
rapport with him. We felt that if we spared his life,
he would supply us with arms, which were essential for
our survival. We tried to convince him that we did not
intend to harm him, that all we asked of him were arms,
but he insisted, "I do not have arms." Suddenly, he
jumped up and leaped through the window. One of the
men was just able to wound him in the leg with his gun,
but he kept on going. The men who were surrounding the
house caught him, tied him up, and brought him back

into the house. We started to torture him, and he
insisted, "You're not going to get anything out of me,
so let it be and just shoot me, for you're wasting your
efforts ...." A Jew, one of his fellow villagers, shot
him.

In the town of Tzruvishitz we killed the head
official who had collaborated with the Germans and was
known as a hunter of Jews who had escaped the "actions"
and were hiding in the villages.

In the town of Oziritz, we liquidated a peasant
who had volunteered to lead Max's men -- partisans who
were disguised as policemen -- to Kruk's Jewish brigade, and, indeed, he "very willingly" brought them
directly to us. He managed to escape but was later put
to death in his home, in his town.

These operations served as a warning to the peasants from the surrounding villages to not harm the Jews
that were in hiding.

In the village of Lishnivka we shot an officer of
the local police whom we had forced to give us arms.
Initially he refused, but then he agreed to bring us to
a warehouse where the arms were hidden. Upon leaving
the house, he started to run away. The first bullet
that was shot, hit him and killed him instantly.

In the village of Novi Roda, we captured the town
leader and brought him to our base for interrogation.
After several days of interrogation, we killed him.

In the town of Griva, we rounded up eight men who
had collaborated with the Germans, including a few that
had served on the Kamin Kashirsk police force. They
received the punishment they deserved.

We carried out more retaliatory operations in the
area. Whoever we captured who had collaborated with
the Germans paid for it with his life. We did all that
we could to obstruct the Germans from moving about
freely in the area and prevented them from obtaining
horses and cattle.

We burned down bridges along the Stockode River
during operations. We burned the agricultural land
holdings (Falvarkim) that the Germans had confiscated,
along with the cattle and grain in them. These holdings had belonged to Polish landlords during the Polish

rule; with the Soviet takeover in 1939, they had been confiscated and turned into work farms. The Germans made them into an important supply station for the German army.

In the vicinity of the town of Refalovta and others nearby, we burned down large storehouses full of grain that the Germans had confiscated from the peasants and had prepared to send to Germany. We also burned down a vodka refinery that operated continuously in order to supply whiskey to the soldiers. We severed all the telephone lines in the area, thus depriving the Germans of any means of communication. They were unable to repair the telephones.

The Germans did not dare enter the places where we were stationed. We controlled wide areas of the forests and villages. The partisan guards made rounds and carefully watched over all that was going on in the area. We young Jews were the first to be in Kruk's partisan unit. There were fighters in it from every region of Rovno and the surrounding area. The command from our relatives, fellow townsmen, and woodsmen was always with us: revenge!

We began to carry out this command on Ukrainian criminals. We knew the names and addresses of many of the murderers who had openly collaborated with the Germans. We systematically surrounded their homes in the dark of night, interrogated them, sometimes at length, sometimes briefly, sometimes demanding arms from them. We tried to convince them to cooperate with us, and we promised that no harm would come to them if they carried out our requests. But most of them did not do as we wished. When we were convinced of the abundance of their crimes, we shot them to death. We searched their houses and took arms, food, clothing, and Jewish possessions (that they had stolen).

Among those we killed were nine peasants from the village of Griva, the former chief of police in the village of Lipniski, the leaders of the villages of Zirba, Truz Tzruvishitz, and Novi Roda, and other peasants in the villages of Sarchov, Uzuriz, and others. Our operations created fear among our enemies, as well as respect.

We moved on to operations against both the Germans and the Ukrainians. We burned, as was previously mentioned, all of the bridges on the Stockode River, grain storehouses, cattle, and the like. We caused severe damage, and in time we adjusted to fierce hand-to-hand battles, and we succeeded in taking booty.

Similar to the partisan unit, was the citizens' camp, a "town in the woods." This camp was made up of old people, women, and children who managed to escape. They lived in the woods and we took care of them.

This Jewish camp created a conflict between us, the Jewish fighters, and the non-Jewish fighters who were mostly Russians. But thanks to our heroic operations, we succeeded in overcoming the manifestations of anti-Semitism; they disappeared for the most part, from the area without causing damage to the town. We came to be appreciated, and in the surrounding area the word spread that the strongest partisans were the Jews, that since the Jews had a particular account to settle with the murderers, their operations were the most dangerous.

The period of using wooden mock-rifles passed; we had gotten booty of arms and ammunition and could now function effectively.

One time we attacked the police station in the village of Krasin. We burned down the building and killed several policemen. We carried out a similar operation in the dark of night in the village of Vivzer. There we called on the policemen to surrender. They replied, "We won't surrender to Jews." They hid themselves in their brick protective building, and we did not have any explosive materials with which to blow it up. In spite of this, we stayed in the village the entire night. We took as booty a lot of food, clothing, and medicine, and we took or destroyed everything that was in the courtyard of the police station.

I was very familiar with the town of Vivzer. My grandfather Yaakov had managed the property affairs of the poritz (landowner). We continued liquidating German collaborators in every area, and scores of them were killed. From our headquarters we received an order not to shoot without a specific command. We evaded this order when we were convinced we had to attend to the murderers of Jews. I would like to mention an incident in the town of Troyanovka. In the summer of 1943, we attacked the German police station in this town. Many of the Germans were killed in an ambush, and the rest fled. My friend Yosef Halpshtein approached a peasant in order to look for Jewish possessions, and the peasant called him a "dirty Jew." Yosef shot and killed him. At headquarters I maintained that Yosef had shot the peasant after the latter had attacked him with an ax.

There were many more events in Partizankeh, including the killing of many German soldiers. I have listed only a portion but through these events it is possible to show our humble part in the revenge against our enemies -- the murderers of our people.

ABOUT KRUK -- THE SECRET IS OUT

Dov Lorber

I first met Kruk in 1942, two weeks before Rosh Hashanah, at midnight, when he, along with Yosef Zweibel from the village of Griva, which is near Kamin Kashirsk, came to the village of Lishnivka to encourage the village youth to go to the woods and establish a Partizankeh.

Nikolai Konishchuk (Kruk) was a poor peasant, who lived in the village of Griva, and was very familiar with the area and the surrounding woods. In 1939, when the Russians had control of the western Ukraine and Byelorussia, Kruk was an active Communist and leader of Griva, even though he lacked education and had no military training.

In 1941, with the invasion of the German armies into Russia and the occupation of our regions, Kruk fled to Kiev, the Ukrainian capital. There the Russians organized all the Communist refugees from the western regions, trained them, and sent them back to their home towns so they could organize and establish a partisan movement.

Upon returning to his village in the occupied region, Kruk encountered many difficulties in carrying out the task the Russians had given him; the townsmen were anti-Communists, and he greatly feared that they would hand him over to the Germans. Because of this, he was unable to appear openly in the village, and he hid with relatives. In order to stay in touch with

-212-

Yosef Zweibel, Kruk met him and set up a time when Zweibel would go with his family to the woods. As was expected, right before Rosh Hashanah, 1942, the Germans began to round up all the Jews from the towns and villages surrounding Manievich; it then became clear to the Jews of Manievich that the hangman's noose was tightening around their necks. Yosef Zweibel immediately contacted Kruk, and the two decided they had to go to the young Jews in Lishnivka and urge them to join them in going to the woods to organize a partizanke group. That night they arrived at Lishnivka, met with Shimon Wolper, and presented their plan to him, but he rejected it. The same night, they came to see me in my hiding place in the barn. (As I mentioned, this was my first meeting with Kruk.) I agreed to their proposition without hesitation and suggested that we go at once with all the families to the woods. My plan was to save as many Jews from Manievich and the surrounding area as possible.

At first, Kruk's behavior was decent and reasonable. The reason for this was clear: All of his officers were Jews. The Ukrainian youths not only did not like him, but they presented a moral threat. Because of this, and because he wanted things to go well, he suggested to me that I be the group commander. I refused, because I thought he would be a better person than I for the position. He had military training from his guerilla warfare in the woods, he was familiar with the local forest paths and villages, and he was a Ukrainian. I agreed to be his second in command.

In time his friendly behavior changed, and he began to show some antagonism toward the Jewish fighters in spite of his knowing full well that without them he would not be a commander for very long. After a number of months in the woods, his personal behavior changed a lot; he chose for himself one of our women fighters to be his "house secretary," despite the fact that he was married and a father.

Most of the time he was in the base in the woods, thanks to the fact that I had taken it upon myself to tend to the needs of the two units -- the combat unit and the unit made up of the old people and women.

Later on we met a man wandering in the woods who was hiding from the Germans. He had been an active Communist in the village of Vivzer during the Russian rule. We decided to take him into our unit. After a

number of weeks, Kruk decided to make him his second in
command, appointing me the unit's sergeant-major.
Several months passed. Kruk again honored his friend,
the peasant from his home town, and appointed him in my
place as the division sergeant-major; he made me the
commander of the combat division. Later, when the combat division was divided into sections and I was its
commander, Russian soldiers who had fled from imprisonment were added to our company, and our otryad took on
a different character. Yet it did have several Jews in
it, and Kruk, despite his showing from time to time an
impatience toward them, was made to see that the Jews
were a force to be reckoned with. His behavior was
much different from the time of his first organizing
efforts.

He began to live a life of ease in the woods, the
life of an "omnipotent" ruler. A dismantled house was
brought from the village of Lishnivka for him and was
set up in the woods. His "wife's" mother was the head
cook, and she managed, with difficulty, to supply him
with food that he liked.

One day his true face was revealed. With his own
hands he shot in the woods a twelve-year-old Jewish
boy, whose only sin was that he had requested to go
with this relatives, the Wolper family, when they had
to leave the base, because the Germans and Ukrainians
surrounded our woods. This event shocked us deeply.
Kruk clearly did not feel at ease on account of this.
His only explanation was that he was obligated to act
as he did for the sake of discipline, that he had to
show that reality was truly harsh in the woods.

After a number of weeks in the Sirnik woods, we
returned to our original bases. There we found the
youth's corpse, still laying in the same spot where
Kruk had shot him; because of the pressure of circumstances he was forced to report this incident to
headquarters. To justify his deed, he ordered me to go
with him and serve as a witness to his merit, in case
Dadya Petya, the headquarters commander, declared him
guilty. But Dadya Petya only reprimanded him with
harsh words, and with this, the matter was closed.

After a while a similar incident occurred; Kruk
shot a young Jew from Kamin-Kashirsk, because he stole
some bread from the kitchen to give it to the camp
where the old people and women lived. For this theft,
Kruk killed him. He went up to him and filled him with
a round of bullets. The youth died instantly.

-214-

During these days, a personal clash took place between Kruk and me. I went out at the head of my division in order to mine the dirt road leading from Kamin Karshirsk to the large village, Vivzer. German convoys and police passed daily on this road to and from the village whre the Ukrainian police forces' main building was set up. The Ukrainians' assignment was to confiscate livestock and food from the local villages for the German army.

On a clear morning, we reached the dirt road that was on the edge of the village of Darchi, and we planted the mine. We took a position behind bushes along the road, in tense anticipation of the arrival of the executors of oppression and destruction. And in fact, after several hours had passed, the motorized column loaded with Germans arrived at the site of the mine. We pulled the cord -- but, Aha! The column passed by and the mine did not explode. After we checked the mine, we found that the cord had in fact been pulled. We didn't understand exactly what had happened and decided, come what may, to remove the ineffectual mine with the utmost care, so that, heaven forbid, it would not deceive us a second time.

Yitzchak Kuperberg and I succeeded in removing it. Disappointed and embittered, we returned to our base in the dark of night, with "His Highness," the mine. We wanted to inspect it, find out why it did not explode, and learn a lesson for the future. Because of this embarrassing incident, we did not want to report to Kruk about our failure that same night, and I decided to report to him in the morning. But two Russians in our division went ahead of me and immediately reported the failure to Kruk, because I had, so to speak, ruined the mission. Kruk, in a rage, drew his pistol and ran toward my trench. Luckily for me, his "wife" preceded him. Endangering her own life, she ran to tell me that Kruk was about to shoot me along with her brother Yosef, who was our unit's "politruk" (political commissar). I was ready to meet Kruk, gun in hand, and then, the same woman who had risked her life for us, appeared. She ran out to meet him and persuaded him to calm down. And, indeed, he calmed down, went into their house, and spoke insolently to me, "I know that you ruined the mission. If it had been anyone but you, I would have shot him, on the spot. From now on, you will not serve in the position of division commander." He appointed in my place one of the two Russian informers.

Kruk ordered that the horses be bridled, and he went to the staff commander, Dadya Petya, to submit a report on the failure, and also on my removal from the post. The staff commander, after listening to his complaint and decision, ordered that the mine be brought to him. With characteristic patience, Dadya inspected the mine and discovered that the explosive material was not of good quality; for that reason the mine had not exploded. He ordered Kruk to immediately reinstate me as division commander, as the unit was completely composed of Jews.

Kruk summoned me, and embarrassedly told me to compile a list of thirty men I wanted. I requested that my division include two Ukrainians, very familiar with the surroundings, for the sole purpose of reconnaissance. I picked my friends Yitzchak Kuperburg and Zev Verba as section commanders. Each one of our thirty men faithfully carried out his asignment; together we performed great and sensational acts, comparable to that of David battling Goliath, as we struck out against our enemy. Our concern was to keep alive every Jewish fighter and every person from the "family camps."

Besides the murders of the two Jews mentioned above, Kruk also caused the death of a Jewish family from Kamin-Kashirsk, that of a young Jew from Warsaw, and others. With these deeds he placed himself, in my humble opinion, in the same category as his Ukrainian brothers -- a murderer of Jews.

THE FIRST ACTION: MAHMED-MELAMED'S CHARACTER

Yisroel Puchtik

The first German patrol, thirty men on motorcycles, wearily entered the town of Manievich. The Ukrainian population gave them a festive welcome. The Germans left their arms unguarded by the "Kauntor," confident that they were among a sympathetic population -- Ukrainians and Poles.

The Ukrainian police quickly organized and inspected the stolen goods and booty of the town's Jews.

Six weeks passed, and 375 Jews, mainly heads of families, were forcibly gathered together and led to their deaths, into pits that had been prepared beforehand by the local peasants in the "Horses' Graves" sector. We do not have much evidence on what happened in the valley of death. From peasants who took part in this action, and from others who were spectators, we learned that the Ukrainian police beat people with beastly cruelty. All were stripped naked, dragged by the neck, and then pushed into the opening of the pit.

There were attempts at escape and struggle. It was told that Binyamin Eizenberg, a locksmith, killed two policemen, but then a third emptied an entire magazine into Binyamin's body -- he was still walking until he fell dead, wallowing in his own blood, into the pit.

After this "action," the Jews were called upon to organize a Judenrat that would direct the affairs of the town's Jews, and would strictly concern itself with implementing the Germans' directives.

I left this place and went to my hometown of Horodok. The town's peasants intervened on my behalf, so that the Gavitz Komissar permitted me to stay with my wife, two children, and mother. My father had been killed in an "action."

* * * * *

At the beginning of our time in the forest, we carried out a number of punitive operations against Ukrainian nationals (zlinovtzim), the Ukrainian police force, and other collaborators. But our dream was to carry out a serious operation against the Germans themselves. The opportunity for such an operation soon arrived: a mine, that was sent from Moscow to the partisan command, was brought to our company. A Soviet partisan also arrived, who taught us how to activate the mine on railroad tracks. Six Jewish partisans and the one Russian went out to execute the operation on the railroad tracks in the vicinity of Manievich-Tzruveka. We attached the mine to the tracks, rigged up a long wire, and hid ourselves in a grove, ready to detonate the mine by means of the wire the instant the train passed. All of a sudden, we spotted from afar German troops coming directly toward us, and the young, strong partisan, "Vlodya" Zweibel was ordered to quickly dismantle the mine.

The mine exploded in Vlodya's hands, and he cried out for help. The Russian officer blocked our way to him, pointed his gun at us, and ordered us to quickly retreat to the forest. Our helplessness to save our friend and our abandoning him on the railroad tracks jolted us into shock. Vlodya's cries echoed in our ears for a very long time.

The next day a Ukrainian liaison informed us of Vlodya's fate. The mine had severed his leg and wounded his entire body, but he hadn't lost consciousness. The Germans cruelly tortured him, but he did not betray his comrades nor did he reveal the location of the partisan base.

After this tragic event with the mine, the anti-Semitic chief of staff, Kartuchin, decided not to give the Jewish brigade any more mines, based on the claim that they were cowards. This attitude caused a bitter mood to fall on the company, especially since we knew that the one who was at fault for the failure of the mission, and the loss of a dear partisan was the Russian instructor.

During this time, there was on the staff a captain by the name of Mahmed -- he was dark-skinned, tall, and handsome. He had served during the years 1939-41 in the townlet of Poboresky in an artillery unit with the rank of captain-engineer. As the Russian's retreat, he decided to remove the cannon shells, so the Germans would not be able to make use of them. With the help of his soldiers, he buried them in pits in the surrounding forests. He himself was captured, but escaped and wandered about the forests alone, until he organized a unit of partisans. Once, when they were near the town of Kovel, they were attacked by Germans and caught in thick and continuous fire. Captain Mahmed successfully covered his men until they extricated themselves from the siege. This was one of the outstanding operations of Mahmed, but even this act of heroism did not serve to elevate him in Kartuchin's, the anti-Semite's, eyes. Kartuchin was suspicious of him because he was a Jew, although this was never proven the entire time he was in the forest.

Mahmed was transferred to the Jewish company called Kruk.

Here, too, Mahmed did not reveal his identity, assuming his Kavkazit identity. In spite of this, he did not refrain from proving to his Gentile friends the great ability of the Jewish partisans. Mahmed organized the removal of cannon shells and their transport to Kruk Otryad, and under his personal supervision and direction, the extraction of explosives from the cannon shells and the preparation of mines began.

This work was carried on intensely, with great expertise and no tools by Jewish youths from the civilian camp ("the family camp"). The process of melting down the explosive material was a very dangerous one. It was necessary to take apart the front piece that was made of copper and to remove another three metal rings to reach the metal explosive, that was as hard as cast cement. All of this work was done using only a chisel and hammer, thus creating a high risk of an unwanted explosion; accidents did in fact occur. Two youths, Syomkeh and Feyskeh were torn to pieces by explosions. They put the cannon shells in a barrel of boiling water, heated them until the hard explosive material melted, and then baked them into wooden molds that were smeared in a paste of flour and water so that the liquid would not stick to the wood. They baked sabotage-bricks that weighed two to five kilograms and used the explosive materials for mines. The girls of the camp made detonators from flashlight batteries they had obtained from Polish "Konductors" in exchange for pork and other commodities.

Mahmed significantly improved the extraction of explosives and the activating of mines, making it no longer necessary to use a long wire to detonate the mine. Instead, a clock was used, and the danger in this operation was greatly reduced. These types of mines were activated with great success by Malenka (Dov Lorber), Vova Verba, Itzik Kuperberg, and many others from the Kruk Otryad; the bombings of twenty trains, bridges, boats, and more were credited to these "cowards." In light of these operations, many partisans, our "comrades at arms" were compelled to recognize the ability of the Jewish company and to change their attitude toward them. The Jewish partisans and the "civilian camp" knew how to set up Mahmad's operation in every situation, and his contributions were always for their benefit.

With the victories of the Red Army and the approaching of the battlefront to our area, many partisans from the otryad joined the army, among them Zev Bronstein, Avraham Merin, Zecharia Viner, Schmuel Lupa,

Avraham Gorodetzer with his two daughters, and many others. All of them died a hero's death in the capture of Konigsberg, Warsaw, and Berlin. (Gorodetzer's two daughters live in Israel.)

Mahmed, too, joined the army and went to the ford at the Bug River, while the Germans continued to hold the city of Kovel, where they had been for several months.

My wife and I settled with partisans in the township of Rafalofka. One day in the train station, I saw Mahmed in a major's uniform of the Red Army. In the forest his rank had been that of captain, even before the war. I ran over to him and called out excitedly, "Mahmed, Mahmed! What a hero of a soldier you are -- already a major!" The officer looked at me in amazement. "Who are you? I don't know you." I apologized. I told him of the strong resemblance between him, the major, and Mahmed the Kavkazi, the captain that was with us as partisans.

The officer did not leave me and asked that I tell him even more about Mahmed. I told him briefly all that I knew of him. "He is my brother," the major cried excitedly, tears welling up in his eyes. "His name isn't Mahmed, it's Melamed. Our family lived in Kavkaz before the war, and he's my twin brother. We assumed that he was no longer living ,and, here, he's alive and goes by the name of Mahmed." We parted with a handshake, <u>shalom aleichem</u> and "God be with you." The Jewish officer Melamed from Kavkaz was forced to conceal his Jewish identity not only from the Germans, but also, and especially, from his comrades at arms -- the Russian partisans.

INTERVIEWS WITH JEWISH PARTISANS

Jack Nusan Porter

Irving Porter (Yisroel Puchtik)

This is an interview with a Jewish partisan leader, my father. Most interviews are carried out with people whom you don't know and with whom it is fairly easy to be objective. However, when you interview your father and when you talk about the destruction of your sisters (daughters) or uncles (brothers), all objectivity in thrown out the window.

It becomes a chronicle of tears and a necessary but painful task. This article is an edited version of an interview that lasted nearly four hours and took place in the living room of our home in Milwaukee, Wisconsin. Several times I had to stop the tape recorder when my father and I broke down into tears. Yet the chronicle continued because he understood how important it was that people, especially young people, know the true story of Jewish resistance during World War II. It was a story that I had to know. As his son, as a young Jew in America, and as a young adult living in this post-Holocaust era, I too had to know.

There are so many myths, falsehoods, and half-truths associated with the Holocaust. One of the most arrogant of these lies is that all Jews were cowards and that they all walked passively to their deaths.

Raul Hilberg in his book The Destruction of the European Jews arrived at the conclusion that "the reaction pattern of the Jews was characterized by the almost complete lack of resistance." Hannah Arendt in her book Eichmann in Jerusalem described Jewish resistance as "pitifully small, incredibly weak and essentially harmless." Psychiatrist Bruno Bettelheim in The Informed Heart pleadingly asked: "Did no one of those destined to die fight back? Did none of them wish to die not by giving in but by asserting themselves in attacking the SS Nazis? Only a very few did."

The myths continue, but what is the truth? Bettelheim says the resistors were "very few" in number; Arendt calls this resistance "pitifully small" and "essentially harmless."

Yet, it was these "very few" who, in the Warsaw Ghetto, held off General Jurgen Stroop and his command of 1000 SS-tank grenadiers, 1000 men of the SS-cavalry, plus two units of artillery for over two months in the spring of 1943, with only a few guns, hand grenades, molotov cocktails, and plenty of Jewish guts.

It was this "essentially harmless" nature of Jewish resistance that forced even Goebbels to admit that "now we know what Jews can do if they have arms."

It was this "pitifully small" number of 25,000 Jewish partisans who fought in the forests and mountains -- of Poland, Russia, Hungary, Czechoslovakia, France, Greece, Belgium, and Italy. Some of them formed autonomous Jewish national units --Jewish partisans led by Jewish commanders. However, most of the partisan bands were mixed groups wherein Jews fought alongside Poles, Russians, Ukrainians, Frenchmen, Italians, and others.

Of the 25,000 partisans, there were a large number of survivors. My father was one of them. Irving Porter (Yisroel Puchtik), called "Zalonka" in the underground, was a leader in the famous "Kruk Division," led by the Ukrainian leader Nikolai Konishchuk (Kruk). They fought from mid-1942 to early 1945 in the vicinity of Manievich, Volynia, Ukraine, U.S.S.R.

This is my father's story. It could well have been the tale of his comrades now residing in America, Canada, or Israel and including such partisans as Dov Lorber (Seattle), Avrum Lerer (Cleveland), Moshe Kramer (Philadelphia), Isaac Avruch (Denver), Moshe Flash (Montreal), and Abba Klurman, Itzik Kuperberg, Vova Verba, Josef Zweibel, Charlie Zarutski, Avrum (Abraham) Puchtik, David Blaustein (Tel Aviv), Avrum and Berl Finkel, and many others.

My father was born in the little town of Horodok in 1906, the same year and a similar shtetl to that of the fictitious Anatevka in the popular Fiddler on the Roof. In fact, after seeing the film I jubilantly asked my father: "It was a great picture, Dad, no?" He punctured my enthusiasm by saying: "Great? That's the way it was. It was no picnic."

We live at a time when our affluence and freedom lead us to glorify and romanticize the European shtetl, but it was nevertheless a hard and dangerous life. My father was one of eight brothers and sisters; his father was a poor shoemaker. After one major upheaval, World War I, he joined the Polish cavalry at the age of 21, one of the few Jews in that Army. After four years there, he worked as a textile worker, saving dowry money for his older sisters.

This delayed his own marriage to his childhood sweetheart Faygeh (Fay) Merin. They finally got married in 1937, two years before the Nazi Blitzkrieg into Poland. He later worked for the Russian Communists in a collective workers' union until 1941. The Germans came to the area in that same year and in 1942 he had to make the painful decision to leave his family, go into the forests, and join the partisans. I was born later in a bombed-out hospital, in Rovno, a small town near Manievich, on December 2, 1944, a few months before the war ended.

This interview deals mainly with the years in the partisans and those soon after the war.

* * * * *

When the Nazis came, I was living in the town of Manievich, a town of 2000, at most 2500 people. They first came in to kill the men; later they came on a Friday night to surprise us and took the women, children, old people, and the few men that remained.

We thought they were going to work camps, but found out that they were marched outside the town, told to dig a big hole, and then the Nazis killed and buried them.

When did you escape?

On Wednesday, two days before they came, I decided to escape. I threw away my jacket with the yellow piece of cloth that all Jews had to wear. I tucked my pants into my boots like a Ukrainian peasant, picked up a pail, and passed by the Ukrainian guards as a farmer -- and then ran into the woods.

The Germans first came in 1941 to take just the men. They killed 375 of them. Later, in the summer of 1942, they came again -- this time pushing women and children into the street.

They drove them out on Friday night. They knew the families were together and they would surprise them. They would kill the Jews, then have an orchestra and a big party, while they took Jewish property. When they finished one job, they'd go on to the next little town.

At this point, I made up my mind that I was not going to go like an animal. I was going to take revenge (<u>nekumah</u> was the word he used). I would run away even thought it meant leaving my family.

On that Friday night in 1942, the Germans killed my two daughters (your sisters), my mother, my father, my four sisters, my grandparents --twenty-five members of my family. (His brothers, Morris, Boris, and Leon, had left home in the 20's and 30's for Chicago and Buenos Aires, Argentina).

How did you feel about leaving your family?

To this day, I feel guilty. I don't feel bad about killing Nazis or taking revenge on the Ukrainians (who collaborated), but I do about leaving my family. Am I no different from my parents or daughters that I lived and they died? No, we are the same. I may not have helped them if I stayed, but at least we would have been together.

What happened after you escaped? Did you find a group of partisans right away?

After I escaped into the woods, I hid for a few weeks, with a Gentile friend -- a Ukrainian who lived in a different town. He gave me a rifle and 150 bullets. A rifle was worth gold; you couldn't pay a million dollars for one!

I told him I was not responsible over myself -- I wanted revenge. My life was worthless. I would burn his house and kill him if he didn't give me a gun. He was scared so he gave me the gun.

I soon found a group of about 50 people who had just two rifles among them. Within three months, this group grew until it included 200 fighters (about 180 Jews and 20 Russians or Poles), 200 men who guarded the others, and between 500-600 women and children. We had a big job -- to find food for nearly 1000 people and to fight the Nazis.

How did mamma escape?

I found her two months after I escaped. When I was with the partisans I asked all the farmers in the area about my family. Did any live? One said that my sister's husband was hiding nearby. I went there, expecting to see a tall man, my brother-in-law, but it turned out to be a "little man" who weighed only 60 pounds.

This "little man" turned out to be my wife. She was so small. She had escaped by hiding in a stall in a nearby barn. The Nazis didn't find her. By a miracle, she was alive. In the partisan camp, she became the chief cook. A miracle! Her whole family was killed. Everyone. She's the only one who survived. I took her in my hands. She was so light.

Why was the leader a non-Jew if most of the group was Jewish?

It was good to have a Gentile as commander because the Jews lived in small towns or big cities. They were tailors, butchers, business people; they didn't know the woods. Our commander, like other Gentiles, knew how to hunt and fight. He knew the woods. Later we wouldn't need him, but at the beginning he was needed.

What did you do in the partisans?

At first, we didn't do too much. But one day, a captain from a Russian partisan group about twenty miles away came over to us. He had done something wrong and his "punishment" was to be sent over to the Jews.

This captain (Mahmed-Melamed) -- who was later found out to be a Jew in disguise -- told us that when the Germans invaded in 1941, they left behind piles of huge artillery shells, which the captain had found and buried. Each shell weighed over 100 pounds and was filled with gunpowder. With this gunpowder, we could make mines.

I was put in charge of this project, along with twenty other men. We carefully took the shells apart so they were no longer dangerous, put them in long barrels, lit fires under the barrels, and heated up this powder to a liquid state. With this liquid, we made mines.

I would go out with a small band of men, and we would place these mines under railroad tracks, water or fuel depots, and bridges, and blow them up. All day long we would sit quietly in the woods; at night we would go out to set mines. There was not too much face-to-face contact with the Germans; we could only slow them up and slow down the trains going to the Russian front.

We got food from the Gentile farmers, whom we threatened to shoot if they didn't give us potatoes, flour, or salt in good will. You must be careful in war. One is bitter and a little crazy. You do many wrong things in order to survive.

During the time of the underground, there is no law. It is like the Old West in America. We had to take food or rifles from the farmers. You had to use the gun to get food, to take his boots.

The farmer had enough food and three pairs of boots, and they probably stole them from the Jews anyway. So we had to use force, even kill a few if they didn't give, or maybe burn their barns. Most of them gave. They were so surprised to see Jews with guns. They were scared of us. They gave.

This is what we did for over two and one half years. We survived.

What happened after the Germans retreated from your area (in late 1944 and early 1945)?

After the war, I worked for the Russians for a little while, but I wanted to leave Russia and go to Israel. I loved the Russian people; they saved many Jewish lives during the war. They even honored me with a medal for heroism.

I got forged passports from the Breicha, the Israeli underground, and began my journey to Palestine. I'll never forget my leaving. I told a Russian officer, maybe he was even a Jew, that I had fought for Russia and now it was time to fight for my own country, for Jews.

He shook my hand and wished me well and then he said: "Puchtik, go in peace, but remember, the Russian boot is a big one; the heel of Russia is here in Moscow, but in twenty years, the toe might be in Palestine." I'll never forget that.

My wife, child and I went by train from Poland to Austria. It took over a month and it is a complete story in itself. We went as Greek citizens and it was a long and dangerous trip. (I understand that the present day exodus from Russia follows a similar route, by rail and the "Chopin Express" from Warsaw to Vienna, but it's much less than a month to travel.)

From Vienna we went to an American displaced persons camp near Linz. There, we waited to go to Israel, but it was going to be a long wait because the British blockade was in operation and the illegal aliyah was starting. My wife was sick and I had a baby boy and the Hagana told us that the trip would be too dangerous for us. They were only taking single people or childless married couples.

In the meantime, we met an American captain who spoke good Russian. He asked me if I had relatives in America. I told him I had a brother, Morris Porter, in Chicago. The American had someone who was going to New York put a picture of me in the Yiddish newspaper --The Daily Forward. My brother saw the picture, got in touch with the Jewish authorities, and sent me money and a boat ticket. I came to American in 1946, first to Chicago, then moved to Milwaukee. I've been here ever since.

I still want to live in Israel, but my children are unmarried. When they get married, I'll move to Israel.

How can you still believe in God after all that's happened to the family?

I can understand if young people don't believe any more in God, but I have reasons not to give up my belief. In fact, unlike some, I believe in God even more now than when I was younger. I saw miracles happen. Ninety-nine percent of the time my life hung on a hair! Bullets would fly all around me, but my body was never touched. Today, I am a strict Orthodox Jew. I don't work on Shabbos or on Jewish holidays.

Now let me ask you a few questions about today's generation of Jews. First, what do you think of the Jewish Defense League?

-227-

They make mistakes, but they do plenty that I like. They should search out and protect Jews. If an old woman is mugged, show the muggers your fist and they won't bother you again. But they should stay out of Israel's politics. They don't need them there. We need them here in America to take care of Jewish enemies.

America needs Kahane more than Israel does. We need protection, self-defense groups, in the parks and in the schools. People are afraid to walk the streets of the city. There's plenty of work for a JDL here in America, but not in Israel. Israel has its own police and army; they don't need the JDL's protection. And give the muggers a fist in the face. They'll think twice.

What can young Jews learn from the Holocaust and the Jewish Resistance?

First, our most bitter lesson is that a Jew can send no one else to take his place. When it comes down to it, no one except a Jew really cares about Jewish problems.

Second, the Holocaust is our history. Young Jews must know their history. They must know their own history before they learn another's.

Third, they must be proud to be a Jew. We must respect every human being; but first of all we must respect ourselves! Our own dignity and our own self-respect must come first!

Reprinted from <u>Davka</u>, Winter-Spring 1973

* * * * *

Moshe Flash and Jack Melamedik

Both Moshe Flash and Jack Melamedik live in Montreal today. Flash (called "Ivan") fought the Nazis from September 1942 to February 1944 and was awarded the "Hero of the Soviet Union" medal. (See Volume I for a picture of Flash and his medal). Melamedik was a young boy during the war and lost both parents and most of his family. He fought under Captain Yanishtikov who

was second in command under Colonel Anton Brinsky
(called Dadya Petya during the war). Dadya Petya was
the Russian commander under whose control were such
groups as Max, Kruk, Kartuchin, and others. These
excerpts of an interview took place in Montreal on
August 28, 1974:

What was it like to join the partisans?

> Flash: Joining the partisans is like a lottery --
> one never knows what life will throw you. The
> important thing is to help your fellow man. We
> had to take revenge against all the killings. But
> we knew nothing about fighting. I was a baker
> before the war. It was Kruk (Nikolai Konishchuk,
> a Uraininian partisan leader) who taught us how
> to fight. He was a mayor of a town there; he knew
> the people; he knew the forests; we needed him at
> first, but not later. He wasn't perfect either.
> He shot a Jew once.

> Melamedik: We (Jewish fighters) made Kruk into
> what he was.

After all the killing and all that you saw, do you
still believe in God?

> Flash: I don't believe in "gott" (God).

> Melamedik: I believe in something or someone that
> guides us. I still believe because I survived.
> It was like a miracle.

> Flash: You can't believe in God after seeing
> young babies shot in the mouth. I'm saying that I
> believe in Judaism, in the Jewish people, and in
> Israel, but not in God. Because of God, many Jews
> died. The religiously orthodox Jews kept the
> people from fighting. They told us we were guilty
> of something so that we were being punished. They
> told Jews not to fight. The religious leaders
> kept a strong hold on the people. I respect them
> today but I do not respect the religion. I go to
> shul (synagogue) for the sake of the family, for
> yahrtzeit (memorial services for the dead) ... not
> to pray to God but for the sake of the memory of
> my family. A partisan was a hefker mensch
> (Yiddish term): he did not care about anything.
> The Jews became partisans to take revenge and to
> save lives -- no politics, no ideology, no

-229-

nothing. God was on vacation, but I didn't have
time for a vacation then. A young Jew must learn
to give a patch (Yiddish for a "blow") to those
who wish to harm us. I admire (Rabbi Meir) Kahane
of the JDL for this. But I don't know. Your
father (referring to Jack Nusan Porter's father)
came from a religious family and he sat at a
Yiddish tish (a "Jewish table"), but I was an
orphan and I never had a good Jewish education.
Maybe if I did I would believe in God today like
your father. (See prior interview with my
father.)

* * * * *

Morris (Moshe) Kramer

Morris Kramer fought in the Kruk otryad (fighting
unit) together with my father. They were very close
friends both during and after the war, when my father
and mother lived im Milwaukee and Moshe Kramer lived in
Philadelphia, where he still lives with his second
wife, Sophie, and his two children. Kramer's first
wife was also in the forests, active in the "family
camp" and she had a child who died in the woods. His
first wife was killed in a tragic accident in
Philadelphia. The interview was carried out in his
home in Philadelphia on October 15-16, 1981, but will
have to wait for another time to be published.

Faygeh Merin Puchtik (Faye Porter)

As can be imagined, interviewing one's own mother
is very difficult, especially concerning the deaths of
her two daughters (my sisters) but here it is. My
father is referred to by several names: Tateh (dad in
Yiddish), Srulik, or Yisroel Puchtik. Compare this
account with several others in the book. The interview
took place in November, 1981 in Boston.

Could you please describe our family's social status
before the war?

My father and mother and all my brothers and
sisters were religious people. I had four sisters
and four brothers; there were sixteen grandchildren and even one great grandchild. I grew up

-230-

in Horodok, a small town near Manievich, Ukraine, until 1939. We were middle-class. My father Nusan Merin was a teacher before World War I; after the war he had a flax and wool machinery shop, but later, together with my brothers, we built a vegetable oil manufacturing firm. We weren't poor but we weren't rich either. My mother Beyla Merin (nee Singerman) was a housewife.

You grew up in a shtetl?

Yes, it was a little shtetl, a town, Horodok, of about 500 people, Ukrainians and Jews. Until 1939. Erev Yom Kippur (the evening of the High Holy Day) in September 1939, the Soviet Army came, and they wanted to surround the Polish Army which was based in Horodok. But first they sent planes to drop leaflets asking for their surrender. The Polish Army said no so the Soviets later came with twenty-five planes and bombed the Polish Army camp, and all the houses, and killed many people. We escaped through a window and fled to the safety of the forests. The next day we returned. Everything was ashes. The only thing alive were the cows, waiting in the fields for us. So we had milk. We sold the cows for clothes and money and moved away to Manievich. I was then living with my husband, Yisroel (Srulik) Puchtik and my parents.

When were you married?

We were married in 1937. We had two children, one daughter Chaya Udel, two years old, and Pesel, born later in Manievich.

Could you describe them? Did they look like (my son) Gabriel?

No. The oldest one looked like you; the other one like Shlomo (my brother -- JNP). They were both dark, brown-haired but with a light skin. The oldest was dark; the youngest light, but with dark hair and dark eyes.

Were they cute?

Don't ask me too much, please.

Did you encounter anti-Semitism before World War II?

> Oh yes, from the Ukrainians. They were
> anti-Semitic. We had a baker once who lived next
> door to us. He used to bake white bread and
> challah. One day, a Ukrainian told me: "If I
> could kill this Jew, I'd kill him." No reason.
> Just like that.

Any other experience with you or Tateh?

> Altogether, no. Tateh had good relations with all
> the Ukrainians. They liked him. He was friendly
> with them. For example, when they needed a
> "peckel michorkeh" (small packet of smoking or
> chewing tobacco), he would get it for them. Maybe
> we were an exception but we had good relations
> with the Ukrainians.

Let's move on to another issue. When war became
imminent, what options were open to you and your
family? What did you do in response to the coming war?

> I understand the question. When the war started,
> the Soviets were pushed back by the Germans, and
> when the Germans started bombing the railroads
> near our town, I said to my husband: "Srulik,
> let's rent a horse and wagon and follow the Rus-
> sians in their retreat. Let's get out of here."
> So I went to Berl Bronstein (see his memoir in
> this book) and said: "Berl, you have horses and a
> wagon, let's go away." But he said no we
> shouldn't go.
>
> Right away, the Russians started mobilizing
> people for the war effort and they came for my
> husband because he had once been in the Polish
> Army as a "Cavalryist", a member of the Polish
> Cavalry and he knew about horses. So they wanted
> to put him on a train which carried horses.
>
> It was a mixed-up crazy situation. We didn't
> know what to do. My mother- and father-in-law
> (Srulik's parents) said to Srulik: "You're going
> and leaving us alone? and your wife and children,
> too?" So, he felt very guilty and left the hor-
> ses, and the train went away without him. It was
> later bombed by the Germans and many people and
> horses died. So, my husband stayed with us. I
> guess, in a way, he was lucky he didn't go on that
> train.

How old were you when the war broke out?

> I was twenty-eight years old and had been married only one year.

How did news of the war first reach you?

> By radio and newspaper.

Polish newspapers?

> No, we had a Jewish magazine (a Yiddish magazine). It was called, I think, the <u>Tog-Morgen Journal</u>. We found out what was going on from that.

What was the first change that occurred in your job, your home life, or social life because of the war?

> When the Germans arrived, the most important change was that they didn't allow us to slaughter cattle anymore. They said we Jews were "punishing" the cattle, "hurting" them. No <u>shochet</u> (ritual slaughter) was allowed to kill even one chicken.

What about your school or job?

> I didn't have a job and I didn't go to school. I was a full-time mother and housewife.

Was your religious life disrupted?

> From 1939 until September 1942, we had our <u>shul</u> (synagogue) and a full religious life -- rabbis, services. Only in September 1942 was it disrupted.

And your social life?

> Oh, what kind of a social life. What a question.

So, what did you do day to day?

> It was a sad life. We just stayed home. We couldn't go out. We had to wear these yellow patches on our clothes (to mark them as Jews). From the beginning we had a white strap with a <u>magen david</u> (Star of David) on it. Then, they made us take off the white straps and we put on yellow patches of cloth -- eighteen inches in

-233-

front and eighteen inches in back . . . and a
fifteen-inch yellow patch on every Jewish house.
This was in Manievich.

When did the patches start?

Right from the start of the German occupation,
September 1939.

And your possessions?

They gave permission to the Ukrainians for three
days to rob the Jews. For three days. Like an
open market. The pillows, the sheets, everything.
They came and took it all away.

And what could you do?

Nothing. Nothing at all. They laid us out on the
floor and came in and took whatever they wanted.
And we had no ammunition to fight them off.

Did you think that this was the end of the world, of
your lives? What was in your mind to do?

(Sadly, with head bowed.) We didn't know what to
do.

Did you have a feeling that the Holocaust, that the
killings, were coming?

We had a feeling that things were going to get
worse but we didn't think it was going to be such
a Holocaust. We didn't believe that because we
knew from the Germans during World War I that bad
things might happen but they didn't kill us back
then. We didn't think they would kill us all now.

What about the Manievich ghetto? Who were the leaders?

We had a Judenrat (a ghetto leadership) set up in
the summer of 1940. They were high-class people,
many newcomers from Poland, teachers, educated
people. The first thing the Nazis asked the
Judenrat to do was collect fur coats, gold,
silver, jewelry as "contributions" for the Third
Reich. There were about 2000 people crushed into
Manievich by then.

Were you surrounded by soldiers?

No.

So, it was easy to escape?

Yes, but you had to wear the yellow patch. If you were caught without a patch .... My brother Zisya was caught without a patch one day. He was taken to the police station and beaten black and blue. I don't know how he survived.

How did you get food?

You couldn't go outside the town, and you couldn't buy food openly from Gentiles. But some people hid clothes and jewelry and exchanged them for food. There was a lot of underground smuggling.

And what did Tateh do?

When he found out that the Nazis would take men "out to work" (meaning to kill them -- JNP), he ran away to Horodok, a small town about eight kilometers away, and I was left in Manievich with the family. He ran away eight days before they took all the men to a place called Ferdishe Mogiles (Horses' Graves), a field outside of town, and killed all the men. That was in late summer 1941, the third of Elul, 1941. This was the first "action", killing the men.

And the second action? (The second action was where they killed the remaining women, children, and any other men still alive. My two young sisters were killed in this action).

The second "action" took place around September 23, 1942, about a year later. Some men, like my father, were still in hiding. The Germans, SS, searched for men, including Tateh but didn't find them. Tateh heard about the action that very same night, and he went into hiding in Horodok. They killed all the men -- Judenrat leaders, rabbis, anyone they could find.

How did they kill them?

They lied to them, said they were going to work. They collected them in a kind of dormitory or auditorium first. I saw them take the men out of the houses and collect them in this dormitory.

-235-

That's all I saw. Then, they put them on trucks and took them outside the town to a field where pits had already been dug. They forced the Ukrainian peasants to dig the pits. They took Tateh's father (Yankel Puchtik), my brothers Zisya and Yankel, Yehuda Merin's father, and many, many others.

And so they took them out to Ferdishe Mogiles, lined them up, and shot them?

Yes.

Did the men know what was to happen to them?

No. (Long silence)

Did they have to dig their own graves?

Some peasants told us later that they had to dig their own graves in some cases, but pits were dug already by the Ukrainians.

So, they lined them up, killed them, covered them with dirt and lime, and then went onto the next town?

Yes. (Deep silence)

Was there any resistance?

No. Yes, Yehuda Merin's brother-in-law (his sister's husband) fought back before they shot him. There may have been others too but I don't know.

And what happened to Tateh?

They liked him in Horodok. He was a good shoemaker. Even the mayor of Horodok liked him and prepared special papers for him to stay, stating that we was needed in Horodok. The mayor even got permission for us to leave Manievich and rejoin Tateh in Horodok. There we were re-united. The Laniz family was there; so too the Nesanel family. (My mother then tells me the story of how the two Nesanel boys, age eighteen and twenty, were killed by a Ukrainian policeman and several others. The boys were taken out to a field, told to dig their own graves, and shot for breaking the

curfew for Jews. They were out too late at night.
Before he shot them, the policeman said: "So, you
were trying to run away and join the partisans,
eh?")

Did you know the name of the policeman -- or the
peasants -- or anyone who did this?

No. The farmers were good people by and large but
their sons became Nazis. Uneducated, stupid boys.
The Nazis said shoot people; they shot people.
Just followed orders. Most were Ukrainian
nationalists, Banderovsty-types.

Did any Ukrainians try to stop this action or even
question it?

I don't think so. Maybe some but it happened so
fast. I think though we should have asked them
for help, but we didn't. They might have saved
some Jewish men if we had asked but we didn't ask.
That was stupid of us (as Jews) -- we didn't ask.
We could have done something ....

What happened later?

We worked in Horodok for a while. Then one day, a
Ukrainian commandant and police (no Nazis) came
and said to take all our things, that we were
going back to Manievich, all three families, the
Puchtiks, Laniz's, and Nesanel's. We knew then
that this was the end. We were going to die.

They drove us from Horodok on trucks. We
wanted to jump from the truck, but your father's
mother, Yenta, said no. So, first they took us to
a jail, all three families in a little room, and
we stayed there overnight. The Judenrat heard we
were in jail and got us out. They took Tateh to
work packing hay, very hard labor. Your father
asked the Nazis: "What will happen to us?" and
the German said: "Der Besteh Jude vil zein der
lesteh" (The best Jew will be the last to go). He
worked in the hay fields for two weeks.

Then, on Wednesday, September 20, 1942, the
police surrounded the entire town and said they
were making a ghetto and started pushing people
into one street. The Tateh said -- "No, I'm not
staying. Enough already. I'm going to try to

-237-

escape." He took off his yellow patch, in fact his whole jacket, and said: "Fayge, should I go?", and I said: "Srulik, do what you want. It's up to you."

He went through the police lines disguised as a Ukrainian farmer and fled past a church. A Polish priest saw him and said: "Are you running away from the devil? The devil will catch you!". He saw that Srulik was a Jew because he looked frightened, but luckily nobody else recognized him. He went into the forest, to Slovik's house, and Slovik, a good man, hid him. I too went and took both children to a Polish neighbor and begged her to help me, but she said it was too dangerous. "Go to the barn and hide there". I decided to return to my parent's house.

After Slovik hid him, Srulik walked back to Horodok and went into hiding. The Ukrainians, even the mayor, couldn't help him anymore. It was just too dangerous so he hid in a Jewish cemetery, slept there, and begged for food at night.

On Saturday evening, September 23, 1942, some Ukrainian friends of his came to the cemetery and told him: "There is no one left alive in Manievich. They are all dead." The Tateh started to cry. He went to a friend Ivan, a sympathetic Ukrainian, and said to Ivan: "Give me a gun. I know you have arms. Let me go and take revenge". Ivan gave him a rifle, 150 bullets, and two grenades. He wished him well and my father left; he went into the forests to join the partisans.

Ivan trusted Tateh so much he gave him the ammunition. Ivan also told him another Jew Abraham Lerer was also hiding somewhere in an abandoned house in the woods. So Tateh went to find his friend Lerer. They hugged and cried. "Now we have to look for others and form a fighting group. We can't stay here any longer." Some Ukrainian friends helped them find Kruk (Nikolai Konishchuk, leader of the Kruk Fighting Group) and others from the towns of Griva and Lishnivka.

Who was in that group that's alive today or who I know?

In this group were the Avruch's, the Zweibels, Vova (Zvi) Verba, the Wolpers, the Blausteins,

Abba Klurman, Sasha (Charlie) Zarutski, the Zaicheks, and others.

So most of the people who escaped and joined the partisans survived? Isn't there a lesson in this?

Yes, if more would have tried to escape, they'd be alive today. You had a much better chance to survive fighting with the partisans. But people were afraid; some didn't want to go into the forests (it was a hard life); and many didn't want to leave their families. Better to stay together in the ghetto.

And what of the rabbis? What was their role?

I'm afraid the rabbis were not much help. Some said it was God's will; most shook their head and did nothing; but a few warned us to leave and to fight. One of them, the Tateh's rebbe said: "Yidn, escape to Russia", but few of us listened.

Were there any other stories you failed to tell me?

Yes, there are a few that I remember well. On Wednesday, when the Germans surrounded the shtetl, Senkeh Melamedik, Jack Melamedik's father, tried to spring over a fence and escape. In that minute, a Ukrainian policeman shot him on the spot. Senkeh was thirty-five years old; Jack was only ten. Chunek Wolper saw it.

My sister Elka, thirty-six years old, had a son, a nice boy by the name of Chunah. He was on his way to work at the parquet (wood) factory. He saw a Ukrainian policeman; he got scared and started running; the policeman shot him. He was only seventeen years old. That was Wednesday, September 20, 1942, a few days before the second action.

Elka's husband, Mordechai Wool, was another example. They lived in a Ukrainian village, Nova Ruda. The police came one day and said to him: "You're a Communist; we have to take you away." They tied him to a wagon and dragged him on the ground for a half a mile. He died. Elka and her four kids ran away into the woods. Her young son, Shlomo Wool, got so sick in the stomach from the shock the doctors had to come and apply leeches to his body.

-239-

The mayor of Nova Ruda, a good man and a Ukrainian, brought her and her children to Manievich at our request. That was a big mistake. She should have stayed in the woods hiding. She might be alive today if she had.

Now, _Momeh_, let's go to your story ....

On Wednesday, September 20, 1942, the Germans made a strict ghetto, and on Friday afternoon, they went from house to house, shouting at us to come out and go to the road, about 300-400 of us, and we saw that this was the end. Everyone started crying and praying "Shma Yisroel" (Hebrew prayer for "Hear O' Israel").

They took us over a railroad track and shoved us into the street and packed us into houses on that street. We didn't know what to do. I was with my sisters Elka and Rivkeh and my two little daughters, Chaya Udel and Pesel.

I noticed that one woman in the crowd had sleeping pills, and I saw her give her child one so she could escape (without the child crying). It was evening and escape was still possible. But she wouldn't give me a pill. It didn't help. Her child awoke anyway.

I said to the people let's make a fire and burn down the ghetto and escape, but they didn't listen to me. We knew we would be killed the very next day, Saturday. Still, they wouldn't believe me.

So, I told my sister Rivkeh that I was going to Velvel Bronstein and Pesel Librant-Bronstein, to their home. (See Pesel's memoir in this book). I went outside but I was afraid. I didn't go back to the house. Instead, I remembered what the Polish lady told me and I went to the barn. I sat in a corner all night Friday and all day Saturday, in the barn, near the hay. I didn't even cover myself, just sat in the corner alone.

And what was your purpose for doing this?

I don't know. I didn't know what to do. But early in the morning on Sunday, I saw Pessel hiding too, and I said: "This is Faygeh. Show me

where you are." And they showed me and I climbed
into, like an attic in a house near the barn, and
there was Pesel, Velvel, and their four children.
It was getting lighter all the time, and the
Ukrainian police were looking for us. I saw them
but they didn't see me. I said we better escape
or they'll come back and find us. So all of us
crawled maybe two blocks over the railroad track
on our hands and knees and came into the forests.
We sat and rested and then went to the forester
Slovik. Slovik helped us to hide just like he
helped Tateh. It was raining. We had no food, no
good shelter, and the lice were all over us. It
was terrible.

A couple days later, three boys (Vova Verba
and two others) from Kruk's group came and told me
that my husband was still alive. I begged them to
take me to him. But it wasn't easy. On the way,
some police started shooting at us, but eventually
we came upon a group of twenty-five young people,
armed with only one short rifle. They welcomed
us. They even had food. I weighed maybe 75-80
pounds. The group had no name. It was outside
the town of Lishnivka.

In a few days, the Tateh came with Kruk,
David Blaustein, and several others. And he found
me. The feeling was overwhelming. We hugged and
cried. But I felt like falling into a grave. I
was so ashamed to be alive.

Did you feel guilty about leaving your two daughters?

Yes, very guilty. Even the Tateh felt guilty
that he had left me, his children, and mother and
father; and I felt guilty for leaving my family.

But, why did you leave your daughters and hide in the
barn?

Oh, I only left to see Bronstein and Pesel. I
wanted to go back home, but there were police
everywhere. I couldn't go back. (Long Pause)
.... That's what God planned for me ....

I eventually joined the Kruk Partisan Group.
However, just two days later, the Nazis and
Ukrainians came to the woods and found us. Chunek
Wolper however saw them and fired at them. They

-241-

opened up such a fire on us. When we heard the
first round, we scattered everywhere. Later we
regrouped and continued the hard partisan life.

And my two little sisters?

You know, Yankele, what happened. Why do you ask?
They were taken out on <u>Shabbos</u> (Saturday), taken
outside the town, only four years old and two, and
... I can't speak anymore.

Editor's Notes

1. This was the term used by the Germans to denote the mass killings of the Jews -- usually men first, the leadership of the ghetto and those able to give the most resistance. The German spelling is "aktion".

2. This was an area, a field really, outside Manievich where horses were buried. Today it is a military cemetery. The editor's family was killed and buried there.

3. This is Jack Nusan Porter's mother. The original name was Puchtik. Today, Faye Porter lives in Milwaukee, Wisconsin. Her husband was Irving Porter (Yisroel Puchtik, known as Zalonka). She is also a cousin to Yehuda Merin.

4. Today, he is alive and living in Tel Aviv, Israel and is a relative to both editors of this book.

5. These are underground bunkers built in the woods to hide the partisans and their belongings.

6. "Daven" means praying in Hebrew; "minyan" is a religious quorum of ten men.

7. "Chametz" means unleavened bread, forbidden on Passover.

8. The Banderovtzy were Ukrainian nationalist gangs, feared by Jews, Poles, and Communists alike.

9. An _otryad_ is a Russian term for a partisan fighting force, often named after its leader.

10. Atlit is a small seaport in Israel and a prison camp. This story itself should be expanded since this is part of the history of the illegal immi-

gration by Jews into Palestine, then ruled by Great Britain.

11. The 22nd day of Elul, 5712 is the Hebrew calendar day for September 21, 1942.

12. Kruk is the nom de guerre for the controversial Ukrainian leader of the partisan fighting group described in these pages, Nikolai Konischuk.

13. Slovik is the family of father Yazenty and his son Casimir, Polish foresters and farmers, who saved several Jewish lives during the "action" in and around Manievich. He saved the life of the mother of the Jack Nusan Porter.

14. It was getting too "hot to handle" for these Russian (Dadya Petya -- Anton Brinsky), Polish (Max -- Jozef Sobiezek), and Ukrainian (Kartuchin and Kruk) leaders. Too many collaborators were being executed and it was becoming too prickly an issue politically.

15. Blaustein was probably too much of a "Zionist" for the authorities to tolerate. The "escape" was the Breicha organization, which helped people emigrate to Israel.

16. Ethnic Germans living in the Soviet Union, Poland, Ukraine, and other areas.

17. The masses of Jews were killed in "actions" from May to October 1942.

18. From the Hebrew term for benevolent Gentiles, non-Jews that treated Jews kindly.

19. The 19th of Elul corresponds to the third week of September in the Hebrew calendar, in 1942, the time of the mass killings (the "action") of the Jews in this town.

20. In Hebrew there is a play on the word "Karah". This pun is an example of the black humor that developed among the partisans, as, usually, one would see "Zeh Karah," meaning, "This happened," and here we hear "Karah," but the meaning is "tore apart." (Ann Abrams, Hebrew translator).

21. Breicha movement -- the movement to rescue Jews from Europe to go to Israel.

22. A group of friendly partisans led by A. P. Feodorov.

23. From the Yom Kippur prayer "who shall die by strangulation."

24. Mourners' prayer for the dead.

25. Probably a displaced person (DP) refugee camp.

26. The Jewish community in Israel.

ANNOTATED
BIBLIOGRAPHY

ANNOTATED BIBLIOGRAPHY

A. Books (English)

Ainsztein, Reuben, Jewish Resistance in Nazi-Occupied
     Eastern Europe, New York: Barnes and Noble
     (Harper and Row), 1974. One of the finest books
     on the subject; see especially pp. 353-360 and
     389-393 for information relevant to this book.

Armstrong, John A. (ed.) Soviet Partisans in World
     War II, Madison, Wisconsin: University of
     Wisconsin Press, 1964. While Jewish participation
     is often overlooked, this is still a most valuable
     compilation of articles on the military and poli-
     tical role of the Soviet partisans during the war.

Barkai, Meyer (ed.), The Fighting Ghettos, Philadel
     phia, J. P. Lippincott, 1962; New York: Tower
     Publications, 1962.

Bartoszewski, Wladyslaw and Zofia Lewin, The Samaritan:
     Heroes of the Holocaust, New York: Twayne, 1970.
     Accounts of Poles who risked their lives to save
     Jews from death during the Nazi occupation.

They Chose Life -- Jewish Resistance in the Holocaust,
     New York: American Jewish Committee, 1973.

Eckman, Lester and Chaim Lazar, The Jewish Resistance,
     The History of the Jewish Partisans in Lithuania
     and White Russia under Nazi Occupation, 1940-1945,
     New York: Shengold, 1977.

Foxman, Abraham, H., "Resistance -- The Few Against the
     Many" in Judah Pilch (ed.) The Jewish Catastrophe
     in Europe, New York: American Association for
     Jewish Education, 1968. Not only was this one of
     the first comprehensive accounts of resistance

-249-

written for students, but the entire book is an
excellent classroom tool.

Friedman, Phillip, Their Brother's Keepers, New
    York: Shocken Books, 1978; Crown, 1957. A moving
    account of the Christian heroes and heroines who
    helped Jews during the war. For a section rele-
    vant to this book, see pp. 130-142, dealing with
    the Ukraine, Latvia, Estonia, and Byelorussia.

Guttman, Yisrael, The Holocaust and Resistance,
    Jerusalem: Yad Vashem; see also Yisrael Guttman
    and Efraim Zuroff (eds.), Rescue Attempts During
    the Holocaust, New York: KTAV, 1979.

Kowalski, Isaac, A Secret Press in Nazi Europe,
    New York: Shengold, 1969, 1972, 1978.

Porter, Jack Nusan (ed.) Jewish Partisans:
    Jewish Resistance in Eastern Europe During World
    War II, Lanham, MD: University Press of America,
    1982. Memoirs of non-Jewish Russian and Ukrainian
    army officers, telling of the bravery of their
    Jewish soldiers and partisans. This is based on
    original Russian and Polish sources and is the
    English version on Binyamin West's Hebrew version.
    Two volumes.

Prager, Moshe, Sparks of Glory, New York:
    Shengold, 1974. Inspiring tales of the often
    overlooked role of Orthodox rabbis and Jews during
    the Holocaust.

Samuels, Gertrude, Mottele, New York: Signet,
    1976. A good book for children based on true epi-
    sodes in the lives of Jewish partisans in Russia
    and Poland told through the story of a young boy
    who joins them in their struggle.

Shabbetai, K. As Sheep to Slaughter?, New York:
    World Association of Bergen-Belsen Survivors,
    1963. A short booklet aimed at discrediting the
    myth of Jewish cowardice.

Stadler, Bea, The Holocaust: A History of
    Courage and Resistance, New York: ADL/Behrman
    House, 1974. Another book on the subject geared
    to young people.

Suhl, Yuri (ed.), They Fought Back: The Story of
    the Jewish Resistance in Nazi Europe, New York:

Schocken Books, 1975. A wide-ranging collection
of resistance on many fronts and in many
countries. One of the best collections around.

Tenenbaum, Joseph, Underground: The Story of a
People, New York: Philosophical Library, 1957.
An early, popular historical account of Jewish
resistance in Eastern Europe.

B. Books (Hebrew and Yiddish)

Granatstein, Yehiel and Moshe Kahanovich, Lexicon
Ha-gevurah (Biographical Dictionary of Jewish
Resistance), Jerusalem: Yad Vashem, 1965, Volume
1, parts 1 and 2. A compilation of names and pic-
tures of Jewish partisans and other fighters in
the western Soviet territory.

Kahanovitch, Moshe, Der Idisher Onteyl in der
Partizaner Bavegung fun Soviet Rusland, Rome,
1948.

_____, Di Milkhome fun di Yishishe
Partizaner in Mizrakh-Eyrope, Two volumes, Buenos
Aires, 1956.

_____, Milchemet Ha-Partizanim
Ha-Yehudim B'Mizrach Europa (The Jewish Fighting
Partisans in Eastern Europe), Tel Aviv: Ayanot
Publishers, 1954. These three books are basically
the same, some are abridged versions, either in
Yiddish or Hebrew, of the role of Jewish
partisans. They are probably the best and most
comprehensive books on these fighting forces in
Hebrew and Yiddish and should be translated into
English one day.

Livneh, Natan (ed.), K'Oranim Gavahu: Partizanim
Yehudaim B'Yaarot Volyn (Like Pines They Grew:
Jewish Partisans in the Forests of Volyn,
Givatayim, Israel and New York: World Union of
Volynian Jews in Israel and in the USA, 1980.

Kantarowicz, N., Di Yidishe vidershtand-bavegung
in Polin, (The Jewish Counter-Movement in
Poland), New York, 1967.

West, Binyamin, (ed.), Heym Hayu Rabim: Partizanim
    Yehudim B'brit Hamoazot B'milchemet-Haolam
    Hashniya (They Were Many: Jewish Partisans in
    the Soviet Union During the Second World War), Tel
    Aviv: Labor Archives Press, 1968. This is a very
    rare collection of memoirs of Jewish partisans in
    Russia written by non-Jewish Soviet army and par-
    tisan commanders. See also Porter, op. cit. for
    the English version.

C. Books (Russian and Polish)

Begma, Vasilii and Luka Kyzya, Shlyakhy Neskorenykh,
    (The Paths of the Unsubjugated), Kiev, 1962. An
    important partisan memoir, Begma was commander of
    one of the major roving bands and since the war
    has occupied key posts in the Communist party in
    the Ukraine.

Brinsky, Anton P., Po etu storonu fronta (On that Side
    of the Front: Memoir of a Partisan), Moscow,
    1958. An important account by one of the leaders
    of organizing teams sent by the Russian Central
    Command to organize and revive the partisan move-
    ment in West Byelorussia and later to the West
    Ukraine. He was called "Dadya Petya" in this
    book.

Feodorov, A.P., Podpolni obkom deistvuyet (The
    Underground Obkom in Action), 2 vols. Moscow,
    1947, plus later editions in 1950 and 1957. An
    English translation appeared as The Underground
    Committee Carries On, Moscow: Foreign Languages
    Publishing House, 1952. Valuable memoirs since
    Feodorov was a high-ranking official of the
    Communist Party of the Ukraine as well as a major
    partisan leader.

Glieder, Mikhail, S. Kinoapparatom v tylu vraga (With a
    Motion Picture Camera in the Rear of the Enemy),
    Moscow: Goskinoizdat, 1947. Written by a Jewish
    cameraman working alongside the partisans, this is
    an interesting account of partisan sidelights and
    partisan propaganda in the Ukraine. Several par-
    tisan films, including those of Jews, were made
    and are found in Russian archives. Hopefully,
    they will be brought to the attention of English-

speaking countries one day. See his account in
Volume I.

Kisilen, K.B., Zapiski Sovetskogo Diplomata, Moscow:
Politizdat, 1971.

Kovpak, Sidor, Ot Putivlya do Karpat (From Putivl to
the Carpathians), Ed. by E. Gerasimov, Moscow,
1945. English version: Our Partisan Course,
London: Hutchinson, 1947. Kovpak was one of the
most famous partisan leaders, respected by many
Jews as well, and his is a fairly accurate account
of military action though not very revealing on
political affairs.

Linkov, Gregory, Voina v tylu vraga (The War in the
Rear of the Enemy), Moscow, 1951, 1959. Linkov
was an engineer and important Communist Party
official who organized and led one of the parachu-
tist detachments that played such an important
role in reactivating the partisan movement in
Byelorussia in 1941-42. He was well-liked and
admired by Jewish partisans, and he spoke well of
them too.

Sobiezek, Jozef and Ryszard Jegorow, Ziemla Plonie
(The Earth is Burning), Warsaw, MON, 1963.

_____, Burzany (Wild Weeds), Warsaw: MON,
1964.

_____, Brygada Grunwald (The Grunwald
Brigade), Warsaw: MON 1964.

_____, Przebraze, Waraw, MON, 1964.
Sobiezek, called Max or Maks, was the well-known
partisan leader in the western Ukraine who made it
a point to save as many Jewish lives as possible.
A man well-respected in Jewish partisan circles,
today he is a Polish rear-admiral. He worked closely with the Kruk Detachment under Nikolai
Konishchuk, a Ukrainian partisan leader also
friendly to Jews.

Strokach, Timofei, Partyzany Ukrainy (The Partisans of
the Ukraine), Moscow, 1943. Strokach was a promin-
ient NKVD official and Chief of the Ukrainian
Staff of the Partisan Movement.

Torzecki, Ryszard, _Kwestia Ukrainska w Polityce III Rzeszy (1933-1945)_, Warsaw: Ksiazka i Wiedza, 1972.

Vorshigura, Pavlo, _Lyudi s chistoi sovestuy_ (_People With a Clear Conscience_), Moscow: Sovetskii Pisatel, 1951. Vorshigura was a motion picture director in Kiev before the war and an aide to Commander Kovpak. He later commanded a roving band himself. He too was sympathetic to the Jewish plight.

_____, _Reid na San i Vislu_ (_The Raid on the San and the Vistula_) Moscow, 1960. Deals with his operations in Volynia and Poland and is especially revealing on Soviet attitudes toward Communism in Poland.

D. Other Languages:

Darashczuk, Dymytrii, _Die Ukraina und das Reich_, Leipzig: Verlag Hans Hirzel, 1941.

Iankyvsky, Kost, _Roky Nimetskoi Okupacii_, New York and Toronto, 1965.

Ilnytskyi, Roman, _Deutschland und die Ukraine 1934-1945_, Munich: Osteuropa Institut, 1958.

Liebrandt, George, _Ukraine_, Berlin: Verlag Otto Stolberg, 1942.

E. Articles

Fein, Barbara, "Not to Go as an Animal", _Wisconsin Jewish Chronicle_, May 5, 1971. A moving account of Irving Porter (Yisrael Puchtik), a partisan leader in the Kruk Detachment in Volynia -- his escape, military exploits, and after-thoughts on the struggle.

Janz, William, "Say Shalom to One Who Fought Dearly", _Milwaukee Sentinel_, March 21, 1979, pp. 5-6. Another account, written on the death of Irving

Porter, on his life with the Ukrainian and Russian
partisans. See also "One Who Fought Back:,
Wisconsin Jewish Chronicle, April 19, 1979, p. 9.

Kahanowitz, Moshe, "Why No Separate Jewish Partisan
Movement was Established During World War II", Yad
Vashem Studies, Vol. 1, Jerusalem, 1957. A good
analysis of the political and military factors
that led to the disbanding of strictly Jewish
groups and their merging into the general partisan
movement in Russia.

Konishchuk, Nikolai, They were Many, in Binyamin West,
(ed.), Heym Hayu Rabim, op. cit., pp. 143-147. A
short description of the Jews who fought in the
Kruk Detachment under the author's command.

Porter, Jack Nusan, Four-part series on the Holocaust
and resistance, in the Wisconsin Jewish Chronicle,
Dec. 1, Dec. 15, Dec. 22, and Dec. 29, 1972.

_____, Zalonka: An Interview with a
Jewish Partisan Leader in Davka, 3,2,
Winter-Spring, 1973, pp. 14-20. Jack Porter
interviews his father Irving Porter (called
"Zalonka" in the underground).

_____, Jewish Women in the Resistance:,
Women's American ORT Reporter, Nov.-Dec. 1978, pp.
7-8

_____, Some Social-Psychological Aspects
of the Holocaust in Bryon Sherwin and Susan Ament
(eds.), Encountering the Holocaust: An
Interdisciplinary Survey, New York: Hebrew
Publishing Company and Chicago: Impact Press,
1979, pp. 189-222. Treats the impact of the
Holocaust on the survivors and their children
regarding both psychological and social responses
to the traumatic events.

Shuelevitz, I. I. "Der Yichus Fun Dem Futer", Jewish
Forward (NYC), Shabbat, January 13, 1973. Another
account of the life of Irving Porter in the Kruk
Detachment including the role played by Porter's
wife, Faye Merin Porter. Also contains a picture
of Porter and his family.

F. Other Sources

Litopysets (psuedonym), Ukrailntsy ta Shydy (Kilka Zamitok po Shydiwskii Spravi), Lvov, 1937.

General Tokarzewski do Gen. Sosnkowski e go, Ammja Krajowa W Dokukmentach, Sept. 1, 1940.

Ulas Samchuk, Zanymem Mista, Lutsk, 1941, Volyn", No.1, Str. 2.

Der Chef Der Sicherheitspolizei und des SD, Berlin Ereignissimeldung, UD, SSP, No. 100 -- Oct. 1, 1941; No. 187 -- Mozz 30, 1942. Meld (No. 4).

Szymon Datner, "Zydowski Ruch Oporu We Wschodniej Europie W Czasie Okupacju Hitlerowskiej; (O Pracy R. Ainsztein)", Biuletyn Zydowskiego Instytutu -- Historycznego W Polsce, Warsaw: Jan.-March, 1976, No. 1 (97).

* * * * *

I am grateful to the following sources for this bibliography: Canadian Jewish Congress, National Holocaust Remembrance Committee, The Holocaust: An Annotated Bibliography, Montreal, Canada, Jan. 1980: and John A. Armstrong (ed.) Soviet Partisans In World War II, University of Wisconsin Press, 1964, bibliography on Soviet publications on anti-Nazi resistance, pp. 770-777.

Compiled by Jack Nusan Porter and Yehuda Merin

PHOTOGRAPHS
AND MAPS

Yisroel Puchtik and his wife Faygeh Merin Puchtik
(Porter) and their infant son Nusan Yankel,
now Dr. Jack Nusan Porter.

Nikolai Konishchuk,
Ukrainian leader of Kruk Group

Captain Jozef Sobiezek,
Polish leader of the Max Group

Polkovnik Anton Brinsky
(Dadya Petya)

General V.A. Begma,
Russian Partisan Commander

Righteous Poles
From left, Yazenty and Casimir Slovik,
father and son from Koninsk, near Manievich.

Left to right, sitting, Berl (Dov) Lorber, known as
Malenka and Alexander Abugov; standing,
David Dichter, Vova (Zev) Verba, Isaac (Yitzchak)
Kuperberg, Isaac Avruch.

Alexander Abugov, commander of the scout unit
and a founder of the partisan movement
in Volyn and Polesia.

Berl Bronstein (Zuk)
Manievich

Berl (Dov) Lorber

Misha Edelstein

Rivka (Irena) Guz,
Max's wife.

Rachel (Raiya) Flos
Povorsk

Vova (Zev) Verba
Manievich

Joseph Zweibel

David Blaustein

Micha Gazit

Shlomo Zweibel and son

A demonstration of Partisan Forces in Village
of Holoziya, Volynia, Ukraine

Near the Sarchov Woods, Volynia

Youngsters in the Woods
From right to left, Yoseleh Melamed,
Berl Finkel, Avrum Finkel.

Moshe Finkel
(Died in 1956 in Israel, the Galil,
by Arab terrorists)

From left to right, Alan Rubin,
Yideleh (Jack) Melamedik, Berl Finkel

Moshe Laniz from Horodok.
He died in 1948
Israel War of Independence.

From left to right,
Yidele Lorber (cousin to Dov Lorber)
and Berl Finkel, from Max's Group

The boy from Kruk's group,
Vova (Zev) Avruch, worked with explosives

Joseph Shneider (on the left) from Troyanovka
and his friends from Povorsk; Rubin Kirzner (Slivka),
is on the right.

Yitzhak (Isaac) Guz
Povorsk

Chunek Wolper
Manievich
fought in Kruk's group.
Emigrated to Israel.

A group of partisans from the Sidor Kovpak Unit.
At top right is Zusia Chajuck.

Shmaryahu Zafran (Vierni)

Alexander (Szika) Grushka (Agas),
also known as Zashka,
from Kartuchin's Partisan Group

Liba, mother of the Grushka's.
Disguised as a Ukrainian peasant woman, she brought
weapons and food into the forests for the partisans.

Merl (mother of Joseph Shneider). She withstood
torture but did not reveal the hiding place.

A unit of partisans from Max's group, which specialized
in exploding mines. Sitting upright, facing camera,
with rifle and cap is Moshe Kramer.

A partisan unit on their journey through
the piney woods of Volynia.

Partisans on horses crossing the Stochod River.

The partisans help the women cross the Styr River
during a retreat from German forces.
Either Kruk or Max Group.

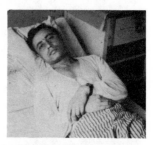

Israel Flash, died from tuberculosis, contracted as a direct result of his work with mine explosives. Kruk's Group.

Moshe Flash from Manievich. Kruk's Group. Today lives in Montreal.

Asher Flash from Manievich, Kruk's Group, uncle of Moshe Flash.

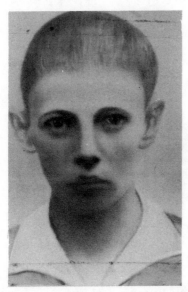

Yehoshua (Joshua) Kanonitz, the boy who brought
the first pistol from the Manievich ghetto.

Shimon Mirochnik, from Manievich, Max's Group.

Binyamin Grushka from Povorsk, Kartuchin's Group.

Yaakov Bronstein from Manievich.

Children from Kamin-Kashirsk, Young Partisans.
On the right is the late Yaakov Shuster of Tel Aviv.

Abraham Gorodetzer, Max's Group and the family camp.
Fell in battle in the Russian army, near Berlin.

The young boy, Ephraim Natanel, from Kruk's group.
Fell in battle in 1948 Israel War of Independence.

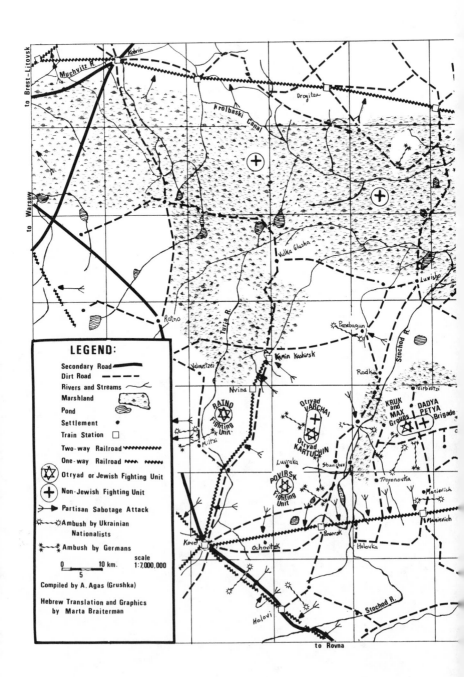

LEGEND:

▬▬▬	Secondary Road
‒ ‒ ‒	Dirt Road
∿	Rivers and Streams
	Marshland
●	Pond
•	Settlement
☐	Train Station
∿∿∿	Two-way Railroad
∿∿ ∿∿	One-way Railroad
✡	Otryad or Jewish Fighting Unit
✛	Non-Jewish Fighting Unit
➤	Partisan Sabotage Attack
✸∿✸	Ambush by Ukrainian Nationalists
✳∿✳	Ambush by Germans

scale
0   10 km.   1:7,000,000
   5

Compiled by A. Agas (Grushka)

Hebrew Translation and Graphics
   by Marta Braiterman

Map labels: to Brest-Litovsk, Kobrin, Muchvitz R., to Warsaw, Krołbaski Canal, Drogitzu, Ratno, Vulka Glusha, Luvisho, Turia R., Valmetzei, Penebagun, Stochod R., Kamin Kashirsk, Rodka, Nvina, Tzirbistzi, RATNO Fighting Unit, Otryad VARCHAI, KRUK and MAX Groups, DADYA PETYA Brigade, Miltzi, Otryad KARTUCHIN, Luvraka, Stawishra, Troyenovka, Manievich, POVIRSK Fighting Unit, Manievich, Kovel, Ochovitzk, Povirsk, Helovka, Holovi, Stochod R., to Rovna

-284-

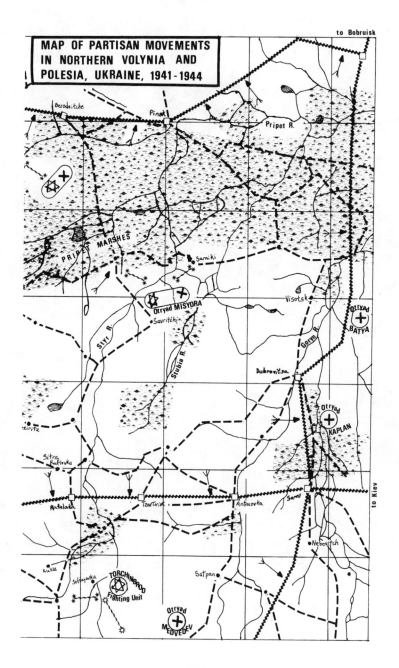

MAP OF PARTISAN MOVEMENTS
IN NORTHERN VOLYNIA AND
POLESIA, UKRAINE, 1941-1944

to Bobruisk

Berodaitche

Pinsk

Pripet R.

PRIPET MARSHES

Sarniki

Otryad MISYORA

Savritchi

Visotsk

Otryad BATYA

Styr R.

Stubia R.

Gorin R.

Dubrovitsa

Otryad KAPLAN

Iziritz

Sitra Ruflovka

to Kiev

Rafalovka

Tzartirsk

Antonovka

Saral

Nebovitch

Kukla

Softayovka

TORCHINBROD
Fighting Unit

Satpan

Otryad MEDVEDEV

-285-

INDEX

To Partisan Fighters and Groups

INDEX

Partisan Fighters

Note: In some cases, only the last name is mentioned; in others only the first or the occupation. Such were the times. I have also included names of relatives of partisan fighters mentioned in the book.

Brat, Moshe, 83,130
Brat, Rachel, 81,83
Brat, Simcha, 83
Brat, Zisla (Zisel), 81,83,130,172
Bredyekovich, 51
Brenson, 51
Brinsky, Anton, photo section, 106,148-150,156,166,167,
    179,195,201-202,214,228,243. See also Dadya Petya.
Bronstein, Berl (also Dov, called Zuk), photo section,
    137-187,219,232,240
Bronstein, Yaakov, photo section, 179
Buzruk, Nikolai, 173

Chapnik, Liza, 43
Chazon, Urtziya, 84
Chernisheyev, 20
Cohen, "Witty", 37

Dadya Malishov, 159
Dadya Petya, see Brinsky, Anton
Damados, 21
Davidov, Gregory, 63-65
Davidovsky, S., 62
Dichter, David, photo section

Edelstein, Misha (Moishe), photo section, 109-110
Ehrenburg, Ilya, 109
Eizenberg, Binyamin (Niyoma), 124,217

Feldman, Nachum, 56-62
Felman, Victor, 59
Feodorov, Major-General A.P., 173,243
Finkel, Avrum (Avraham), photo section, 81,222
Finkel, Berl, photo section, 222
Finkel, Kahat, 81,99,110
Finkel, Moshe, photo section
Fismyeni, A., 56
Flash, Asher, photo section, 84,135
Flash, David, 103
Flash, Isroel, photo section, 115
Flash, Moshe, photo section, 222,228-229
Flash, Shaiya, 145,152,171
Flos, Rachel (Raiya), photo section, 109
Friedlander, Sima, 38

Galfend, S., 38
Galperin, Alexander, 38
Ganzinko, Simon, 60-62
Garchik, Gregory, 36-37
Gazit, Micha, photo section, 92

Partisan Groups

ABOUT
THE AUTHOR

ABOUT THE AUTHOR

JACK NUSAN PORTER is a sociologist, author, editor, and political activist. Born in the Ukraine and raised in Milwaukee, he graduated cum laude from the University of Wisconsin-Milwaukee, and received his Ph.D. in sociology from Northwestern University in 1971.

He has published fifteen books and anthologies and nearly 150 articles, including Student Protest and the Technocratic Society, The Study of Society (contributing editor), Jewish Radicalism, The Sociology of American Jews, The Jew as Outsider: Collected Essays, Kids in Cults (with Irvin Doress), Conflict and Conflict Resolution, Jewish Partisans (two volumes), and Genocide and Human Rights. He has made many contributions to reference books and journals including The Encyclopedia Judaica, Encyclopedia of Sociology, Society, Midstream, and Writer's Digest.

He is the founder of The Journal of the History of Sociology and the Sociology of Business Newsletter and the winner of the John Atherton Fellowship from the Breadloaf Writers Conference as well as fellowships from the Memorial Foundation for Jewish Culture and the World Jewish Congress. He is listed in Who's Who in the East, American Men and Women of Science, Who's Who in Israel, and Contemporary Authors.

Dr. Porter has lectured widely on American social problems and political/religious movements. He has testified before several government commissions including the White House Conference on Families and the National Peace Academy hearings. Long active in Israel and Jewish communal activities, he is considered one of the founders of the Jewish student movement in the USA and Canada in the late 1960's.

He lives in Boston with his wife Miriam and their son Gabriel.